Praise for *Earth-Friendly*

"Adrian Hofstetter's earth-friendly collection of essays is compelling and hard to put down. I found myself not wanting to stop reading. One is carried away by the vision, the passion, the insights. Her affection for science, her critique of it, the connections between ancient wisdom and the new cosmology, between Thomas Aquinas and Rudolf Steiner, the implications of a holistic approach for education, for today's world all reflect a sage at work. Some of the essays ought to be required reading for every Dominican, for every educator."

— **DONALD GOERGEN, O.P.** —
member, Friends of God Dominican Ashram

"A testimony to teachers who instilled in her a love of learning, and to parents who animated her abiding care for those in need, these essays reveal just how liberating learning can be for one who allows what Bernard Lonergan identified as the 'unrestricted desire to know' to direct her life. May her witness inspire other generations to let a vision of faith open the human dimensions of science, as mentors like Owen Barfield and Rudolph Steiner guide us to a contemporary Thomas Aquinas. The convergences are nearly miraculous but never forced, showing how much a personal search for understanding can realize for others."

— **DAVID B. BURRELL, C.S.C.** —
Hesburgh Professor of Philosophy and theology, University of Notre Dame

"In his 1998 encyclical *Fides et Ratio,* John Paul II called for a recovery of philosophy as an authentic wisdom capable of nurturing the contemporary search for truth and meaning. Sr. Adrian's book is just such a recovery. In the integrative spirit of her Dominican brother Thomas Aquinas, she courageously tests the frontiers of current knowledge in areas ranging from food to spirituality. Inspired by Rudolf Steiner's living thinking, she provides us with sound directions for creating a peaceful, life-enhancing, and earth-friendly worldview."

— **TYSON ANDERSON** —
Professor of Philosophy and Religion, Saint Leo University

"The 'signs of the times' that so motivated St. Dominic to launch an entirely new form of apostolic religious life must also move Dominicans to help re-create, in the words of Thomas Berry, a new vision of a mutually enhancing human-Earth relationship. Adrian Hofstetter is doing just that. In her essays, Adrian reflects on the science of Johann Wolfgang von Goethe and his great interpreter Rudolph Steiner, whose vision of nature underscores the interconnection between science and spirituality. More importantly for us Dominicans, she points the way back to our brother Thomas Aquinas, whose teaching on creation provides a philosophical base, not only for Steiner's work, but for all who are committed to bringing about this new vision."

— **SHARON THERESE ZAYAC, O.P.** —
Director, Jubilee Farms
author, *Earth Spirituality in the Catholic and Dominican Tradition*

"Earth Friendly invites us to follow Adrian Hofstetter's explorations of a new kind of science, one rooted in a clear and profound epistemology that allows the wholeness of nature to become visible. These essays let us participate in a personal spiritual journey to overcome the rifts between philosophy, religion, and science that characterized the twentieth century. We can learn much from them."

— **CRAIG HOLDREGE** —
Director, The Nature Institute
author, *Genetics and the Manipulation of Life: The Forgotten Factor of Context*

"These luminous essays reflect the thought and deep work of a woman whose long and brilliant life has engaged some of the most profound revelations of our time. As mystic-activist, spiritual-scientist, and endless enquirer into the workings of the world, she brings fresh and radical perspective that stuns as it awakens the reader. Earth-Friendly is at once an education for the new century and an inspiration for those who would make a difference, and even, a new creation."

— **JEAN HOUSTON, PH.D.** —
Director, The Foundation of Mind Research
author, *A Mythic Life: Learning to Live our Greater Story*

For Alida

Earth-Friendly

Re-Visioning Science & Spirituality through Aristotle, Thomas Aquinas, and Rudolf Steiner

& Adrian M Hofstetter

Adrian M. Hofstetter, O.P.

 Lindisfarne Books
2004

Published by Lindisfarne Books
400 Main Street, Great Barrington, MA, USA
www.lindisfarne.org

LIBRARY OF CONGRESS CATALOGING-IN-PUBLICATION DATA

Hofstetter, Adrian M.
  Earth-friendly : re-visioning science and spirituality through
Aristotle, Thomas Aquinas, and Rudolf Steiner / Adrian M. Hofstetter.
  — 1st ed.
    p. cm.
  ISBN 1-58420-023-5
  1. Religion and science. 2. Aristotle. 3. Thomas, Aquinas, Saint,
1225?-1274. 4. Steiner, Rudolf, 1861-1925. I. Title.
BX4705.H64A5 2004
261.5'5—dc22
                                                        2004009534

10 9 8 7 6 5 4 3 2 1

Printed in the United States of America

Contents

To
the memory of
Oscar Bernard Hofstetter
Marguerite Sanders Hofstetter
Vincent Edward Smith
Aquinata Martin, op

Adrian Hofstetter: An Introduction

Foreword by CHRISTOPHER BAMFORD

*Led by the Spirit, we will emphasize **study**;*

***contemplation** of the interconnectedness*
of all God's creation;

***living** simple, sustainable community;*

***working** against the violence*
that alienates and marginalizes.

We will collaborate with others,
sharing our gifts and resources.[1]

Often, when we think of the lives of religious—those monks and nuns who dedicate themselves to God—we think of their lives as outwardly uneventful and hidden from the world. This may be true of some orders but, if Adrian Marie Hofstetter is in any way typical, it is probably not true of Dominicans. This tall, apparently unassertive, eighty-five-year-old has led a life *in the open*, on the cutting edge—the trenches—of the major spiritual, intellectual, and social issues of the twentieth century. Listening to her speak of her life, one is initially overwhelmed by its fullness and complexity. Then, gradually, three threads emerge: inner development, social action, and the epistemological foundations of an earth-friendly science. Finally, all the threads become one— a passionate concern and love of the world. Appearances are certainly

---

1. From the "Vision Statement" of the Dominicans of St. Catharine, Kentucky.

deceptive. Beneath Sr. Adrian's mild exterior lies a stubborn will for the good and a heart cocked for justice, truth, and beauty.

One of six surviving children in Nashville, Tennessee, of Swiss, German, English, and Irish stock, Harriet (her given name) grew up during the Depression. Her father was a lawyer of great compassion and conscience. He saw the practice of law as service, a form of healing. This meant that money was always tight. But there were other things. There was love and there were books, including the great row of Harvard Classics. But her mother was strict; she did not hold with too much reading! Nevertheless, in defiance of her mother's watchful eyes, Harriet, already an avid reader, managed to get "unacceptable" books in through the window! Already, she was on a search. Like all sensitive teenagers, she wanted to know why she was alive.

She attended Siena College in Memphis, a small Catholic school run by the Dominicans of St. Catharine, Kentucky. Dating back to 1822, when nine young women answered a plea to teach the children of pioneers in an abandoned still house, the Dominican sisters remained true to their mission "to teach, to heal, to serve, and to transform oppressive structures." One Sister in particular, who transformed life for many of her friends and students, stands out in Harriet's memory. Her name was Sr. Aquinata, and she was a true mentor. She was a historian, pursuing Eastern and Western wisdom in all its forms. Harriet never forgot her great love of St. Dominic, Dante, Bergson, and the historian Christopher Dawson. Teilhard de Chardin and Carl Gustav Jung would come later. Drawn initially to psychology, Harriet found the approach too physiological. She majored instead in mathematics, graduating in 1941.

There were other influences. Dorothy Day of the Catholic Worker Movement had visited Siena. She had her own catechetical ministry among migrant workers in Arkansas. Harriet found Day's message of a life radically committed to Gospel peace and justice, as well as its practical application among the poor and marginalized, enormously inspiring. It moved her that, whenever Dorothy Day visited the South, she broke the law by staying with black families. After college, therefore, Harriet found herself faced with a choice: Dorothy Day or become a Dominican. In 1939, her father took her to the World's Fair in New York. They went down to Mott Street, where the Catholic Worker had its headquarters. The poverty and squalor were too much—they didn't stop. When they returned home, Harriet decided on St. Catherine's.

After time spent reading deeply in the lives of Dominican saints and mystics, as well as in the Carmelites Theresa of Avila and John of the Cross, Harriet finally left for the convent. At first, she was disappointed. The novice mistress was little prepared for her independent older charges and only the most pious selections were available for reading and study in the novitiate. This aridity notwithstanding, Adrian showed the resolution that was to be her hallmark throughout her life. She persevered in the regular life of prayer and study; and she learned a great deal about her new way of life. Then, after two years of novitiate, she was sent to her first mission in Jefferson, Indiana. This was followed by a summer of teaching Sisters in Brooklyn, before she returned to teach high school biology and mathematics in Memphis.

In Memphis, Adrian's friendship with Aquinata, now a colleague, deepened. Together, they read and discussed literature, philosophy, mysticism, as well as the state of the Church, and religious life and the world, all as part of the Mystical Body of Christ. Aquinata had spent years meditating St. Paul. Now, she initiated Adrian into the depth Paul's knowledge and understanding of the mystery of Christ.

There was also a growing opportunity for fieldwork. Helen Caldwell Day, a young black woman, had opened up a Blessed Martin House of Hospitality in Memphis, fashioned after the Catholic Worker Houses in New York. (She describes the experiences that led her there in her book *Color Ebony*.) At Blessed Martin House, Helen cared for homeless women and children. A nurse and a Catholic convert, she was a tireless, determined, and courageous challenger to racial separation (as she describes in another book, *Not Without Tears*.) She led mostly by example—as when she attended St. Patrick's Church, a "white" Church, located in what had become a mostly black neighborhood.

In 1953, Adrian received permission to go to Notre Dame for a doctorate in zoology. It was a turning point in her work as a scientist and philosopher of science. Her mentor in this was Vincent Edward Smith, the editor of *New Scholasticism* and a master of the philosophies of Aristotle and Thomas Aquinas. It was on the basis of the study of these philosophers (with a dawning awareness of the work of Teilhard de Chardin as well as the pioneering earth-centered theology of Thomas Berry), that Adrian began to understand the necessity of creating a truly organismic, participatory, holistic and ecological, living science of life.

By 1956, she had a Ph.D., and was back in Memphis. Her life now unfolded on two fronts. She continued to teach and pursue her science interests, working on stress research with Hans Selye at the Institute of Experimental Medicine in Montreal, in phycology (algae) at the University of Texas at Austin, and in phycological research with her Siena students (in collaboration with Edward Doody, C.S.C. at Christian Brothers University in Memphis). At the same time, she became increasingly active in social issues, particularly those having to do with race, poverty, and gender.

Through her concern for the poor and the marginalized, she met Jim Lawson, a Methodist pastor who had studied non-violence with Gandhi and who brought Martin Luther King, Jr., into a struggle for a decent livelihood for the sanitation workers in Memphis. In 1966, she joined the civil rights movement in Memphis, marching with Martin Luther King. Invited by her friend Frances Loring, Adrian stood behind King at Mason Temple, on the night before he died when he gave his "I have a dream" speech. After his death, she became a volunteer organizer and, in the summer of 1969, codirected project NAME, a three month program which brought nuns from seventeen states and Canada to Memphis to confront white racism there.

At this time, Adrian also met and later became a close friend of Margaret Ellen Traxler (1924–2002), one of the great advocates of the oppressed in our time. Margaret Ellen marched with Martin Luther King in Selma, attended the Paris Peace talks during the Vietnam War, and was detained for protesting in St. Peter's Square in Rome. An early spokesperson for women's rights, she founded the National Coalition of American Nuns—"a group of sisters united to study and speak on issues related to human rights and social justice"—the Institute of Women Today, and the Women's Ordination Conference. After meeting Margaret Ellen when she came to speak in Memphis after marching in Selma, Adrian became intensely involved in civil rights work, both locally and nationally. Later she would expand this work, doing workshops and traveling around the world with Margaret Ellen.

After working with a Brookings Institute regional planning group at Rhodes College, Adrian was finally led to ecumenism and peace studies, especially in relation to the Middle East. She prepared for this mission by a retreat in the Holy Land which included walking barefoot and penniless, carrying only the Blessed Sacrament, from Jerusalem to Bethlehem. In 1972, with the Rev. Ramzi Malik, she founded Center for Ecumenicism and Reconciliation at St. Catharine's and later undertook six peace missions to the Middle East.

During this period (the 1970s) Adrian was a Board member of the Southern Christian Leadership Conference, the American Civil Liberties Union, the National Coalition of American Nuns, and the Concerned Women of Memphis—these were busy times!

Meanwhile, after a stint in Clinical Pastoral Education—of inestimable importance, as she says, for her inner growth as a more human and feeling individual— she returned to teaching. Her biology and science classes, primarily in black colleges, were a source of her deepening knowledge of ecology and philosophical questions relating to the organism. She began to lecture on Teilhard de Chardin and slowly—it did not come easily to her—she began to write articles in which she could begin to work out the fundamentals of a new view of nature.

A long life of continuous learning is a near miraculous thing. Adrian Hofstetter never stopped learning. As the century aged, she moved from Savannah State University to Knoxville College, and, in 1980, became a Chaplain at Creighton University in Omaha, Nebraska. While there, she got a Master's in Ministry—her first theological degree. Then, in 1983, Barbara McClintock won the Nobel prize. It seemed the moment for the organism had arrived. Adrian had by now moved to New York, where she was involved with the Center for Corporate Responsibility. But her journey was by no means over. As always, one thing led to another. Pursuing her inner path and peace work, she contacted Clare Danielsson, a godchild of Dorothy Day, whom she had met in the 1960s at a Pax Christi meeting at Graymoor, New York, which Dorothy Day also attended. Inspired by her godmother, Clare had visited the town of Geel in Belgium where, from medieval times, the Beguine community had evolved so that now all the townspeople opened their homes to the mentally disturbed.

Adrian now joined Clare as codirector of a Home Sharing project at Clare's home in Boughton Place, in Ulster County, New York. There they found homes for and with the elderly and began to give workshops in dream, myth, and fairy tales. Clare, a psychodrama trainer, initiated Adrian into psychodrama practice, which she continued for many years with Zerka Moreno. Adrian's own home-sharing experience evolved into her sharing the home of Laura Miller, a Dominican Associate where she now lives, writes, and gardens. During this period, too, Adrian further expanded her horizons by participating for three years in Jean Houston's Mystery School. But her activism did not stop. She continued to protest injustice and violence wherever she found them. During the 1980s she was arrested five times—each time on Good Friday before the Riverside Research Institute in New York City—for protesting America's nuclear weapons program.

The next and perhaps final stop was the discovery of anthroposophy and the work of Rudolf Steiner. She was introduced to biodynamics by Miriam McGillis, at the Caldwell Dominican's Genesis Farm, "a learning center for re-inhabiting the Earth." Immediately, Adrian sensed the next stage of her journey. From Genesis Farm, she was led to the Threefold Community in Spring Valley, where, in the bookstore, she discovered the works of Owen Barfield, Georg Kühlewind, and Rudolf Steiner. It was Steiner's work on Aquinas, *The Redemption of Thinking*, that opened her eyes to the profound realization that anthroposophy's participatory, non-dualistic epistemology and "Goethean" approach to nature was what she had been looking for all her life—a fulfillment of her promise to God to let no obstacle stand in her way. The journey and its fruits are in these pages. May they continue!

Introduction

Why did I decide to publish these articles written over many decades, which include sixty years as a Dominican religious woman, thirty-five as a science teacher, and more than thirty-five as a civil rights activist. My commitment to leave this testament to a revision of science teaching, to the necessity of the liberal arts for a true education, followed on the tragic death of Vincent Edward Smith, my mentor and friend at the University of Notre Dame. This truly great teacher, whose life was cut short by a hit and run driver in 1972, left me the burden of ensuring that his vibrant thinking and teaching about a more meaningful, organic, pre-experimental approach to the science of nature would not be lost to a Western world of science dominated and desecrated by excessive mechanization and militarization. Added to my dedication to a renewal in science teaching is a second commitment, following the Church's Second Vatican Council, to a more engaging, experiential spirituality. These objectives for the re-visioning of science and spirituality have received amazing new life through my coming to know the nature-based science and embodied spirituality of Johann Wolfgang von Goethe (1749–1832), his great interpreter, Rudolf Steiner (1861–1925) and a few of Steiner's eminent commentators. Their vision of nature as a basis for true knowledge of science, spirituality and God in its relationship to the thought of Thomas Aquinas brings me to a third objective—to make Steiner's thought and his total dedication in the pursuit of truth more known and understood by readers who reverence and appreciate the heritage of Thomas Aquinas, especially the men and women of my Dominican Family, whose motto is Veritas, or Truth.

The first two objectives—re-visioning science and spirituality—are the subject of the chapters making up the body of this book. In this introduction I develop my third objective—indicating the valuable interdependence of the thinking of Rudolf Steiner and of Thomas Aquinas, and to invite those who love and appreciate St. Thomas to envision the creative future that Steiner and several of his commentators bring to his rich heritage. I am encouraged in my understanding of Steiner's gifts by academics in the United States who have discovered and written about and/or are now writing, publishing, teaching and lecturing about Steiner's little-known legacy. Among these editors, publishers, historians, educators, scientists, poets and philologists are Robert McDermott, Richard Tarnas, M. C. Richards, Owen Barfield, Georg Kühlewind, Christopher Bamford, John Barnes and others who have realized Steiner's unique talents—praised by Barfield as a "priceless gift ... for those who have felt out of the depths of their being the fearful need of this living creative thinking."[1]

All of these advocates of Steiner's legacy have used some aspect of this multifaceted genius's work as a creative resource in their own fields. In amplifying some area of Steiner's thought, they make it more accessible and easier to comprehend, though at the same time several admit the challenge it presents. Owen Barfield, a British sage who held professorship in several U.S. universities, admits his years of trying to comprehend Steiner "with resistance...then gradual acceptance with the one changing into the other by innumerable gradations or convictions, ending in a firm conviction that the findings of Rudolf Steiner's spiritual research are far and away our most reliable avenue in the direction of truth."[2] After years of similar reflection, Georg Kühlewind, a scientist, poet and linguist, came to accept the truth in Steiner's works only after contemplating again *The Philosophy of Freedom*, which he had not fully understood. Robert McDermott, former president of the California Institute of Integral Studies, writes about his chance discovery of Steiner's two works on the Bhagavad-Gita. These books, "fascinating and impressive," so captured his imagination that they led to many years of study, culminating in his writing introductions for some twenty-five of Steiner's works, published as *The Essential Steiner*. M. C. Richards, a potter, teacher and poet, brings the Steiner philosophy of education to life in the poetic language of an artist in her book *Toward Wholeness: Rudolf Steiner Education in America*. In *The Crossing Point*, Richards explores ways of connecting physical life with inner growth to bring each person to full humanity—a basis of Steiner education. John

Barnes's translation of Steiner's work, *Nature's Open Secret,* and Christopher Bamford's forewords in several Steiner books indicate that these authors are advocates of Steiner's spiritual science and kindred spirits to my interpretation of the science of nature of Aristotle and Aquinas.

It was in Steiner's book *Goethe's World View* that I first discovered the wealth available in the thinking of both Steiner and Goethe in support of an organic, nature-based science like that of Aristotle and St. Thomas. The reality of the world of nature and communion with its creative living processes was a legacy left to future generations by both Aristotle and Goethe. These gifts—recognized, assimilated, nurtured and enriched by Thomas Aquinas and Rudolf Steiner—are now ready for cultivation and fruition for a renewal of Western science in the twenty-first century. Though separated in time by centuries, Steiner's relationship to Goethe is strikingly similar to that of St. Thomas to Aristotle. After seven years as editor of the Weimar edition of Goethe's natural science, Steiner came to his own life work of designing a disciplined path by which humans can "find the path that leads from the earth to the spirit," which he named Anthroposophy.[3] In approximately the same length of time near the end of his short life, St. Thomas wrote twelve Commentaries on the thought of Aristotle, clarifying and illuminating it with new layers of meaning to leave a rich epistemological legacy for the Western world and provide the basis for his own radically embodied psychology and incarnational theology.

The way to truth for these intellectual and spiritual geniuses was rooted in human knowledge as an integral part of a real world of nature. Steiner knew in his own life the truth of Goethe's deep experience of the living world—the fruit, in Goethe's case, of years of contemplating plant life in Germany and Italy. Goethe expressed the creative and active powers of nature in both science and literature. Nature revealing itself through the human was Steiner's own experience, which brought him the further realization that human creative, "living" thinking is nature's primal and highest gift. More will be said later about "living thinking" as a treasure left to the West by the Greeks. It was Steiner's determination, through his major writings, especially through his often recommended book *Intuitive Thinking as a Spiritual Path: A Philosophy of Freedom,* to invite humans to the full realization of the human spiritual capability of thinking as a great gift in the unfolding of nature.

Thomas Aquinas, "unquestionably one of the most influential think-ers of western civilization,"[4] throughout his extensive writings was also intent on explicating what a full human life and personality entails for each individual. Like Steiner, Goethe and Aristotle, he called for and wrote much about a life of virtue as "a necessary condition for recogniz-ing truth, for seeing reality."[5] St. Thomas early in his search for truth courageously moved beyond Augustine's alignment with the shadow and symbolic world of Plato to embrace the reality of the sense world of Aristotle. This provided a base for his understanding of nature as a rev-elation of the Divine: "In the making of the very least creature there is manifested the infinite power, wisdom, and goodness of God because every single creature leads us to knowledge of the first and highest One, which is infinite in every direction."[6]

Goethe was also deeply aware of the presence of God in nature and referred to a "pure, deep, inborn and trained way of knowing things, which had taught me absolutely to see God in Nature and Nature in God, such that this way of picturing things constituted the foundation of my whole existence."[7] Living six centuries after St. Thomas and one after Goethe, Steiner also finds the divine to be reached through nature, but his spiritual science has a characteristic emphasis on human know-ing. For Steiner, the world of nature was a means through which humans moved into the world of the spirit. He wrote that "the highest activity of man, in his spiritual creativity, is incorporated organically, into the general working of the world." The human, he explains, "is the active co-creator of the world process, and his activity of knowing is the most perfect part of the organism of the universe."[8]

Steiner recognized and acknowledged that the intellectual and spiri-tual gifts of St. Thomas had a close affinity to his own and those of Goethe. In his lectures on Thomas Aquinas, published as *The Redemp-tion of Thinking,* Steiner explains, "In the world outlook of Goethe is to be found what Thomism must become if it is to rise to the highest pos-sibilities of the present time and play a real part in the evolution of [humankind]." Later in the same lecture on "Thomism in the Present Day," he points out once again that Thomistic philosophy, which was expressed in abstract form in the thirteenth century, can be rekindled from Goethe to live on as his own Spiritual Science. Steiner cites an inci-dent affirming his thinking about St. Thomas when a Cistercian priest "highly trained in Thomism," present at one of his lectures, remarked that the germ of Steiner's remarks on Goethe are to be found in the thought of St. Thomas.[9]

Steiner knew that a renewal of the thought of St. Thomas could contribute to a greater acceptance of his own work: "Once we realize all that Thomism can be for our time and for our modern age, and that its revival must spring out of its great achievements in the Middle Ages, then we shall see Thomism in Spiritual Science, Thomism in its twentieth-century form."[10] In closing the three lectures on St. Thomas, Steiner explained that they were "given in order to demonstrate that one of the peaks of European spiritual evolution is manifest in the Scholasticism of the thirteenth century, and that this present age has every reason to study this period and will discover that there is an endless amount to be learned from it. This is especially so in what we must call, in the full sense of the words, *the deepening of our thought-life*, so that we may…experience the permeation of our thought-life by Christ."[11] *The Redemption of Thinking* was required reading for several workshops that Laura Miller and I gave in several parts of the country on deepening the earth story to awaken Dominicans to the depth of Steiner's thought and his hopes for reviving the thought of St. Thomas as a basis for his own spiritual science and for a renewed Christianity.

I hope it is now evident why I want to awaken those who love and appreciate the thought of St. Thomas to the good news of the heritage left by Rudolf Steiner. As I ponder the neglect of Steiner's legacy among Thomists, I find it helpful to consider the views of two eminent Steiner advocates who are deeply concerned about his being generally ignored outside of anthroposophical circles. Robert McDermott opens *The Essential Steiner* with this consideration: "If, as his followers claim, Rudolf Steiner is a genius in twelve fields, why do we not come across his name in colleges, in scholarly writings, and in the popular press? Experts in each of the fields in which he worked—including history, philosophy, science, art, social sciences, education and Gospel commentary—seem equally unaware of his work." McDermott leaves no doubt that he does not consider Steiner's work in any way inferior or idiosyncratic but, on the contrary, provides an impressive account of the depth of truth—intellectual, practical and spiritual—to be found in Steiner's voluminous works. That his clairvoyance and esotericism have caused skepticism among academicians and other informed American readers McDermott finds understandable, but he points out that close examination indicates "the intimate relationship between Steiner's spiritual power, his original teaching, his richly varied contributions, and his increasingly effective successors."[12] Owen Barfield in his book *Romanticism Comes of Age* expresses little patience with the repugnance that artists and scientists alike displayed toward Steiner. He explains,

> Indeed, for those few who have as yet been brought by the circumstances of their lives to comprehend how desperately Europe needs what anthroposophy can give her, it is an experience more moving and at the same time very much more bitter than the spectacle of high tragedy to see the indifference, misunderstanding, antipathy and cold suspicion with which Rudolf Steiner's works are met on every side.[13]

I resonate with his feeling but rejoice in the fact that there are now artists, educators and other scholars in the United States that are committed to making Steiner's work known.

Of special interest to me are those commentators on Steiner's works who were or are equally interested in the works of St. Thomas. In a chapter on "The Texture of Medieval Thought" in his best-known book, *Saving the Appearances: A Study in Idolatry*, Owen Barfield claims the sole purpose of the book is to show that the lost world, the spiritual wealth of medieval thought, "can be, and indeed, if incalculable disaster is to be avoided, must be regained." The participatory language of St. Thomas is his model for this lost world in which "the word conceived in the mind is representative of that which is realized in thought." In this world so obviously at one with the spiritual for Barfield, "The human word proceeds from the memory, as the Divine Word proceeds from the Father."[14] Our present difficulty in understanding medieval language, in which words actually participate in the things to which they refer, results from a modern philosophy of science that has left moderns with what Barfield calls an "idol infected language" in "islanded consciousness."[15] He originally conceived this book to help readers realize that our current idolatrous language is one of the principal obstacles to the understanding of Steiner's teaching.[16] Barfield traces the evolution of consciousness from the alive thinking of the Greeks to the Middle Ages, in the writing of Thomas Aquinas, then to the work of Goethe and of Steiner. To the credit of readers in the United States, Barfield, before his writing and teaching career ended at ninety-nine years of age in 1998, admitted his work had ten times better reception in the U.S. than in his own country. In the 1988 edition of *Saving the Appearances,* Barfield sadly acknowledged that this book, which had a sustained distribution in the United States, was never reprinted in England.

Another Steiner advocate, Georg Kühlewind of Budapest, at seventy-nine years of age continues to give conferences on Steiner's thought in various retreat centers in the United States. Like Barfield, Kühlewind casts new light on Steiner's "living thinking" in relationship to the thought of Thomas Aquinas. In his "Meditations on Zen Buddhism, Thomas Aquinas and Anthroposophy," Kühlewind correlates the thought of Thomas Aquinas and the Eightfold Path of Zen Buddhism with the insights of Anthroposophy, providing an understanding of the similarity in the spiritual disciplines in these traditions. The Church's Second Vatican Council acknowledged that non-Christian religions that preceded Christianity "often reflect a ray of that Truth which enlightens all."[17] Kühlewind, like Barfield, is trying to awaken seekers to the great, unacknowledged Anthroposophical spiritual path. His meditations provide me with further hope for a re-visioning of spirituality to follow the widespread practice among Christians in the United States of Buddhism and other Eastern religions.

One of the most believable and convincing of the Steiner advocates is Richard Tarnas, whose best-selling book, *The Passion of the Western Mind: Understanding the Ideas That Have Shaped Our World View,* records the gradual evolution of the Western mind, its changes in the conception of reality over the grand archetypal vista from the ancient Greek, Roman and Christian worlds to form the modern and postmodern Western mindset. It covers the evolution of consciousness during the last four hundred years from the "mind-forged manacles" of the Newtonian fragmented worldview and Kant's furthering the disjunction between the objective physical world and subjective human knowing into the now budding good news of a blossoming advent into a Steinerian vision of a more human and cosmic participatory world.

My interest in *The Passion of the Western Mind* was greatly enhanced by Tarnas's understanding of the enormous contribution of St. Thomas and St. Albert to the wisdom heritage of the West. He ended the chapter on "The Scholastic Awakening" by acknowledging that, "In Aquinas, the forces at work in the immediately previous centuries came to full articulation. In his relatively brief life he would forge a worldview that dramatically epitomized the high Middle Ages' turning Western thought on its axis, to a new direction of which the modern mind would be the heir and trustee."[18]

Tarnas described at length the genius of St. Thomas in developing the concept of participation from Plato rather than Aristotle, who missed its full implication. Aquinas, he says, takes the truth from Plato's world of spirit and Aristotle's world of nature that possessed real being and becoming with humans having a pivotal role in mediating the two realms of spirit and nature, both participating in the real existence communicated to them by God. In the Epilogue to the book, Tarnas looks again at the role of participation in the awakening evolution of human consciousness.

This reawakening of the Western mind to a more participatory world Tarnas records as "first visible in Goethe with his study of natural forms, developed in new directions by Schiller, Schelling, Hegel, Coleridge, and Emerson, and articulated within the past century by Rudolf Steiner."[19] Steiner's writing is now receiving more recognition in the United States, as the growing ecology movement gives us greater insight into the earth revealing itself through the human. Some ecologists are rediscovering the intimate human relationship with nature and with the whole cosmos.[20] Steiner's dedication to making the scientific works of Goethe known has certainly been a key to the current interest in Goethe as a scientist. Goethe's influence can now be recognized in the works of such scientists as Rupert Sheldrake, Henri Bortoft, John Barnes, Craig Holdrege and Arthur Zajonc, among others. This gives me renewed hope that my writing will be a part of the post-modern science now coming to life among these authors, and that with them I will contribute to a renewal of our heritage of wisdom in the West.

My Collection of Essays

To demonstrate how my writing has received new life through the nature-based science and spirituality found in Anthroposophy, I open this collection with an essay about food and education, both of interest to anthroposophical agriculture and education. "Food: A Lost Mystery of Creation" begins with an insight into my childhood in a city in the South. Unfettered by the electronic media that strips the modern child of her imagination and creativity, I was free to explore the natural world with children in our neighborhood. I could only wish that Thomas Jefferson's dream for a meaningful education for Americans, explored in this article and complementary to Steiner's approach to education, had been realized in my early education. During the fifth decade of my life I spent a year and a half in clinical pastoral education in order to begin to recover the feeling side of my nature, which I had lost in the drive to succeed in modern science. This recovery allowed me to return to the classroom with the ability to hear students' own creative answers to problems presented, instead of expecting them to repeat the textbook jargon or even the less-understood intellectual insights I hoped to impart. It was only after engagement in the feminist, ecological and environmental movements that I developed a fuller understanding of the mystery of food and the other gifts of the earth.

Both Steiner and Barfield have called for a return to the great wealth of the medieval scholastic education, with its close link to the riches of ancient Greece. "Liberal Education, A Dominican Challenge" is a call to Dominicans to a deeper understanding of the unique contribution of our Dominican brother Thomas Aquinas to such a liberal arts education. As Barfield has said, "In the mind of Aquinas, with his enormous erudition, the whole corpus of medieval thought is in a manner recapitulated."[21] Despite the noble efforts of Robert M. Hutchins to establish the liberal arts for the education of the youth in America, Hutchins's fear that the loss of the liberal arts in education would also be the loss of a democratic way of life is unfortunately becoming a frightening reality of the twenty-first century. My plea to interest others in Mortimer Adler's *Reforming Education: The Opening of the American Mind* was not heard, and my membership in and hopes for the Albertus Magnus Lyceum at the Dominican House of Studies in River Forest, Illinois was another failed attempt to see the gift of Aristotle and St. Thomas to modern science realized; the Lyceum closed in 1969. My hope now is to make known Steiner's spiritual science as a continuation of the liberal arts heritage from the Greeks and medieval scholasticism. Ita Wegman, a disciple of Steiner, finds an echo of the ancient mystery religions in the *Physiognomy* of Aristotle and "a last reflection of this inspired knowledge in the Seven Liberal Arts."[22]

The articles collected here are not presented in the order in which they were written, but rather an order indicative of my breakthrough in understanding Rudolf Steiner's prophetic spiritual science.[23] "Ancient

Wisdom and Modern Science" was prepared at the invitation of an anthroposophist, Dr. Douglas Sloan, for discussion in his and Dr. Mary Boyd's seminar for doctoral candidates at Columbia University Teacher's College and Union Theological Seminary. I intended it for prospective teachers as an invitation to consider the classical understanding of education as a comprehensive approach to making a person good both as a person and as a citizen. Certainly the *Great Books of the Western World* provide an excellent introduction to the unique place that the Greeks hold in the world outlook of the West. Rudolf Steiner is introduced as the author of the biodynamic gardening movement now being popularized in the United States. Organic and biodynamic agriculture and Waldorf Schools have been the means by which some farmers, teachers and parents in the United States have been attracted to Steiner's thought.

"Science, Education and the Christian Person" was presented to religious educators at the 1964 Conference on Christian Humanism at Mount Mary in Asheville, North Carolina, and published in the book *The Divine Synthesis*. It argues for a nature-based education to replace the mechanical approach to living organisms predominant in schools in the United States. Such a reformation is available in Waldorf Schools for children and their teachers, and for other adults in much of Steiner's writing. "To be sure," Steiner intuits, "we have torn ourselves away from nature, but we must still have taken something with us into our own being. We must seek out this natural being within ourselves, and then we shall also discover the connection to her [nature]."[23]

The awakening of religious women to the challenge science and technology present to our survival on planet earth came to a great extent through the insights of Thomas Berry and Brian Swimme. Their book *The Universe Story* was in the 1990s a kind of Bible for religious women interested in stopping the technological assault on the earth. Since the Berry and Swimme book was basically an espousal of an earth story based on modern science to replace the traditional Judeo-Christian one, I wrote "New or Traditional Earth Spirituality" to remind religious women of the wealth of earth concern in our early Christian tradition. It is notable that Rudolf Steiner, in *The Origins of Natural Science*, does not oppose our dehumanized modern science but rather is intent on discovering "seeds of spiritual life in the highly productive modern methods of scientific research."[24] In the foreword to another Steiner book, *Mystics*

After Modernism: Discovering the Seeds of a New Science in the Renaissance, Christopher Bamford paraphrases Steiner as prophetically saying "if we are to redeem the one-dimensional scientific worldview of modernism, we must do so by picking up where the mystics and humanists of the late Middle Ages and early Renaissance left off, integrating their insights and way of knowing with what we have gained from modern science to create a new "spiritual science," at once "mystical" and scientific."[25]

The article "Thomas Aquinas and the New Cosmology: Faith Encounters Science Anew" makes an appeal to environmentally involved persons for a philosophy of science more in keeping with the biodynamic farming methods that most endorse. It is certainly understandable that Rudolf Steiner, with his creative insights into thinking as the primal gift of nature, finds a kinship between his work and that of St. Thomas. He has this to say about the value of the Scholasticism in the Middle Ages:

> For, quite apart from the question of content, whoever has a sense for the form and manner in which any scientific or other subject should be set out with absolute accuracy of thought and who can appreciate how the relationship between things should be expressed in logically related ideas, will realize that thought was never so exact, so logically consistent, either before or afterwards, as in the age of Scholasticism. The essential quality in it is that pure thought runs with such mathematical certainty from idea to idea, from judgment to judgment, from conclusion to conclusion that these thinkers account to themselves for the smallest, even the tiniest step.[26]

In another reference, Steiner explains that modern scientists find the method of the Scholastics so tedious and unpleasant that they condemn them as learned pedants. Yet he points out these scientists are "totally unaware that true Scholasticism is naught but detailed elaboration of the art of thinking, in order that thought may provide a foundation for the genuine comprehension of reality."[27]

I wrote "Viruses: Are They Alive?" soon after finishing graduate school as an antidote to the tragic inability among biologists to define life. The alive thinking of the Greeks that persisted in the language of the Middle Ages permitted Aristotle and St. Thomas as participants in the living processes of the natural world to define life and thus identify the essence of what it is to be alive. They, unlike the static thinkers among scientists today, would not attempt to define life by the chemical composition of an organism or its characteristics. Their general science of nature is an approach to the scientific study of nature that respects and credits the "becoming" apparent in the world of living beings. Such an approach would in no way denigrate the triumphs of modern science. In fact, Steiner and recent historians of Western thought admit that modern science, despite its dehumanizing limitations, has tremendous technical achievements and is a necessary step in the evolution of consciousness of the independent human individual. Richard Tarnas has optimistically taken this development another step: in his "understanding the ideas that have shaped our world view," humans seem to be at the birth of a reconnection with "the cosmos in a mature *participation mystique.*"[28] He thus predicts a possible recovery of the rich heritage left by the Greeks and the Scholastics of the Middle Ages, which Barfield often reminds us must take place if our civilization is to continue.

"Nature's Law: Competition or Cooperation?" was written as an antidote to the biased emphasis on competition in biology textbooks that I examined for student use. Aristotle's commonsense argument for the cooperative principle operating in nature should appeal to any scientists willing to test the waters of ancient science. Notice the simple language of his science, without the jargon in which modern science is so deeply engrossed. St. Thomas takes this principle operating in nature into a theological realm and thus brings Aristotle's natural wisdom under the light of the divine.

"The Cell and the Organism: A Re-Examination" was presented in the St. John's University Philosophical Series in 1964. It questions current attitudes toward the cell theory as an adequate or inadequate way to study living organisms. Experiments provide evidence of the need to keep the organism itself in focus when studying its parts. This experimental approach is certainly in keeping with the thought and practice of Aristotle, who used all the experimental knowledge available to him. More than forty years before this presentation, Rudolf Steiner looked into the same problem from a philosophical standpoint. He had no difficulty in referring to the "whole dreadful" cell theory of Schwann and Schleiden as leading to atomism and thereby losing any real idea of organisms. He concluded, "We were not aware that by conceiving the organism as divided up into cells we atomized it in our minds, which in fact signifies killing it. The truth of the matter is that any real idea of organisms has been lost to the atomistic approach."[29]

For many years following my presentation at St. John's, there was no outlet for articles about an organismal approach to the philosophy of biology. For several years, teaching and researching as a phycologist, I published, with students, articles about numbers and kinds of algae in the Mississippi River and surrounding land. The summer after Martin Luther King was killed I joined Sr. Margaret Ellen Traxler, Director of the National Catholic Conference for Interracial Justice (NCCIJ), in codirecting a project in Memphis that brought nuns from seventeen states and Canada to confront white racism. I spent one summer in the Traveling Workshop of the NCCIJ to reduce racial tensions across the U.S., and began teaching in a black college as part of Margaret Ellen's plan to send five hundred Sisters to minority colleges. I left Memphis, teaching, and involvement in civil rights in 1972 to become the director of the Center of Ecumenism and Reconciliation for my Kentucky Dominican community. Its purpose was twofold: the reconciliation of Jews, Christians and Muslims (working with HOPE Seminar in Jerusalem) and the reconciliation of men and women in ministry. My preparation for this ministry was a trip around the world with Margaret Ellen to study U.S. foreign policy, women's issues and spirituality. I spent a year and a half in Clinical Pastoral Education, mentioned earlier, for personal renewal, and then returned to teaching in two other black colleges as part of the NCCIJ project. When "the honkies" were no longer welcome in the black college I spent three years as a campus minister for peace and justice issues at Creighton University. At Creighton I taught a course on dreams and during a semester break participated in a seminar at the Jung Institute in Zurich, Switzerland. Leaving Creighton, I became the community representative to the Center for Corporate Responsibility in New York and moved upstate to join Clare Danielsson, a godchild of Dorothy Day, in coordinating a home sharing project for Ulster and Dutchess counties. During these years I continued as co-director of the Center of Ecumenism and Reconciliation, went on six peace missions to the Middle East and was active in Star Wars and antiwar demonstrations in New York.

The year 1983 supplied a biological breakthrough, when Barbara McClintock won the Nobel Prize for her work in cytogenetics. Now that her radical revelations about genes and chromosomes in corn plants was recognized, I and other women would be more likely to get a hearing for articles outside those currently in vogue. At the invitation of Father Thomas Berry, I presented the paper "The New Biology: Barbara McClintock and an Emerging Holistic Science" at a 1991 American Teilhard Association meeting in Riverdale, New York. McClintock's revelations of the genetics of the corn plants was a fulfillment of Goethe's statement that "nature has no secrets that it does not somewhere *place naked before the eyes* of the attentive observer."[30] McClintock certainly knew her corn plants intimately and thus fulfilled Steiner's remark that in Goethean science, "We have the prospect of arriving at objective knowledge because we are allowing the object itself to speak."[31] When McClintock claimed to see more than others because she "goes down into" her corn plants and "looks around," I hear Steiner observing that when one is conscious of standing within a living thing, "it brings its principles along with it."[32]

When Beverly Rubick, the editor for the Center of Frontier Sciences at Temple University, read the McClintock article, she asked me to write one for her Center's publication. "Universe Coding, Not Genetic Coding" was sent to her in 1993 but was not published, as Rubick found it too political (but granted that "further development of [such an] idea is critically needed"). Further development was not long in coming, for that same year *Exploding the Gene Myth: How Genetic Information Is Produced and Manipulated by Scientists, Physicists, Employers, Insurance Companies, Educators, and Law Enforcers*, by Ruth Hubbard and Elijah Wald, was published. The title is a good summary of the threat that our new information on the genetic makeup of natural beings, especially of the human, can be to all of us.

Several visits with Dominican sisters to the Fellowship Community, a Rudolf Steiner retirement residence, were intended to interest them in the depth and wonder of Steiner's multitudinous projects, and the outstanding fruit flowing from his philosophy. As Jesus said, "By their fruits you will know them." The alive, healthy, and flourishing approach to a village community seemed to me an amazing model for developing a modern form of religious communal living. The article "A Rudolf Steiner Sustainable Community" was written to interest other community members in the gift that co-workers like those at Fellowship Community could be for our community in view of our declining membership. They could provide rich resources for sharing the fruits of the Dominican way of life.

"Is This the Time? was written to awaken psychodramatists to the much-neglected philosophy of J. L. Moreno. My many years of psychodrama training with Zerka Moreno, whose husband J. L. founded psychodrama, prompted this article. Psychodrama, for Moreno, was a way of life much more than a therapy. He was committed to the development of the creative potential of each individual in the hopes of bringing about a new social order in which the human has priority over the machine. For him, the gifts of creativity and spontaneity are the anti-dotes to best counter the mechanized culture in which we live. His heal-ing ministry of love and mutual sharing was based on that of Jesus, Buddha, Socrates and Gandhi. Moreno's goal for a new social order based on the creativity of each individual is not unlike that of Rudolf Steiner, whose anthroposophy is also a creative way to a new social order.

I wrote "Women Scientists, Ancient Wisdom and Modern Science" for a projected issue on women scientists for *Hypatia* magazine. It was not accepted, but I am glad it has been in this volume, as I believe it offers much to women scientists looking for a more organismal and less patriarchal approach to modern science. Rudolf Steiner was again ahead of his time when in 1906 he gave a lecture on "Women and Society" and pointed out the absurdity of those writing that women were less intelligent than men or that they should be denied access to any field of scholarship. Women scientists know the struggle that is still required to win a semblance of equality when they attempt to penetrate the patri-archal power structure of modern science.

My concluding article, "A Call to Dominican Religious Women," was written from deep concern for the divisions in religious communi-ties following the Church's Second Vatican Council. It was intended to promote discussion among members of communities to help heal the bad feelings resulting from the many religious women who became involved in Zen Buddhism and other Eastern religions. Their participa-tion in other traditions could be the good news of living out the Council directives that Karl Rahner interpreted as having the potential for the Church to become World Church. My own dream is that women, now winning their right to contribute their God-given gifts for full equality in a participatory world coming to birth, will be channels of the Spirit into "this new reality [which] is itself a creative act."[33]

The need for the church to recover its basis in the mystery religions is quite apparent in the writings of Rudolf Steiner. A study day of his book *Christianity as Mystical Fact* with Dominicans and friends in Gloucester, Massachusetts, was my way of introducing them to this need. My three years in Jean Houston's Mystery School in Port Jervis, New York, provided me an experiential knowledge of what Rudolf Steiner revealed about the connection of these schools to a deeper faith and a richer spirituality. My trip to Greece and to Africa with Mystery School participants helped me understand what Ita Wegman learned from Steiner about mystery religions, especially about the Elusian Mysteries. In the Port Jervis Mystery School we reenacted the Elusian healing ceremonies, not only at the school but also at the original site of these mysteries in Greece. Ita Wegman's writing about the Mysteries after Steiner's death illuminates the much greater significance these mystery centers had on Aristotle and the depth of the extraordinary heritage he left for the West. Challenging research could now uncover what Wegman and Steiner revealed about the fruits of the mystery religions being found today in the liberal arts and in Anthroposophy.

I hope that readers will find the short descriptions that I have provided for the following essays to be helpful in selecting articles in which they would be most interested. I am grateful for this opportunity to bring together this testament to my commitment to liberal education, and to a re-visioned science and spirituality for the twenty-first century.

1.

Food
A Lost Mystery of Creation

$\mathcal{M}$ost of the time, in today's mechanistic world, the deeper mysteries of creation are lost. Partaking of food, which those of us in middle-class America are fortunate to have each day, is one of these mysteries that has become routine. Why has such a gift of creation become a thoughtless ritual? The artificial world of industrialized nations, with its well-obscured dependence on nature, has changed not only our relationship to food and sustenance but our connection to all of creation. Has our food become one more commodity of commerce? I propose to challenge us to take responsibility for our daily bread—its source and production—and for a mechanical worldview that threatens not only the quality and availability of food, but civilization and even life itself.

"The world we have lost was organic," laments Carolyn Merchant, a professor of environmental history and philosophy at the University of California in Berkeley, in her book *The Death of Nature*. Sounding the alarm for the magnitude of the loss of a primal organic world, Merchant tells us that until the seventeenth century and the "scientific revolution," people of the earth lived "in daily, immediate, organic relation with the natural order for their sustenance."[1] In their close-knit cooperative communities, the earth was reverenced as alive and numinous, as a home for humans and all creatures. In this world, food was gift, manna in the desert, a profound mystery, a sacrament. This sacrament of food is provided basically by plant life nourished through the spirits of the sun, the water and the earth.

In the early part of the twentieth century, I experienced the remnants of this world. Although we lived in a city, my mother purchased fruits and vegetables in front of our home from a farmer who peddled his produce on a horse-drawn wagon. Fruit and nut trees in our small yard provided peaches, pears, cherries and walnuts for our family, with enough to share with neighbors. We had chickens for food, pet rabbits and a dog. In summer, I joined neighborhood children in waiting for the iceman to chip ice from the large blocks on his truck for our iceboxes. We eagerly collected the small chips to cool us on hot days. My brothers walked with milk cans several times a week to a nearby dairy farm for unpasteurized milk.

After college I entered a community of religious women whose motherhouse was located on a 640-acre farm in Kentucky. The farm supplied most of our food: milk from the cows, eggs from the chickens, meat from the hogs and other animals. In summer we had an abundance of fresh vegetables from our gardens; in the fall, apples from the orchard; in winter, those foods that could be stored in our cellar. Two lakes supplied water that was purified by our own plant and pumped into a water tower for later use.

Living thus in close contact with nature, we were not threatened by contaminated food, chemical pesticides, bacteria, radiation, genetic tampering, meat from confined animals kept alive by antibiotics, or milk from cows injected with hormones to increase milk production. We did not need vitamins to supplement food grown in depleted soil. All this has changed during my lifetime.

The loss of this organic world began in the seventeenth century as scientists and philosophers discovered new ways to think about and manage nature. Control over nature continued to evolve over the next three centuries, resulting in the addiction to science and technology that characterizes our lives today. Research and development for and after World War II gave us all kinds of synthetic pesticides and means for killing, not limited to insects and weeds. Now, in this machine world, we accept food as one more consumer item on our shopping list, a supermarket commodity, divorced from its natural origin. It is difficult to understand why a country founded to free people from the oppression they fled from in other lands, under the guise of "progress," would now subscribe to a dehumanizing and unhealthy form of agriculture and life.

The industrial production and processing of food is the subject of a remarkable Sierra Club book, *The Unsettling of America*, by Wendell Berry. A Midwest farmer, writer, poet, educator and concerned citizen, he recounts the history of the change from established rural agricultural communities in the United States in the 1940s to the loss of 26 million family farms by the 1970s.[2] "In one decade, 1980–1990, 1,746,320 people left the farm, a decline of thirty-one percent."[3] With the development of agribusiness, five percent of the people can now produce all the so-called "cheap food" for U.S. consumption and for export. Berry sees the exodus from the farm as stemming from the loss of Thomas Jefferson's educational ideal. "In the mind of Thomas Jefferson," Berry explains, "farming, education, and democratic liberty were indissolubly linked."[4] This Jeffersonian ideal corroborates Berry's own thinking and serves as a basis for his critique of the "potentially totalitarian" agribusiness now controlling and producing our food.[5]

Thomas Jefferson dreamed that a country of small landowner farmers with a liberal education could provide the leadership needed for a democratic form of government. He wrote, "Cultivators of the earth are the most valuable citizens. They are the most vigorous, the most independent, the most virtuous, and they are tied to their country, and wedded to its liberty and interests by the most lasting bonds."[6] In a letter to James Madison in 1785, he wrote, "It is not too soon to provide by every possible means that as few as possible shall be without a little portion of land. The small landholders are the most precious part of a state."[7]

Less than fifty years after Jefferson's death, his aim of universal liberal education was tragically betrayed through the unfortunate addition of the word "practical" to "liberal," describing the kind of education Congress prescribed for land-grant colleges. Congress passed the land-grant acts "to promote the stabilization of farming populations and communities and to establish in that way a 'permanent' agriculture, enabled by better education to preserve both the land and the people."[8] But agriculture literally lost ground when Jefferson's ideal was rapidly replaced by a "practical" form of education. Vocational training became the order of the day in colleges and universities. Thus began the invasive science and technology that came to be the basis for industrial American culture, including food and agriculture. Congress aided and abetted this new order by accepting industrialists' claims that American lives would be improved by replacing farmers with machines, thus making food cheaper and more abundant. Funds intended for farmers, agriculture and rural communities were then allocated to machine production of food by profit-driven entrepreneurs. The family farm was destroyed by a rapidly growing, rapacious agribusiness. Its promise of more efficient monoculture food production on vast acreages has resulted in decreased fertility of the land and a catastrophic loss of topsoil. The accompanying tragedy of uprooted farmers and rural communities has not yet been figured into the cost of our "cheap food."

All of us experience the fruits of this mechanized world in our declining health, our poor education, the stupidity of our entertainment industry, in our whole way of life. The impact of agribusiness technology on our culture is well documented by such writers as Rachel Carson, Carolyn Merchant, Joanna Macy, Elisabet Sahtouris, Theodore Roszak, Thomas Berry, Thomas Hayden, Morris Berman and others. Our dreams for a better world through science and technology have become the nightmares of the millions who left the farms, many of whom have become the unemployed and unemployable in American cities.

The loss of the sacred that has accompanied the growth of this "mega-technological web" in American life is the subject of another remarkable Sierra Club book, *In the Absence of the Sacred: The Failure of Technology and the Survival of the Indian Nations*, by Jerry Mander. Mander cites the failure of technology as a cause of the cancerous growth invading planet earth, while suggesting alternative paths for restoring healthy ways of living.[9] By listening to the voices of indigenous peoples, Americans may yet learn to respect nature and to live in harmony with our mother the earth. Despite our affliction with "the most advanced strain of ignorance the world has ever developed,"[10] we may still have time to awaken to technology's failure before it is too late to solve the monumental problems it has created.

Mander claims the biggest conundrum we face is our inability to conceive of letting go of our dependence on the extravagant commodities that technology has duped us into making necessities. He is not advocating that all of us return to the simple lifestyle of Native Americans, but that we learn from them healthier ways of living, of producing nutritious food, of taking from nature only what we really need, thus having more leisure. The wisdom of Native Americans could help us to heal our tragic separation from nature, from the sacred, and provide a more human society with the possibility of liberty and justice for all.

A return to the educational ideal of Thomas Jefferson would make our schools less dependent on machines and therefore less costly. It could also educate some of the next generation to evaluate and to demand a change in the insane materialism that threatens their future. By reading and analyzing the works of the great minds of the past, students could acquire the arts of critical thinking, writing, and speaking coherently. They could come to understand the roots of Western culture, which brought this civilization into existence—thus restoring a hope for its continuance.

Such a revolution will demand massive dedication and determination on the part of all those who are aware that our disastrous, high-tech lifestyle is a path to extinction. While environmentalists, ecologists and eco-feminists have led the way, religious communities are lately responding to the prophetic call of Thomas Berry, who urges us to assume responsibility for the fate of the earth. He warns:

> The devastation that is presently taking place through the industrial-technological exploitation of the earth is already so great that future generations are presently condemned not only to live in the ruins of the infrastructure of industrial society but also amid the ruins of the natural world itself. This can be said apart from any consideration of nuclear war.[11]

My hope is that my community of Kentucky Dominicans will soon join other religious men and women who are electing to change their way of life by making their community properties into models of sustainable living. Our 640-acre farm has been influenced over the years by the agribusiness mentality and now has two hundred head of cattle. If our farm is once again to provide a sustainable way of life, those residing there will need to eat lower on the food chain, to eat more organically grown vegetables, fruits, and grains, and less meat. Such a change could enhance the physical, mental and spiritual health of college students, faculty, employees, sisters, and those sick in the infirmary. In addition, by a deeper investment in the liberal arts in our college, we could increase the chances that Jefferson's visionary ideal will be maintained for future generations.

It is remarkable that something as simple as one's way of eating can help begin a journey away from the insanity of the artificial world we have created. When we see vegetables growing in our gardens and those of others, or produced by farmers in our bioregion, food can once again become for us a part of natural agriculture, of nature. My relationship with the earth deepens when I pick a cherry tomato or a snow pea from the garden in my yard, put it in my mouth and slow down sufficiently to let myself realize the awesome truth that this delicacy is now en route to mysteriously become part of me. Like the Native Americans, I can thank the plant for its ability to let go of its life as it becomes part of and sustains mine.

Wendell Berry poetically expresses this mysterious aspect of food: "To live we must daily break the body and shed the blood of creation. When we do this knowingly, lovingly, skillfully, reverently, it is a sacrament. When we do it ignorantly, greedily, clumsily, destructively, it is a desecration. In such desecration we condemn ourselves to spiritual and moral loneliness and others to want."[12]

This chapter was previously printed in *Sisters Today* Vol. 70 No. 5 (September 1998).

2.

Ancient Wisdom
and Modern Science

I wrote this article after reading the book *Ancient Wisdom and Modern Science,* a collection of papers presented at a 1982 meeting of the International Transpersonal Association in Bombay.[1] The conference focused on the ancient wisdom of the East, where the primacy of the spiritual over the material attracts many Westerners. However, it is the ancient wisdom and culture of the West, from which modern science originated, that I claim as a means of dislodging science from the mechanical and materialistic philosophy of the last three centuries so as to free it for a more holistic, integrated course for the future. I will substantiate this claim from my own experiences and insights as well as from others similarly concerned that the creative forces of Western culture have withered and dried up under its domination by science and technology.

My Preparation

My preparation for this task developed during a quarter century of teaching and researching with college science students. During these years I felt myself a loner among biologists in my search for a more meaningful and intelligible, and less mathematical, approach to science education. The textbooks were largely compilations of charts, graphs and inane facts presented with little or no supporting evidence. The books that I assigned to stimulate students to a sense of wonder, awe and reverence were those of organismal biologists like Rachel Carson, Loren

Eiseley, Rene Dubois, and Barry Commoner, who were trying to reverse the dehumanizing trend of modern science. I also recommended humanistic science books such as Martin Gardner's *Great Essays in Science*, Walter B. Cannon's *The Wisdom of the Body*, Sherrington's *Man on His Nature*, Erwin Schrödinger's *What is Life?*, and Libbie Hyman's *The Invertebrates*.

My own passion for the truth about the nature of reality was nourished early in life by my father, who had only six years of formal education but often selected a volume of *The Harvard Classics* from the bookcase in our home and insisted that I read. I was fortunate in undergraduate and graduate school to have teachers whose education was not warped by the fragmenting effect that modern science and technology have had on much of education. They were in touch with the pre-industrial, enchanted world of nature, alive with spirit, with gods and goddesses, with heroes and heroines, a world in which humans were at home on the earth with other living creatures. This motivated me to search for such a liberalizing education for science students in the colleges where I taught.

Resources for The Great Conversation

A significant resource for deepening my appreciation of ancient wisdom was available in the *Great Books of the Western World*, popularized in the 1940s and '50s through the genius of Robert M. Hutchins, president of the University of Chicago and Mortimer Adler of St. John's College in Maryland. Their 1952 edition of the Britannica Great Books was a monumental attempt to stem the loss of these treasures from education and to avert the West's "headlong plunge into the abyss" of a sterile, materialistic philosophy of life.[2] Not only were science, literature and the arts imperiled by a descent into a world stripped of value and meaning, but democracy itself would be doomed without a liberally educated citizenship.[3] It was such an education that nourished the creativity and belief in the human spirit of the Founding Fathers of our country.

The first three volumes of the Great Books set were invitations from Hutchins and Adler to a dialogue between wisdom and science. In the first volume, *The Great Conversation*, Hutchins deplored the calamitous effect of the infiltration of the scientific method into all disciplines, replacing "the Great Conversation" that was the core of Western education until the beginning of the twentieth century.[4] He noted the triumphs of science and technology but found them mixed blessings. As root causes of the deplorable new trends in education, they were a hindrance; but they did provide leisure enough for all to be educated. If all had access to the Great Conversation, Hutchins believed it could "recall the West to sanity."[5] He stated that "No dialogue in any other civilization can compare with that of the West in the number of great works of the mind that have contributed to this dialogue."[6] These books have endured, he said, because persons in every age "have been lifted beyond themselves by the inspiration of their example."[7]

The next two volumes, *The Great Ideas: A Syntopicon of Great Books of the Western World*, are remarkable resources for furthering the dialogue between wisdom and science. They include essays about and outlines of 102 great ideas, with references to the exact location of 2,987 topics in the 54 books in the collection. As a means of following the discussion of any topic beginning with the ancients through twenty-five centuries of the Great Conversation, it is an unparalleled reference, research, and study tool, which merited Hutchins's claim: "When the history of the intellectual life of this century is written, the Syntopicon will be regarded as one of the landmarks in it."[8]

As a college teacher, I usually had several science students who were willing to use the Syntopicon to step into the deep, rich waters of Greek and medieval wisdom. I promised it would expand their vision and stimulate their creativity in exploring nature. I shared Hutchins's dream of universal liberal education and his insight that "The substitution of machines for slaves gives us an opportunity to build a civilization as glorious as that of the Greeks, and far more lasting, because far more just."[9] I agreed that the torpor and apathy of Americans toward democracy was one result of the boredom of routine, meaningless jobs in offices and factories. A creative education could result in a more human way both of living and earning a living. When Hutchins left Chicago to found the Center for the Study of Democratic Institutions in Santa Barbara, he in fact advocated a guaranteed annual income for all Americans. A small percentage of the population could produce all the food, clothing and shelter needed for a good life, he claimed, and the resulting leisure could make possible universal education to replace universal schooling.

Science and Philosophy

As the Great Conversation declined early in the twentieth century, the triumphs of science and technology were enthroning them as the primary arbiters of truth. Some philosophers, artists and scientists sounded the alarm as value and meaning were being lost in a spiritless material world. E. A. Burtt, in the opening pages of his classic work, *The Metaphysical Foundation of Modern Science*, contrasts the worldview of an author from the Great Books with one from modern science. In the following quotation from Dante's *Divine Comedy*, Burtt finds Dante's marvelous poetic description of the universe "reposeful, contemplative, infinitely confident":

> The All-Mover's glory penetrates through the universe and
> regloweth in one region more, and less in another.
> In that heaven which most receiveth of his light, have I
> been and have seen things which whoso descendeth from
> up there hath not knowledge nor power to re-tell;
> Because, as it draweth nigh to its desire, our intellect sinketh
> so deep, that memory cannot go back upon the track.
> Nathless, whatever of the holy realm I had the power to
> treasure in my memory, shall now be matter of my song.[10]

In contrast, Burtt quotes from a contemporary philosopher of science, Bertrand Russell's Mephistophelian account of creation. Burtt's concern was that such views were being thrust on reflective persons with "increasing cogency." The quotation from Russell is typical of the "metaphysical barbarism" with which Burtt characterized the centuries in which modern science developed:

> Such in outline, but even more purposeless, more void of meaning, is the world which Science presents for our belief. Amid such a world, if anywhere, our ideals henceforward must find a home. That man is the product of causes which had no prevision of the end they were achieving; that his origin, his growth, his hopes and fears, his loves and his beliefs, are but the outcome of accidental collocations of atoms, that no fire, no heroism, no intensity of thought and feeling, can preserve an individual life beyond the grave; that all the labours of the ages, all the devotion, all the inspiration, all the noonday brightness of human genius, are destined to extinction in the vast death of the

solar system, and that the whole temple of Man's achievement must inevitably be buried beneath the debris of a universe in ruins—all these things, if not quite beyond dispute, are yet so nearly certain, that no philosophy which rejects them can hope to stand.[11]

In this quotation Russell's view is not only an example of metaphysical barbarism, but of the crippling spell that a mechanical worldview cast over the West. Another philosopher and economist, E. F. Schumacher, in his well-known book *Small is Beautiful* makes the same point:

The leading ideas of the nineteenth century claimed to do away with metaphysics, are themselves a bad, vicious, life-destroying type of metaphysics. We are suffering from them as from a fatal disease.... The errors are not in science but in the philosophy put forward in the name of science.[12]

Science and Specialization

In my view modern science and technology has had a deadening effect in the classrooms. I was bored by the accumulation of factual data presented in biology classes at the University of Notre Dame. The scientists were absorbed in bits of reality disconnected from the world of everyday life, like bees in a hive, learning more and more about less and less, usually without exchange with the scientist next door, much less with those from other disciplines. Their loss of contact with a richer cosmos prompted me to recall William Blake's famous lines "May God us keep, / From Single vision and Newton's sleep."

In 1930, the distinguished Spanish philosopher Jose Ortega Y Gasset, in *The Revolt of the Masses*, confronted this situation with a scathing attack on specialization. He deplored the "astounding mediocrity"[13] of these specialists, whom he saw as "learned ignoramuses."[14] In a chapter entitled "The Barbarism of Specialization" he describes the culture that ensues:

Anyone who wishes can observe the stupidity of thought, judgment and action shown today in politics, art, religion, and the general problems of life and the world by "men of science," and, of course, behind them the doctors, engineers, financiers, teachers, and so on. That state of "not listening," of not submitting to higher courts of appeal, which I have repeatedly put forward as characteristic of the mass-man, reaches its height precisely in these partially qualified men. They symbolize, and to a great extent constitute, the actual dominion of the masses, and their barbarism is the most immediate cause of European demoralization.[15]

The Nobel laureate Erwin Schrödinger also admonished scientists about the evils of specialization, warning that those who do not understand the underlying assumptions of their thought result in "the grotesque phenomenon of scientifically trained, highly competent minds with an unbelievably childlike-undeveloped or atrophied philosophical outlook."[16]

Crisis in Thought and Values

The book that gave me a unique perspective on the scientific devastation of twentieth century culture was *The Crisis of Our Age* by the Russian-born philosopher, historian and distinguished sociologist Pitirim Sorokin. His prediction that a new age was being born as our technological era was dying gave me hope. Sorokin found three systems of truth, proceeding as cyclic phenomena throughout the recorded history of the West. Our present system, based on that which can be seen, heard, felt, smelled, counted and measured, he called a Sensate system. It was characteristic of the heyday of the Roman Empire as well as the Machine Age of the last three hundred years. A Sensate culture is followed by an Ideational phase, which is focused on spiritual reality and values as revealed by God through mystics, prophets and founders of religious orders. The Ideational Christian period lasted from the sixth century to the end of the twelfth century. An Idealistic system is a synthesis of the other two and is based on reason. The supreme examples for Sorokin of Idealistic or Integral culture were the fifth century Greek world of Plato and Aristotle and the Middle Ages, the thirteenth century of Albert the Great and Thomas Aquinas.[17]

Long before others realized that the twentieth century was the end of an era, Sorokin had identified it as the termination of a sensate culture and a time of transition into an ideational one. When a culture passed from one dominant system of truth to another it was always accompanied by a breakdown in values and meaning, with disruption of relationships, loss of family life and a disintegration of culture itself. Sorokin opened the first chapter of his book with the claim that,

on the basis of a vast body of evidence every important aspect of the
life, organization, and the culture of Western society is in
...extraordinary crisis.... Its body and mind are sick and there is
hardly a spot on its body which is not sore, nor any nervous fiber
which functions soundly.... We are seemingly between two epochs,
the dying Sensate culture of our magnificent yesterday and the coming Ideational culture of the creative tomorrow.[18]

Decline of a Sensate Culture

Five decades later we see the metastasis of Sorokin's prognosis of life
in the West. We experience it in our lonely, anxious and stressed lives,
in the homeless, in crime-ridden cities and a ravaged environment. It
seems that the creative period Sorokin expected has been slow in arriving. Over half a century after he wrote these words, there are signs of
renewed interest in the spiritual, not only among the cults and funda-
mentalists, but in mainline churches and in alternative approaches to
the spiritual life, such as home liturgies, group meditation, sweat lodges,
vision quests and shamanic journeys. The ecology movement is even
finding its way into the churches and synagogues and hopefully will initiate the creativity needed to avoid the impending destruction of life on
this planet.

What Ortega saw as European demoralization sixty years ago is
endemic to industrialized nations at the end of this century. For the
most part, the average citizen is still locked into dull, boring occupations
as a spectator. Divorced from nature, we madly and mindlessly control
and destroy the world as extensions of the machine. Students carry guns
and knives to school, corporations label longtime workers as "surplus"
in downsizing their operations. Society in general is afflicted by crime
and greed tearing our cities apart, while drugs, guns and television fill
the vacuum in the lives of the young. Mechanical metaphors are used in
medicine, in describing animal and plant life and in attempting to
replace humans with artificial intelligence. A mechanical philosophy of
life dominates our computerized educational and medical systems. Six
distinguished scientist took part in a twenty-hour PBS program in June
1994 entitled "A Glorious Accident," referring to humans as accidental
arrivals on this planet.

An example of our monolithic, mechanistic thinking in medicine came to my attention recently. The American Cancer Society (ACS) has blacklisted the remarkable work of Gaston Naessens. Naessens, a Canadian biologist, has discovered a very promising, nontoxic treatment for cancer, AIDS and other immune deficiencies. American doctors, rather than exploring his work, remain locked into the powerful money-making tactics of modern medicine. His blacklisting by the ACS and legal restrictions imposed by the Canadian Health Association are indicative of the hold that the profit motive has on our medical system.[19]

The crisis we face was poignantly described by D. H. Lawrence:

> We are perishing for lack of fulfillment of our greater needs, we are cut off from the great sources of our inward nourishment and renewal, sources which flow eternally in the universe. Vitally the human race is dying. It is like a great uprooted tree, with its roots in the air. We must plant ourselves again in the universe.[20]

The Integral Culture of Fifth-Century Greece

My search in graduate school for a more holistic approach to science led me to courses in the Posterior and Prior Analytics of Aristotle. Here I gained insight into the revolution modern science would undergo if it were rerooted in the soil of ancient Greece from which it originated. The world of the ancients was very different from our own. Their integrated pursuit of wisdom and truth, of happiness and the good life, and of concern for the welfare of society is now only a distant memory. They were fed from the myths, epics, rituals and Mysteries (secrets of the initiates into cosmic wisdom), by what D. H. Lawrence called "inward nourishment and renewal, sources which flow eternally in the universe." Aristotle's world, alive with cosmic wisdom, was also intent on a truly scientific approach to the reality of a world of the senses, so as to yield certitude through the observation and experience of nature.

I was encouraged to find confirmation of my thinking about Greek science in Erwin Schrödinger's *Nature and the Greeks*. There he claimed that modern science "very truly revived and continued ancient science and philosophy" and needed "the highly flexible and open-minded spirit that pervaded antiquity." Because Newtonian physics, with its atomistic matter, has been superseded by relativity and quantum theory, he argues, the "present crisis in modern basic science points to the necessity of revising its foundation."[21] In his opinion "the philosophy of the ancient Greeks attracts us at this moment because never before or since, anywhere in the world, has anything like their highly advanced and articulated system of knowledge and speculation been established."[22]

Schrödinger quotes Benjamin Farrington on the disastrous results of disregarding the historical roots of our way of thinking, for "a great part of the…superstition of educated men consists of knowledge which has broken loose from its historical moorings."[23] Reconnecting science with its roots could save it from its frightful limitations which:

> …gives a lot of factual information, puts all our experience in a mag-
> nificently consistent order, but it is ghastly silent about all the sundry
> that is really near to our heart, that really matters to us. It cannot tell
> us a word about red and blue, bitter and sweet, physical pain and
> physical delight, it knows nothing of beautiful and ugly, good or bad,
> God and eternity. Science sometimes pretends to answer questions in
> these domains, but the answers are very often so silly that we are not
> inclined to take them seriously.[24]

Aristotelian Science

In several publications Schrödinger has quoted the Greek scholar John Burnett, who says that an adequate description of science is "thinking about the world in the Greek way,"[25] and Theodor Gomperz on the intellectual necessity of studying ancient science:

> To ignore the past is here not merely undesirable, but simply impos-
> sible. You need not know of the doctrines and writings of the great
> masters of antiquity, of Plato and Aristotle, you need never have
> heard their names, none the less you are under the spell of their au-
> thority. Not only has their influence been passed on by those who
> took over from them in ancient and in modern times, our entire
> thinking, the logical categories in which it moves, the linguistic pat-
> terns it uses (being therefore dominated by them)—all this is in no
> small degree an artifact and is, in the main, the product of the good
> thinking of antiquity. We must, indeed, investigate this process of
> becoming in all thoroughness, lest we mistake for primitive what is
> the result of growth and development, and for natural what is actu-
> ally artificial.[26]

What would it mean to modern science to be reconnected with its origin in the science of the ancients? What would reinstate science as an integral part of the Great Conversation? What would it mean to move from a Sensate to an Ideational or Integral Culture? Certainly it does not mean a return to belief in a geocentric universe or in the spontaneous generation of life or other limited perceptions of the natural world held in the fifth century BCE. It could mean, as it has for Arthur Zajonc, a physicist at Amherst College, appreciating ancient wisdom through "the learned and probing mind of Aristotle," which was "bent on illuminating and enumerating the entire cosmos, its contents, structure and Creator by the methodical brilliance of the human mind alone."[27] Aristotle developed a methodology in his general science of nature, both logical and experiential but pre-mathematical, not dependent on experiments or instruments. Science for him was certain knowledge of things through their proper causes. The causes were not just material and efficient causes, the matter in motion of modern science.

For Aristotle there are four ways to know the "why" of things. The material cause is "that out of which a thing comes to be," as the marble from which a statue is sculpted. The formal cause is the organizing principle or archetype, the design in the mind of the sculptor. The efficient cause is the primary source of the change or coming to rest, the artist who sculpts the statue. The final cause is the end or "that for the sake of which a thing is done"—the finished statue.[28]

Omission of the formal and final causes has left modern science in a fragmented world devoid of mind, spirit and meaning. The need to know all four causes is common sense. Today there are a number of scientists calling for a renewal of such common sense. They are sparking a renewal of dialogue which could contribute to a future Ideational or Integral culture in the West.

Ideational System of Truth

It seems to me that the vigorous growth in our midst of the ecology movement is a sign and a promise of a developing Ideational System. Physicist Brian Swimme and geologian Thomas Berry are frontrunners among advocates of this growing movement to save planet earth. Their book *The Universe Story* is a profound attempt to awaken academia, the Church and all who will listen to a new story of the universe. This story, according to Thomas Berry reveals "the universe as the primary sacred reality," which enables us to "become sacred" by participation in "the sacred dimension of the cosmos." We can recover our sense of the sacred, Berry says, only by appreciating "the universe beyond ourselves and our role in the universe." He claims that the universe itself is "the norm of authenticity of every spiritual as well as every physical activity within the universe."[29]

Biologist Rupert Sheldrake calls for "a new renaissance" to let us be "reborn into a living world". "As soon as we allow ourselves to think of the world as alive, we recognize that a part of us knew this all along. It is like emerging from winter into spring. We can begin to reconnect our mental life with our own direct intuitive experiences of nature."[30] The best selling author and lecturer Joan Chittister expresses a similar appeal in her book, *The Illuminated Life*. "To be a contemplative, it is necessary, to walk through nature softly, to be in tune with the rhythm of life, to learn from the cycles of time, to listen to the heartbeat of the Universe, to love nature, to protect nature. And to discover in nature the presence and the power of God."[31]

An Integral System of Truth

The claim that the universe is a primary sacred reality may seem simplistic in the light of Aristotle's extensive and comprehensive logical, epistemological, structural and metaphysical approach to reality. It begins to dawn on me that the perception of the earth as primary may be the prelude needed for dialogue between and synthesis of Western thought and the monumental achievements of modern science and technology. Could this be a move into the next Integral Culture and the fulfillment of Hutchins's dream of a future civilization "even greater than that of the Greeks"?

The realization of such a vision was the hope of another philosopher and scientist, Rudolf Steiner (1861–1925). This long-neglected scholar, genius in many fields, came to my attention through the ecology movement as the founder of biodynamic farming. Steiner is a guide to two outstanding contributors to the Great Conversation, Johann Wolfgang von Goethe and Thomas Aquinas. Steiner's study of Goethe's scientific work is only now being recognized as a revolutionary alternative to a materialistic, mechanistic worldview.

In his deep appreciation of Thomas Aquinas, expressed in a three-lecture series entitled *The Redemption of Thinking*, Steiner called for a renewal of science that "does not hesitate to reintroduce into our own day the great thoughts which have played so vital a part in the evolution of humanity-such as those of the Scholastics—and apply them to all that the scientific outlook of our own day has discovered."[32]

Thomas Aquinas's enormous contribution to the Great Conversation is apparent in the abundant references to him in the Syntopicon. His summation of the wisdom of the Greeks, especially of the works of Aristotle, integrated with the truths of the Christian faith, made a profound mark on the intellectual life of the West in establishing the one truth of faith and science. Aquinas and his teacher, Albert the Great, are responsible for the integration of ancient science and philosophy with the theology of the Middle Ages into a synthesis that was the seedbed for modern science and made the thirteenth century into a second Integral Culture.

An Integral Culture of the Future?

What are the hopes for such an integration of faith and science today? In the 1980s I saw a sign of hope in the comprehensive and profoundly challenging book of Morris Berman, *The Reenchantment of the World*. R. D. Laing finds in it "the seeds from which a rediscovery and renewed understanding of our enchanted world and of ourselves may grow."[33] In 1991, Richard Tarnas's magnificent book, *The Passion of the Western Mind*, offered another beacon light. His chapter on "The Awakening of the Scholastics" is a timely historical account of the thirteenth-century integration of the Greek and Christian world views, of faith and reason, of nature and spirit, a model for Rudolf Steiner's challenge to apply the "great thought" of the Scholastics to our modern world view. Tarnas explains that "In Aquinas, the forces at work in the immediately previous centuries came to full articulation. In his relatively brief life he would forge a world view that dramatically epitomized the ... turning of Western thought on its axis, to a new direction of which the modern mind would be the heir and trustee."[34] A similar evolution of Western consciousness is Steiner's challenge. Tarnas also responds to D. H. Lawrence's indictment by concluding that "*the deepest passion of the Western mind has been to reunite with the ground of its being.*"[35] A significant contribution to this reunion with the *"ground of its being"* I find in Tarnas's closing recognition of the West's strong feminist movement, which is at the same time a response to Hutchins's dream that we create a civilization far more lasting than that of the Greeks because far more just:

> Today we are experiencing something that looks very much like the death of modern man, indeed that looks very much like the death of Western man. Perhaps the end of "man" himself is at hand. But man is not a goal. Man is something that must be overcome-and fulfilled, in the embrace of the feminine.[36]

Another sign of hope I find among the bestsellers in the *New York Times Book Review*. William Bennett's *The Book of Virtues*, Thomas Moore's *Care of the Soul* and Joan W. Anderson's *Where Angels Walk* have all been on the list for over forty weeks. Bennett wrote *The Book of Virtues*, advertised as "moral stories adapted from the Greeks, the Bible, folklore and elsewhere," to encourage moral literacy among the young. He introduces it with the following remarkable quotation from Plato:

> You know that the beginning is the most important part of any work, especially in the case of a young and tender thing, for this the time in which the character is being formed and the desired impression is more readily taken... Anything received into the mind at that age is likely to become indelible and unalterable, and therefore it is most important that the tales which the young first hear should be models of virtuous thoughts.[37]

There are also notes of hope for a revolution in the way scientists view reality, which I have documented in the chapter "A New Biology: Barbara McClintock and an Emerging Holistic Science."[38] Another outstanding scientist calling for a new consciousness, a new imagination, a new metaphysics is Arthur Zajonc, in his article in the 1994 book *New Metaphysical Foundations of Modern Science*. Zajonc calls for a synthesis of insights from quantum theory and chaos dynamics with the science of Goethe and Rudolf Steiner.[39] In the same volume, Nobel laureate George Wald, at the end of his long career in biology at Harvard University questions his former, commonly held belief that mind is a "late development in the evolution of living things." He concludes that the "universe is life-breeding because the persuasive presence of mind had guided it to be so."[40]

Among the scientists whose creativity seems especially to flow from a rich understanding of Greek science and a desire for a synthesis with modern science is the Nobel laureate, Ilya Prigogne, in his and Isabel Stenger's *Order Out of Chaos*. Their knowledge of philosophy, especially that of the Greeks, is for me a real beacon that the Great Conversation may again become a conscious part of Western culture. I close with their understanding of Aristotle's science, as a portent of the future:

> In any case, for an Aristotelian it is more interesting to know why a process occurs than to describe how it occurs, or rather, these two aspects are indivisible. One of the main sources of Aristotle's thinking was the observation of embryonic growth, a highly organized process in which interlocking, although apparently independent, events participate in a process that seems to be part of some global plan. Like the developing embryo, the whole of Aristotelian nature is organized according to final causes. The purpose of all change, if it is in keeping with the nature of things, is to realize in each being the perfection of its intelligible essence. Thus this essence, which in the case of living creatures is at one and the same time their final, formal, and effective cause, is the key to the understanding of nature. In this sense the "birth of modern science," the clash between the Aristotelians and Galileo, is a clash between two forms of rationality.[41]

Conclusion

The choice is ours. Shall it be a rationality based on matter in motion, on quantity and number, on a world stripped of values, life, mind and the human person—continuing our planetary exploitation and degradation? Shall we continue in our monotonous jobs with lives that have retreated into "the oblivion provided by drugs, television and tranquilizers?"[42] while we export Coke, McDonald's fries, designer jeans and fighter planes into a decaying world order? Do we opt for the delusional world scientists are manufacturing in their computers?

Or shall we choose to recover, nurture, celebrate and share our Western heritage? Shall we seize this unique moment in history for the reenchantment of the world with the colors of the rainbow, the delight of a sunset, the song of a bird, consciousness, the sacred, and the divine? Shall we choose as our model the mysterious and magical progression of a cell dividing and differentiating into the marvel of a chick or an oak tree? Shall we humble ourselves to let nature be our teacher and guide in a relational, interconnected, holistic world so that we can again entertain the idea that it is wisdom, not science and technology that is our human project? I believe with Alvin Toffler that *Order Out of Chaos* can symbolize a "historic transformation in science," can be "a lever for changing science itself, for compelling us to reexamine its goals, its methods, its epistimology—its world view"[43] and thus be a response to wisdom's challenge.

3.

Liberal Education
A Dominican Challenge

$\mathcal{T}$he plight of education in the United States is much in the news these days as politicians, educators and parents propose diverse remedies for a failed system. Advocates for vouchers, magnet schools, home schooling and smaller classes in public and private schools miss the heart of the problem. The loss of liberal education throughout the educational system and the intellectual bankruptcy of universities have left education without real guidelines for reform. Scientism, relativism and nihilism have made the search for truth through education seem futile. This plight is a challenge to Dominicans, as our motto Veritas puts us on record as seekers of the truth. Dominic's bequest to us "to search for truth and to become free"[1] is at the heart of liberal education.

The prophetic educator Robert Maynard Hutchins spent almost fifty years of the twentieth century trying to establish the ideal of liberal education in the U.S. As president of the University of Chicago from 1929 to 1945, he challenged educators across the land to return to the liberal arts as a cornerstone of Western civilization. Hutchins's prophetic writings on this subject were a beacon for me during my years of teaching, and are a guide to me now as I write this article.

The Purpose of Education

"It must be remembered," Hutchins said in a 1935 radio address, "the purpose of education is not to fill the minds of students with facts;

it is not to reform them, or amuse them, or make them expert technicians in any field. It is to teach them to think, if that is possible, and to think always for themselves. Democratic government rests on the notion that the citizens will think for themselves. It is of the highest importance that there should be some places where they can learn how to do it."[2]

"[The] Western devotion to the liberal arts and liberal education," Hutchins concluded, "must have been largely responsible for the emergence of democracy as an idea."[3] This is a call to Dominicans to reflect on Dominic's genius in founding an order devoted to study and to a democratic form of government. We also need to take seriously Timothy Radcliffe's recent reminder: "The time has come to renew the love affair between the Order and study."[4]

Hutchins struggled to make the University of Chicago into a center of learning modeled on the great universities of the Middle Ages. He was convinced that a university can fulfill its mission as "a symbol of human integrity, a trustee for civilization, an intellectual community"[5] only if its students have been well prepared to read, write and calculate, and are introduced to the great heritage of Western civilization. He therefore often addressed the need for universal liberal education to instill the discipline and sensitivity that make the life of the mind possible, to replace the social, recreational and custodial roles now making up much of universal schooling.

Hutchins's mission, "To see knowledge, life, the world, or truth whole," the object of a university,[6] was not understood by a faculty whose specializations had isolated them from one another and made dialogue among them inconceivable. The role of the university in restoring the kind of conversation that prepares citizens to think critically about and take responsibility for issues that make for the common good is also impeded by students and educators who erroneously think education is completed by schooling. Years of boring textbooks, nonsensical tests on factual data, and a deplorable grading system, plus the onslaught of an advertising industry focused on making students into producers and consumers, have left the majority with little or no interest in intellectual concerns.

University presidents did not escape Hutchins's blame for the loss of liberal education in America: "Here the great criminal was Mr. Eliot, who as President of Harvard applied his genius, skill and longevity to the task of robbing American youth of their cultural heritage. Since he held that there were no such things as good or bad subjects of study, his laudable effort to open the curriculum to good ones naturally led him to open it to bad ones and finally to destroy it altogether." Hutchins concluded that it is possible for one to get an education in an American university, but to do so one would have "to be so bright and know so much" that it would not be needed.[7]

Hutchins's heroic and courageous educational reform over sixteen years at the University of Chicago was eliminated by the graduate faculty the year after he left. But it was not without fruit. Together with his colleague Mortimer J. Adler and the staff of the Encyclopedia Britannica, he initiated the *Great Books of the Western World* Program, which resulted in widespread adult study groups. Through such groups and the Center for the Study of Democratic Institutions in California, Hutchins promoted the kind of independent rational discourse and disciplined debate that brought the great universities of the thirteenth century to be true centers of learning, academies of creative thinking.

What a shame that we now allow our country to lose the ideals on which it was founded. For the first time in world history, an affluent country has universal schooling, universal suffrage and potential leisure time for all its citizens to have the kind of liberal education that enabled our Founding Fathers to conceive the Declaration of Independence and our Constitution. Their plan for a democratic way of life can only be sustained by a liberally educated citizenry. As long as schools are primarily engaged in job and career training, they provide little as an antidote to our materialistic twentieth-century culture.

A Call to Dominicans

Hutchins's failure to achieve his dream for the University of Chicago is indicative of the odds against finding an ideal university in the anti-intellectual U.S. His commitment to continue "the brilliant leadership of the University of Paris"[8] is a call to us Dominicans, as it was our brother, Thomas Aquinas, who was the preeminent exponent of that medieval university. Who else than Dominicans should keep this ideal aloft at a time in our history when Hutchins and other prophets of our day warn, "The world is probably closer to disintegration now than at any time since the fall of the Roman Empire."[9]

The exemplary University of Paris, established c.1200, was unique and preeminent among the universities of the Middle Ages. Devoted exclusively to philosophy and theology, it was specially suited to its role of examining the "character of reality as a whole."[10] It was here that St. Thomas grappled with and integrated two apparently polar views of reality: the theology of Holy Scripture and the science of the pagan Aristotle. The German philosopher Josef Pieper claimed "there was no other place in the Western world which offered the young man of twenty more favorable conditions for his own development than the University of Paris. Here the most important teachers were located, the most radical opposition; here was challenge, creative resistance, and immediate resonance."[11]

While teaching at the University of Paris, Thomas "cultivated the oral *disputatio* to an extent hitherto unknown."[12] It seems that he invented a particular form of "free" discussion on subjects chosen by those in attendance. The enormous energy he put into such discussions, which he held twice a week, suggests that he must have enjoyed this form of teaching. Richard Tarnas captures the genius of St. Thomas, who "embraced the new learning, mastered all the available texts, and committed himself to the Herculean intellectual task of comprehensively uniting the Greek and Christian worldviews in one great summa, wherein the scientific and philosophical achievements of the ancients would be brought within the overarching vision of Christian theology. More than the sum of its parts, Aquinas's philosophy was a live compound that brought the diverse elements of its synthesis to new expression—as if he had recognized an implicit unity in the two streams and then set about drawing it out by sheer force of intellect."[13]

Where today is such learning possible? I was fortunate in being introduced to the great ideas of the Western world in the classes of a history professor at our Dominican college in Memphis and in several courses in the philosophy department at the University of Notre Dame. I spent two fruitful years with the Brookings Institute at Rhodes College, in dialogue with teachers and community leaders about improving life in Memphis. The Albertus Magnus Lyceum at River Forrest, Chicago, offered me an opportunity for discussions relative to integrating modern science and philosophy. Through current Dominican planning for "closer union" I hope to find others who will join me in rediscovering liberal education. We could begin by studying the guidelines for a true education in Mortimer J. Adler's book *Reforming Education, The Opening of the American Mind.* [14]

This chapter was previously published in *Dominican Ashram* Vol. 17 No. 3 (September 1998).

4.

Science, Education, and the Christian Person

Those willing to think deeply about the problems of our times, to face the reality of the burdens of fear, of impoverishment, of racial prejudice, of ignorance, of miseries of one kind or another, with which we moderns are afflicted, must admit that modern science and technocracy are not unmixed blessings. Mauriac said he believed in twentieth-century science, in the progress which it promised, until one day he saw a carload of German Jewish children headed for one of the concentration camps and for slaughter.[1] This, he knew, was not progress. It has even been claimed that it is through science that we have fallen into our current plight. Written a century before the advent of jet planes and fifty-megaton bombs, the words of Thomas Peacock sound prophetic. According to him, the results of modern science consist almost totally in elements of mischief:

> See the complications and refinements of modes of destruction.... See collisions and wrecks and every mode of disaster by land and by sea, resulting chiefly from the insanity for speed, in those who for the most part have nothing to do at the end of the race, which they run as if they were so many Mercuries speeding with messages from Jupiter. Look at our scientific drainage, which turns refuse into poison.... Look at our scientific machinery, which has discovered domestic manufacture which has substituted rottenness for strength in the thing made, and physical degradation in crowded towns for

healthy and comfortable country life…. The day would fail, if I should attempt to enumerate the evils which science has inflicted on mankind. I almost think it is the ultimate destiny of science to exterminate the human race.[2]

Short of the actuality of humans destroying themselves with the aid of the instruments provided through modern scientific venture, there are other horrors that humans have contemplated and are in danger of bringing to fruition. "The 'anti-Utopias' and the *Brave New World*s, the *Nineteen Eighty-four*s project into the future a vision of society more dark than the deepest pessimism the ancient world ever conjured up," warns Barbara Ward.[3] These books arouse in us a much greater concern for what modern science and technology have done to humans than for the way they have changed human surroundings. Many persons are now doomed to spend their lives in industrial slums and factories, cut off from contact with the soil, with the sweet-smelling honeysuckle, with the beauty of the brilliant red and yellow autumn leaves, with the playful scampering to and fro of the chipmunks, with the early dawn choruses of mockingbirds, catbirds, and jays, with the silence of forest life at midday away from the frantic hum and buzz of our modern cities.

There are some people even more deprived than those involuntarily cut off from nature. These, Gerald Vann writes, are "the people who do live in contact with Nature, who are free to walk in field and forest, to listen to the voice of river or sea, but who in fact are blind and deaf to these things: having eyes they see not, and having ears they hear not, because psychologically speaking they are dead, and they are dead because, as we shall see, they have lost the faculty of wonder."[4] Rene Dubos observes that "Many generations of scientific discovery seem to have dulled the primeval appetite for wonder,"[5] for, as Walter Grompius has said, in "the triumphal march of the practical sciences, the magic of life has been crowded out."[6] The world does not lack for wonders, but humanity is seriously sick for lack of wonder. Modern science explains a human, a flea and a nasturtium each as a different arrangement of the deoxyribonucleic acid molecule, DNA. The DNA-defined human in turn renounces the childlike attitude of reverent wonder that prompted Blake to write:

> To see a world in a grain of sand,
> And heaven in a wild flower,
> Hold infinity in the palm of the hand
> And eternity in a hour.[7]

As modern science strips the mystery from the grain of sand and takes heaven out of the wild flower, humans blindly turn their dull, dispirited thoughts on themselves and their neighbors. J. B. S. Haldane was thus blinded when he wrote, "I am far more interested in the problems of biochemistry than in the question of what, if anything, will happen to me when I am dead…. When I am dead, I propose to be dissected."[8] How different from the words of Shakespeare: "What a piece of work is man! How noble in reason! How infinite in faculty! In form and moving, how express and admirable! In action, how like an angel! In apprehension, how like a god! The beauty of the world! The paragon of animals!"[9] Is a human an animal, an angel, a god, or is one merely a biochemical? The answer we give to the question "What is a human being?" will greatly determine what we make of ourselves in the brief span of time given to us on this earth. Our outlook on the world largely determines our viewpoint of ourselves and others.

Why are people deaf and blind to their own nature? To the mysteries of a leaf or of a star? How have they come to their present state? Where did they get the drab picture of our twentieth-century world as a meaningless conglomeration of random, moving atoms? It is conjured up as the modern scientist sits watching index needles, revolving drums and sensitive plates. Withdrawn from the nature he attempts to explain, he looks only at the aspect of nature that is heavily controlled by and geared to the artificial environment of his own design. From the pointer readings, the "little shivers and wiggles"[10] of his apparatus, from these symbolic manifestations of the world he wants to know, he sketches the world as it appears to him. The results are strange, to say the least. Here is Bertrand Russell's account: "Academic philosophers… believed that the world is a unity…. The most fundamental of my intellectual beliefs is that this is rubbish. I think the universe is all spots and jumps, without unity, without continuity, without coherence or orderliness…. Indeed, there is little but prejudice and habit to be said for the view that there is a world at all."[11] If scientists accepted Russell's conclusion, actually there would be no point in any scientific investigation or explanation. A non-existent world is scarcely a suitable object of study. The modern scientist seems to be in Alice's dilemma as she asked the Cheshire Cat:

> "Would you tell me, please, which way I ought to walk from here?"
> "That depends a good deal on where you want to get to," said the Cat.
> "I don't much care where...." said Alice.
> "Then it doesn't matter which way you walk," said the Cat.
> ".... so long as I get *somewhere,*" Alice added as an explanation.
> "Oh, you're sure to do that," said the Cat, "if you only walk long enough."[12]

It is of the very nature of the human mind to want to move toward some goal, some end or purpose, even though the person involved, like Alice, denies that he has any particular one in mind. The following fable by William Beck[13] may be a little overdrawn, but it illustrates the point that every human, including the scientist, must at least implicitly have a goal. The main character in this fable is Sigmund, a fairly typical modern scientist, except for the fact that Sigmund has an unusually strong faith in his ability to reach certitude through experimental science. He knows that all experiments, up to his time, have failed in certitude because of some uncontrolled element in the experiment. If sufficient care were taken, if every possible eventuality were foreseen, surely, he believes, an experimental animal could yield the kind of certitude he so devotedly seeks. He proposes to perform a perfect experiment in which every element of uncertainty would be ruled out. The frustrations he encounters with his experimental animal, the amoeba, are carefully recounted, and finally all is in readiness. Months of anxious work have brought on a stomach ulcer, colitis, and he knows that he is near a nervous breakdown, but he must push on, for he is close to his goal. The author's description of Sigmund at this stage seems to me significant of what may happen to anyone who loses him- or herself in the finite: "Sitting there at his desk, Sigmund looked rather like a plant that had been grown in a cave."[14] The dramatic conclusion of Sigmund's experiment comes as two inadequately insulated wires on badly overloaded electric circuits cause a flash of fire to ignite vapor seeping out of a poorly constructed solvent locker. Sigmund and the entire science building are burned to a crisp. Sigmund has given his life in his search for certitude, which according to Beck was actually a search for the Infinite. The fact that Sigmund failed is related to the fact that his knowledge of science was as unsound as his knowledge of himself. Beck says of him: "Had it not been for ill fortune, he might have achieved his mission and immortality—or so it would seem. As it turned out, however, Sigmund's sublime moment turned him into a cinder instead of a saint."[15]

The analogy of the scientist to the saint is not completely unfounded. Isn't there a resemblance, call it a caricature if you like, between the dedication of the scientist and that of the saint? Both are looking for the Certitude that alone can satisfy the human heart. The scientist willingly gives up his time, his dreams, his hopes, in a word, himself, in pursuit of his goal. Is it any wonder that the world bestows on him the role of "wise man, the Magi of our day," provides him money and time to retire to his monastic laboratory to contemplate the mysteries of nature and then accepts him as the seer and the diviner of reality? [16]

Is it not the scientist who today bears witness to the following words of St. John of the Cross?

> To win to the knowledge of all, wish not to know anything.
> To win to the tasting of all, wish not to taste anything.
> To come to the possession of all, wish not to possess anything.
> To win to the being of all, wish not to be anything.

The scientist is willing to give up the knowledge of all except his one tiny specialty; he is willing to forego the taste of pleasure and social life; he is not ambitious for wealth; he will even give up health of mind and body—for what? In order to arrive at Certitude in the one area in which he thinks it is to be found. And It is there. God is everywhere. But the scientist is doomed to failure because he has stripped nature to the dimensions of his own thoughts about the world; he denies that there is any more to her than what he has unearthed and can control. His sense of wonder gone, the modern man next denies that there is any mystery in the natural order and finally repudiates the supernatural, thereby cutting himself off from God. "Where there is no God, there is no man," Berdyaev wrote.

If the modern scientist does believe in God, he is pitifully silent as his colleague Julian Huxley ascends the pulpit: "With the substitution of knowledge for ignorance...and the growth of control...God is simply fading away, as the Devil has faded before him, and the pantheons of the ancient world, and the nymphs and the local spirits.... A faint trace of God, half metaphysical and half magic, still broods over the world, like the smile of a cosmic Cheshire Cat. But the growth of psychological knowledge will rub even that from the universe."[17] We hear in Huxley's words the modern scientist's testimony that he has cut himself off from God." Let us now bring modern science to the witness stand to see what retribution has been demanded of humankind in return. We radically remove God from His creation, but only to be uprooted ourselves in the process. According to the data of some years ago:

> In the United States during 1956, close to one million persons were hospitalized for mental disease, more than ten million were thought to be in need of psychiatric teatment, and there was reason to believe that a good percentage of the total population would spend at least part of their lives in a mental institution. In 1955, 16,760 persons were known to have committed suicide and not a few of those who had died a violent death had directly or indirectly been victims of abnormal or antisocial behavior. On the other hand, it was considered a great medical advance that tranquilizer drugs had become available to all. Three out of ten prescriptions were for these drugs in 1956, and more than a billion tablets of meprobamate alone were sold in a year![18]

Would we not declare a national emergency if any other disease reached such proportions? G. K. Chesterton once observed that it was strange that we should see sublime inspiration in the ruins of an old cathedral and see none in the ruins of humanity. While our skyscrapers go higher and higher, it is time that we look at what our toil and trouble is doing to us as we launch this bigger and better world. We reduce nature to the mechanical models and mathematical equations of the laboratory and classrooms and end up disintegrated ourselves, because our fellow humans measure us by the same yardstick. D. H. Lawrence has well expressed our dilemma: "We are perishing for lack of fulfillment of our greater needs, we are cut off from the great sources of our inward nourishment and renewal, sources which flow eternally in the universe. Vitally, the human race is dying. It is like a great uprooted tree, with its roots in the air. We must plant ourselves again in the universe."[19]

What can education do in the face of such a dilemma? As educators, can we help humans to relocate themselves in nature, to reclaim their sanity and their health? Can we fulfill our own function, to bring humans along the road of the arts and sciences toward the Wisdom that will set them free? One hundred years ago Longfellow wrote:

> Were half the power that fills the world with terror,
> Were half the wealth bestowed on camps and courts,
> Given to redeem the human mind from error,
> There were no need of arsenals or forts. [20]

Where shall we begin? If humans are to reclaim the job of thinking from the machine, if humans are to be free to search for that Truth which makes them free, among the imperatives must be the creation of a different atmosphere in our schools. "The frenzied tempo, the confusion, the activism of modern life, its hatred or fear of silence and stillness" is like a death house for the life of the mind. Gerald Vann says,

> Education could set itself to combat this state of affairs; but in fact it
> is itself too often determined by the prevailing atmosphere; and becomes itself a frenzied rush, a scramble for examination marks, for
> degrees and diplomas; it becomes so activist that there is no time to
> think and live; it becomes itself so utilitarian that it defeats its own
> essential ends; it may provide a great deal of information; it can hardly hope to be a royal road to a deep and vivid culture. [21]

A school that provides a homey atmosphere for students away from home, that concerns itself with human problems, that is interested in the human need for creativeness, that helps one to find roots in nature, is preparing to meet the challenge of the times. If we can lead our students back into the fields to lie again in the rich soft carpet of green grasses that provide so many benefits to humans, or take them to the seashore to see the feeding of the fiddler crab and the stealthy movements of the ant lion, and teach them to rejoice again in the song of the bird, we may bring them to realize that their problem is far less that of fighting nature than of fighting for nature. Joseph Wood Krutch in his provocative book *The Great Chain of Life*, claims that in this age of mass education and conformism, students may even have to relearn the basic lessons of their own dignity and individuality from the animals.

> If we are ever to regain a respect for ourselves it may be that we shall
> regain it by the discovery that the animals themselves exhibit, in rudimentary form, some of the very characteristics and capacities whose
> existence in ourselves we had come to doubt because we had

convinced ourselves that they did not exist in the creatures we assumed to be our ancestors. Even if man is no more than an animal, the animal may be more than we once thought of him.[22]

Life outdoors is healthful for the body and tranquilizing for the spirit. In a recent public lecture Werner von Braun said that if American youth are to be educated, we must create an atmosphere of study in our schools. Televisions and cars must be removed from the campus. Without TV as a constant distractor, students might seek the outdoors for purposes other than the attainment of that much-desired and eagerly sought status symbol, the suntan. They might return from the outdoors with a tranquil spirit that makes study and meditation a possibility again, without tranquilizers.

Contact with nature could also restore to youth a sense of cosmic affiliation that would offset some of their anxieties and tensions. Children need to feel at home in their world, in God's world. They need to know that this is their home—one prepared for them by a loving and tender God. Jean Danielou says that before the time of Abraham, God had already made promises to all people. Through the regularity of the seasons, the promise of rain, through the soil and the fruits thereof, through a kind of cosmic liturgy, God had already made a covenant with humanity. Adults as well as youth could rediscover these truths, if they approached nature humbly and were attentive to her message. As Wordsworth put it:

> And hark how blithe the throstle sings!
> He too is no mean preacher.
> Come forth into the light of things,
> Let Nature be your teacher. [23]

Chesterton is a good example of a man in close contact with the reality of nature:

When Chesterton shook himself out of his reveries and gazed on reality, then miracles happened. Romance is always something brought to a thing, and Chesterton invested the whole world with the great goodness of his heart. Chesterton in contact with a thing, be it a lamppost or an umbrella, was like the fuse that ignites a Roman candle. Anything at all set his intelligence off on a brilliant fireworks of paradoxes that penetrated into the heart of reality. He was a symbolist, and the inner meaning of creatures was never hidden from his concentration. This world diaphanously let through the glories of another order, and Chesterton could see God in a gable. If his world looked like a pasteboard toy theatre created by a father for the sheer joy of his children, Chesterton could demonstrate that the analogy was strictly true. If the toy was out of order and deranged, the contrast fingered more sharply than ever the primeval origin of the world in goodness. [24]

How are the schools to develop leaders of such wisdom and vision who can help humanity to relocate itself in the world? How can individual teachers contribute to this enterprise? Teachers in the elementary schools might take their children out into the fields to discover the burrows of moles, the quick nervous movement of the towhee, the noiseless gliding of the water beetles over the surface of the water. Or, better still, students can be asked to write about their own adventures outdoors, to tell of the antics of the birds and bees that they have observed. The horned toad and the preying mantis brought into the classroom may well serve as invitations to the students to observe other animals in their natural habitats, where they will reveal themselves more fully.

In high school, boys' and girls' interest turns more toward themselves. They want to understand the changes in their own bodies and minds, which are closely related to the rhythms in nature. These changes in the adolescent are not so frightening to one who has seen and understood the natural rhythmic cycles in the lives of animals and of plants from season to season and from year to year. As a result of a deeper appreciation of the natural world, these students will see themselves less in the image of the machine, and more as the highest manifestation of organic life. Firsthand experience with animals and plants in the pond and on the plain will offset some of the effects of mechanization on young people and prepare them to accept themselves and others as creatures fashioned in the image and likeness of God, with some of the Divine freedom and daring to create.

At the college level, students who are re-rooted in the world of nature will again be prepared for the kind of scientific study that the genius of Aristotle and of St. Thomas left them as their heritage. If their lives have been enriched through a participatory encounter with the world of nature, with a basis in nature for their appreciation of the dignity of the human being and of the natural laws that provide for and protect them, students will be ready to undertake a Thomistic and truly scientific approach to the science of nature. This approach does not strip away wonder, but admits of more wonder and mystery as all the causes of natural things are carefully investigated. Humans will never succeed in exhausting the riches of a blade of grass, or of a flower petal, but they can gain much through an orderly approach to their study. Aristotle's and Thomas's conception of the universe as a hierarchical one, as a plenum, is in accord with a commonsense view of the natural world. It is less sophisticated, but not less true, than the highly technical and mechanical explanation of the world in terms of aggregates of atoms in blind and meaningless motion. There is an even greater challenge for college teachers to help students to recapture some of the wonder of childhood, to capitalize on their native curiosity in developing their imaginations, emotions and intellects, ultimately to awaken in them the vision of a Chesterton, a Pasteur, or a Teilhard.

Ultimately, an education in tune with nature and with the best traditions in the Western world will more fully nourish the Christian person who is in danger of becoming only a cog in a wheel of a massive impersonal society, of being regimented in schools, factories, armies and even in suburbia. Christian persons can thus keep alive the faculty of wonder that makes one first a contemplative in the world of nature. For the contemplator of nature, the windows of life will open onto infinite horizons in an atmosphere of mystery. If we bring our students to behold such a world, then the words of Daniel 12:3 will be applicable to us: "But the wise shall shine brightly like the splendor of the firmament, and those who lead the many to justice shall be like the stars forever." No violence need be done to a student's courses in modern experimental science while teachers supply for the deficiencies in a contemporary person's view of the world. Eminent contemporary biologists are trying to reinstate the organism as the focal point of a necessarily multi-level scientific approach to the world of living things. This could be accomplished more easily if graduate students had learned to know and appreciate the world of oak trees and lizards at an early age. Some outstanding scientists in all fields are beginning to realize the necessity of teaching each discipline within a historical and a philosophical perspective. Such a perspective is only acceptable to students who have understood the possibility of more than one view of a human being and of a flea.

This chapter appeared previously in *The Divine Synthesis: Lectures of The Conference on Christian Humanism 1961–1964*, Asheville, NC: Mount Mary, 1968.

5.

New or Traditional
Earth Spirituality?

$\mathcal{A}$t a recent General Chapter in my community, the theme of the keynote address, and a dominant influence throughout the sessions, was earth spirituality. But some sisters were distressed that earth spirituality was presented as though it superseded the gospel message as a basis for our decision making. At a previous Chapter, four years earlier, even more controversy was generated when another keynoter spoke on "the new cosmology," based on modern scientific revelations.

Resistance to this "new genesis" was exacerbated by the stated proposal for "developing our understanding of the earth's revelation of differentiation, interiority, communion" as a Chapter Act. Some felt that the interest of a minority was legislating a new spirituality for the entire community. My intent in this article is to point out the limitations of an empirically based "new cosmology" and to propose a renewal of a traditional "living cosmology" that is integral to both science and faith.

The modern scientific story of the earth is receiving much attention among religious men and women. The prophetic voices and dedicated ministries of Thomas Berry and Miriam Therese MacGillis have awakened religious to the great gift of God's creation, the biospheric earth. They especially alert us to its present plight, to our current and future responsibilities for our community property, and to the contribution we can make to change our outrageously wasteful way of life. According to Berry and MacGillis, we need to perceive the earth itself as sacred and primary, with humans as derivative. But it is the minor passing reference to God in this developing scientific creation story that causes concern and confusion.

Certainly the twentieth-century scientific vision of an expanding universe is impressive. It tells us that fifteen billion years ago, a "big bang" exploded the universe into existence, spawning time and space, energy and matter. A marvelous array of stars, galaxies and supernovas arose from the chaos and order along with our planet of rocks and mountains, springs and rivers, plants, animals and ourselves. This scientific account of a fertile matter evolving into a wondrous vast universe is an invitation for us to image and create new structures to replace our moribund institutions.

It is understandable that such an imaginative cosmic story would attract many religious active in solving the problems of societal and environmental degradation, especially when a silent institutional Church is intent on authority issues such as women's ordination, celibacy, homosexuality and abortion. On the one hand, the Church seems to be caught up in a dying twentieth-century materialistic culture; on the other, science offers an exciting narrative of a living and creative earth. Its enthusiasts propose this vision as a means for avoiding our present catastrophic road to extinction. Modern science and technology, however, have played a significant role in causing both the rise and the impoverishment of Western culture.

Today, modern science has largely displaced religion as the arbiter of truth in our culture. For all its promise, this has caused many religious, myself included, to question a scientific account of the origin of the universe as a replacement for our traditional Judeo-Christian creation story. Despite its popularity, the scientific story is a recent version of the beginning of the universe. It was only in 1992, at a physics meeting in Washington, D.C., that the announcement of the discovery of "ripples" in cosmic background radiation made headline news around the world. Stephen Hawking hailed it as the greatest discovery of the twentieth century. Without this "missing link," the big bang might well have gone the way of other discarded theories of modern science. Scientists greeted this finding with much jubilation, as they had no substitute theory to take its place.[1]

The enthusiasm of the press for the scientific revelation of the "birth of the universe" has contributed immensely to its influence. A burgeoning array of books on cosmology by mathematicians, astronomers and physicists has appeared, with titles such as *The Physics of Immortality; The God Particle; The Mind of God; The Astonishing Hypothesis: The Scientific Search for the Soul;* and *In the Beginning: The Birth of the Living Universe.* But this should raise concern for the prophetic, philosophical and theological roles that scientists now assume. They, like any special interest group, are taking advantage of their current prestige as an opportunity to market their views.

Not all scientists support the present popular story of the birth of the universe. Some are disturbed at the unproved assumptions necessary to sustain this theory; some pose questions of what preceded the big bang. Nobel laureate Leon Lederman aptly reminds us that when space and time tend toward zero at the big bang, "the equations we use to explain the universe break down and become meaningless" and "at this point we are just plumb out of science."[2] As physicist Paul Davies remarks, "if one insists on a reason for the big bang, then this reason must lie beyond physics."[3] Astronomer John D. Barrow acknowledges that the initial conditions of the universe lie beyond science and are "condemned to remain partially always within the realm of philosophy and theology."[4]

Two books challenging the "big bang" were published in 1995. *Beyond the Big Bang: Ancient Myth and the Science of Continuous Creation* by Paul A. Laviolette, president of an interdisciplinary research institute, labels the big bang theory a "positivist cosmology," which he summarizes as follows:

> (a) all that exists is the tangible physical universe; (b) its origin and workings can be entirely described by physical theory; (c) there is no need to invoke the presence of God or a metaphysical beyond in accounting for the existence of this elegant machine; and (d) unless God can be physically measured in some way, he does not exist.[5]

The second book, *Inventing a Universe*, is by Luc Brisson, director of the French National Center of Scientific Research, and Walter Meyerstein, a professor of philosophy at the University of Barcelona. They find a "big bang" cosmology, like Plato's *Timaeus,* an interpretation of the universe based on "remarkable mathematical theory." This kind of "scientific" knowledge, they explain, "ultimately rests on a set of irreducible and indemonstrable formulas, pure inventions of the human mind."[6] Their argument is based on Aristotle's insights about the nature of scientific knowledge. He disagreed with Plato's belief that the world is basically mathematical at its deepest level, and argued that mathematics is a product of the human mind and not a physical reality. Aristotle's empirical approach to a real natural world significantly influenced Western science up until the seventeenth century. An understanding of the difference between a science based on an organic, developing natural world and one constructed from mathematical equations is described in John D. Barrow's 1988 Gifford lectures, published under the title *Theories of Everything.*

> Aristotle draws a sharp dividing line between the activities of the physicist and those of the mathematician. The mathematician limits his enquiry to the quantifiable aspect of the world and so dramatically restricts what is describable in mathematical terms. Physics, for Aristotle, was far wider in scope and encompassed the earthy reality of sensible things. Whereas Plato had maintained that mathematics was the true and deep reality of which the physical world was but a pale reflection, Aristotle claimed mathematics to be but a superficial representation of a piece of physical reality. Such is the contrast between idealism and realism in the ancient world.[7]

The dispute between idealism and realism was fought again in the Middle Ages and continues today between the scientific cosmology based on Platonic mathematical theory and a much-neglected cosmology held by the Christian mystics of the twelfth to the fourteenth centuries. Their writings are replete with the consciousness of the earth as sacred, as a primary gift of God, as a way to knowledge of and intimacy with its Creator.

Fortunately, within the last fifteen years, a living cosmology that draws from these Christian mystics is being celebrated through mystery schools, especially those of Jean Houston and Creation Spirituality, as popularized by Matthew Fox. This movement, like that of the Rhineland mystics in the Middle Ages, erupts at a time when the insular institutional Church allows the laity and religious men and women to take over leadership.

After eight hundred years, the cosmic insights of Hildegard of Bingen are finally being heard. "It is God which humankind is then able to recognize in every living thing."[8] "God has arranged all things in the world in consideration of everything else."[9] Her concern for the earth is no less urgent than that of deep ecologists and ecofeminists today.

> The earth should not be injured. The earth should not be destroyed. As often as the elements of the world are violated by ill treatment, so God will cleanse them. God will cleanse them through the sufferings, through the hardships of humankind. All of creation God gives to humankind to use. But if this privilege is misused, God's justice permits creation to punish humanity.[10]

The twelfth century, blessed with the music, visions and writings of the incomparable Hildegard, was followed in the thirteenth century by the cosmic theology of Thomas Aquinas. These achievements inspired the marvelous poetry of Dante and the prophetic preacher Meister Eckhart. Eckhart's God was surely incarnate in the earth: "We must learn to penetrate things and find God there."[11] "God is a great underground river that no one can dam up and no one can stop." Eckhart was a precursor for a time-developmental universe heralded by "the new cosmology." "Now God creates all things but does not stop creating. God forever creates, and forever begins to create, and creatures are always being created, and in the process of beginning to be created."[12]

Thomas Aquinas, in his great synthesis of science and faith, wrote twelve commentaries on Aristotle's works based on an organic world (and none on Plato). Richard Tarnas, in his luminous book *The Passion of the Western Mind*, explains the significance of St. Thomas's thought.

> In Aquinas, the forces at work in the immediately previous centuries came to full articulation. In his relatively brief life he would forge a worldview that dramatically epitomized the high Middle Ages' turning of Western thought on its axis, to a new direction of which the modern mind would be the heir and trustee.[13]

Tarnas grasps the beauty and depth of St. Thomas's contribution to modern thought at a time when it is being neglected by the Church and by his own Dominican brothers and sisters. Aquinas's ability to integrate faith and the science of his time is a challenge to us, as faith today has little impact on contemporary culture, while modern science, allied to industry, government and the military, is adrift from morality, art and wisdom.

Aquinas is now available as a prophet of the environment in the recently published book *Sheer Joy: Conversations with Thomas Aquinas on Creation Spirituality* by Matthew Fox. He translated for the first time many of the biblical commentaries of St. Thomas and made his cosmic theology accessible "by asking contemporary questions and letting Thomas answer in his own words. The author of the foreword to *Sheer Joy*, the well-known biologist Rupert Sheldrake, finds St. Thomas a "great and visionary thinker" whose "strong sense of the spontaneity of life" "leads into an amazing realm of creative synthesis."[14] A twentieth-century visionary, Rudolf Steiner, calls for a science that "does not hesitate to introduce into our own day the great thoughts which have played so vital a part in the evolution of humanity such as those of the Scholastics—and apply them to all that the scientific outlook of our own day has discovered."[15]

I have tried to show that the "new cosmology" based on mathematics provides only an interim creation story to be replaced when mathematicians come up with equations for a more likely one. It is surely not a replacement for our traditional wisdom stories of creation. When scientists venture to write books about the mind of God, the soul and immortality, we realize that we, like the institutional Church, have neglected to live, love and proclaim the richness of our tradition. Is science invading the territory that the institutional church has deserted, while the laity is awakening to our rich mystical tradition, to a living cosmology integral to science and faith? Through mystery schools, creation spirituality and the wisdom traditions of native Americans and other ancient peoples, we can respond to Christopher Fry's challenge: "It takes so many thousand years to wake, But will you wake for pity's sake?"[16]

This chapter was printed in *Sisters Today* Vol. 69 No. 1 (January 1997).

6.

Thomas Aquinas
and the New Cosmology
Faith Encounters Science Anew

Why ask Thomas Aquinas for enlightenment about the new cosmology, a subject already controversial among religious women? His misunderstanding of women has caused many feminists to reject him altogether as an authority figure. Yet St. Thomas's great achievement in integrating faith with the most advanced science of his day (despite its pagan source) into a numinous medieval worldview is a challenge for any Christian struggling to accept a current cosmology based on modern science.

Few question that the growth and development of modern science and technology have contributed to the global crisis in ecology, sociology, education, economics, religion, and culture in general that now threatens planet earth. The intent of this paper is to bring Aquinas's enduring work on creation to bear on some of the troubling aspects of a cosmology based on modern science, and to consider the way his science of nature could enrich the creation story as a developing myth to move us to a sustainable future.

Before turning to St. Thomas for help in critiquing the emerging scientific story of the cosmos, I want to acknowledge the positive effect that the new cosmology or universe story has had on religious women. Since awakening to the tragic exploitation of our imperiled earth home, we religious women have made notable responses. Ecology learning centers, wilderness and sacred earth retreats, equinox and solstice celebrations, horticulture and permaculture courses, organic and biodynamic gardens, community-supported agriculture, sustainable farming projects and land trusts are among the many efforts toward sustainability now found on the properties of religious communities. These are not only hopeful signs of the changes that religious women are making in their personal lifestyle; they herald a revolution in consciousness that is desperately needed if the Western industrialized world is to be diverted from its suicidal course.

Problems with the New Cosmology

Elsewhere I have discussed problems with the new cosmology that have caused divisions among women religious.[1] Of concern to many is the place of God, of a Creator, in the accepted scientific account of the origin of the cosmos. To understand this problem we need to consider the mechanical philosophy that has developed over the last few centuries as a legacy from Isaac Newton and Rene Descartes. Their world as machine stripped the cosmos of life, mind and consciousness. Their earth, no longer a living organism, became a drab, dead world without color, taste, feeling, beauty, sensibility or meaning. The scientific method became the road to knowledge with mathematics as its language.

In a world in which the origin of the cosmos is explained by a few observations and bolstered by an array of assumptions based on mathematical equations, the need for a Creator is questionable. For Stephen Hawking, God is needed only to "wind up the clockwork" of this mechanical cosmos "and choose how to start it off."[2] Hawking even thinks he knows "the equations that govern human behavior."[3] Other equations, he thinks, can provide "understanding of how the big bang created everything in the universe."[4]

Medieval World View

St. Thomas lived in a different world. The thirteenth century was an age of faith, an age in which humans and nature were in close relationship with one another. St. Thomas's profoundly incarnational philosophy and theology[5] reflected an enchanted world, a cosmos in which human beings were at home on a sacred earth provided by a loving

Creator. In this world, Aquinas taught, theology and science cannot contradict one another; in fact, he insisted, one cannot do theology without science. But his Creator God was not dependent on the findings of natural science. To understand the timeless contribution of St. Thomas to the creation of the cosmos, we need some grasp of the difference between his intellectual background and that of cosmologists today.

The liberal arts were foundational to the medieval university. Students and faculty engaged in disciplined debate and rational discourse in their quest to comprehend all of reality. Much controversy at that time surrounded the introduction of the pagan science of Aristotle, which had found its way from Arabic sources into the European university. It was in such a climate, especially at the University of Paris, that Thomas Aquinas could develop his celebrated work on Creation.

For Aquinas, the science of nature or philosophy of nature (terms he used interchangeably) is a science distinct from metaphysics and theology. From Greek science he accepted the fact that every change in the physical world requires a preexisting cause, that something in the material world cannot come from nothing. But for Aquinas, God's creation of the world out of nothing was not an act dependent on a physical change. It was not a change from one state of matter to another. We may have physical evidence to date the time the cosmos came to be, but not for what caused its creation. Physics alone can not tell us how matter and energy came to be in the first place. God's act of creating was a metaphysical act, a radical act of bringing the whole cosmos into being and sustaining it in being. The natural sciences can account for change from one material state to another, but not for creation itself. No doubt St. Thomas would accept the big bang cosmology insofar as it explains the time of the origin of the cosmos. But this in no way denies the need for a Creator to bring the cosmos into being from nothing.[6]

So when mathematical physicist Paul Davies concludes that "it is now possible to conceive of a scientific explanation for all of creation,"[7] he is just explaining how matter and physical forces account for changes in the content and course of the cosmos. He does not explain what brought matter and physical forces into being. There would be no cosmos for the modern scientist to contemplate if God had not first given it being. Even Stephen Hawking admits that after finding the one possible unified theory, "just a set of rules and equations," there still remains the question, "What is it that breathes fire into the equations and makes a universe for them to describe?"[8]

Neglect of Philosophical Education Today

In comparison with the rich philosophical education scholars enjoyed in medieval times, today the philosophy of nature, theology and metaphysics, are neglected in the impoverished educational system of the United States. Our scientists have little or no philosophical or theological background. The reductive scientific method has infiltrated the whole curriculum and causes much of the stupefying education most of us received. It also accounts for the confused, myopic thinking and writing among cosmologists. This glaring deficit and neglect in the education of U.S. scientists is responsible for their inability to distinguish the origin of the cosmos from its creation. It is regrettable that there is no reference to any of these disciplines, including the wisdom traditions, in the index of the current popular account of the cosmos, *The Universe Story*.[9]

Cut off from Greek and medieval foundational science, our mechanistic world view, so devoid of life and purpose, leaves us with a physicist like Nobel laureate Steven Weinberg concluding, "The more the universe seems comprehensible, the more it also seems pointless."[10] Philosopher Daniel Dennett finds that "evolution is a mindless, purposeless, algorithmic process."[11] This skepticism and denial of an intelligible world of meaning opens the way for such farfetched cosmological speculations as are described by a senior science writer at *Scientific American*:

> Much of modern cosmology, particularly those aspects inspired by unified theories of particle physics and other esoteric ideas, is preposterous. Or rather, it is ironic science, science that is not experimentally testable or resolvable even in principle and therefore is not science in the strict sense at all. Its primary function is to keep us awestruck before the mystery of the cosmos.[12]

Recovery Needed

The search for wisdom about ultimate realities or metaphysics was a preeminent science for the Greeks and for Aquinas. The appreciation and recovery of their legacy to the Western world can reroot our thinking in the fertile soil from which modern science arose. Metaphysics is a fundamental science that "lays the foundation for all the other sciences"[13] and is needed to distinguish the philosophy of nature from mathematics and metaphysics itself.

Aquinas's science of nature, found in his *Commentaries on the Physics of Aristotle*, offers "a universal scientific knowledge about nature."[14] Its universality is indicated by Robert Hutchins, former President of the University of Chicago: "The Physics of Aristotle, which deals with change and motion in nature, is fundamental to the natural sciences... and is equally important to all those who confront change and motion in nature, that is, to everybody."[15] In order to recover the nature we have lost through the controlled experimentation and measurements of modern science, we need its reinterpretation through Aristotle's pre-mathematical and pre-experimental science of nature. Only thus can we rediscover a scientific world of common sense, one again intelligible to the human community.

Women scientists offer strong opposition to the "distortion of nature" that results from the metaphysical view of nature as a machine.[16] Ruth Hubbard, Professor of Biology Emerita at Harvard, claims there is "selective rendering of nature" by the male-dominated priesthood of scientists. She warns that, "The roots of the problem lie in our Western view of nature, which leads us to seek power over nature rather than understanding within it.... When people want to use science in order to dominate and exploit nature for production, their science even sees nature in exploitative ways."[17]

Elisabet Sahtouris, in her book *Gaia: The Human Journey from Chaos to Cosmos*, also exposes the contradictions evident in the male-dominated, mechanical world view of modern science.[18] She claims that seeing Gaia as a mechanism "raises the question of purpose. But purpose is a taboo in scientific descriptions of nature, because God, which Renaissance scientists saw as the Grand Engineer of natural mechanism, is no longer part of scientific explanation. Scientists thus argue a logical contradiction, that nature is mechanical but has no creator and no purpose."[19] She recalls writing shortly after finishing graduate school, "I sometimes think I was awarded a Ph.D. for successfully denying my humanity—behaving mechanically, dissecting nature without feeling or emotion."[20]

Hopes for the Future

A different approach to science is realized in the research of a brilliant woman scientist and Nobel laureate, Barbara McClintock, who died in 1992. She integrated the best of modern science with a commonsense, relational approach to the world of nature but paid a heavy price among her male colleagues. Their cultural myopia resulted from their inability to understand the subtlety of her deeply perceptive research in corn cytogenetics. Her intimate relationship with the corn plants was evident in her patient looking and hearing "what the material has to say" and "let[ting] it come to [her]." Her "feeling for the organism" bolstered this daring challenge to the ruling dogmas of a mechanistic science. Courageously and creatively, she chose a natural, commonsense, indeed mystical methodology that, as I have tried elsewhere to demonstrate, is our legacy from Aristotle and Aquinas.[21]

Another hope for the recovery of the heritage left us by Greek and medieval science is the 1992 republication of Pitirim Sorokin's classic book, *The Crisis of Our Age*. Sorokin challenges the twentieth-century "veritable blackout in human culture" due to an "outmoded unilateral conception of truth."[22] His remedy is the "re-establishment of an integral and more adequate system of truth and values." He finds this in the great integral cultures of fifth-century Greece—the time of Plato and Aristotle—and in the thirteenth century of Thomas Aquinas and Albert the Great. These eras provided the West with "supreme examples, attempting to embrace in one organic whole divine as well as sensory and dialectic truth."[23] Sorokin characterizes the philosophers of the twentieth century as "midgets" in comparison with Aquinas and other great scholastics.[24] Richard Tarnas is another critic of "the philosophy that has dominated our century and our universities," which "resembles nothing so much as a severe obsessive-compulsive sitting on his bed repeatedly tying and untying his shoes because he never quite gets it right—while in the meantime Socrates, Hegel and Aquinas are already high up on their mountain hike, breathing the bracing alpine air, seeing new and unexpected vistas."[25]

Hopes for the future can also be found among the wholistic and naturalistic scientists who contributed to the 1996 publication *New Metaphysical Foundations of Modern Science*.[26] Among them, Arthur Zajonc, a physicist at Amherst College, proposes a metaphysics for the twenty-first century in the neglected works of the poet-scientist Johann Wolfgang von Goethe, who lived almost two hundred years ago, and his able interpreter, the philosopher-scientist Rudolf Steiner, who died in 1925. The philosophy of both of these scientists, like that of Thomas Aquinas, is derived from an intimate communion with nature.

Goethe and Steiner insisted on a new way of seeing. They saw nature in a romantic, wholistic way that included "the workings of the divine within nature."[27] "Lively engagement with a phenomenon is essential for its understanding," Zajonc writes, "because, in Goethe's view, we are changed in the process; we develop faculties adequate to comprehending what is before us."[28] Steiner claims that "because one spirit works both in nature and in man's inner life, man can lift himself to participate in the production of nature."[29] Goethe himself wrote, "My own pure, deep, innate and schooled view of things had taught me without fail to see God in Nature, Nature in God, and this view was the foundation of my very existence."[30]

Steiner envisions a kinship of his own and Goethe's philosophy of science with that of Aquinas, stating: "In the world outlook of Goethe is to be found what Thomism must become if it is to rise to the highest possibilities of the present time and play a real part in the evolution of [humankind]."[31] In the same lecture on St. Thomas in his book *The Redemption of Thinking,* Steiner sees his own natural science as a revival of Thomism. He insisted that "one of the peaks of European spiritual evolution is manifest in the Scholasticism of the thirteenth century, and … this present age has every reason to study this period, and will discover that there is an endless amount to be learnt from it."[32]

A Search For An Enriched Cosmology

Aquinas, like Goethe six hundred years later and Steiner seven hundred years later, would have refused to accept a cosmology based solely on a mechanical and mathematical way of perceiving the cosmos. Whether the cosmos is best understood or interpreted as an organism or as a machine is a metaphysical question. It must be addressed by those who contend that the earth is a living organism while at the same time accepting the thesis that the cosmos can be understood by a mechanistic science explained by mathematical equations alone.

This contradiction presents a challenge to women religious to complement their efforts to manifest and celebrate the wonders of mother earth and all its interdependent inhabitants with a consistent philosophy of nature. Both Goethe and Steiner offer such a philosophy and, as contemplative scientists, perhaps mystics, they contribute to a deeply spiritual cosmology. Barbara McClintock, looking to the East for correctives for the limitations of modern science, claims to be a "mystic" herself. Certainly St. Thomas, a mystic and a saint, left us a valid philosophy of nature within a framework of faith: "A mistake in our thinking about Nature results in a mistake in our thinking about God." And again, "The opinion is false of those who assert that it makes no difference to the truth of the faith what anyone holds about creatures, so long as one thinks rightly about God. For error about creatures spills over into false opinion about God, and takes people's minds away from God, to whom faith seeks to lead them." [33]

Could the legacy of Thomas Aquinas prepare the way to reconsider the cosmic genesis of Pierre Teilhard de Chardin for an enriched twenty-first-century cosmology? [34] Such is proposed by Richard Tarnas, who builds on the cosmic vision of Teilhard as well as that of Jung and Hegel in claiming that the Western mind in its renewed appreciation of mother earth is undergoing an initiatory process into a new paradigm. This transformative initiation he envisions is in process within the Judeo-Christian context of personal sin (the shadow side of humans) and the shadow that humans have cast on the earth in the twentieth century producing the "blackout in human culture" to which Sorokin refers. Tarnas sees the momentous feminist revolution as fundamental and crucial to our turning from a path toward extinction to a twenty-first-century vision of humans and other species as part of a cosmos becoming conscious of itself and of a future sustainable world. [35]

Does this vision of a new paradigm for the cosmos fulfill Sorokin's prophetic hopes for the renewal of an integral culture for the West, one built on the legacy of Greek and medieval world views, one that includes the best of the moral, intellectual and spiritual life of mind and heart? And is the pivotal work of women religious contributing to the ongoing earth and human transformative process at last moving us toward a new creation reminiscent of St. Paul—"the whole created earth groans in all its parts as if in the pangs of childbirth"?[36]

Published previously in *Sisters Today* Vol. 69 No. 1 (January 1997).

7.

Viruses
Are They Alive?

Some workers on viruses have no difficulty in taking a stand on the living or non-living character of the viruses by denying any distinction between the living and the non-living. Stanley ends his discussion of whether or not viruses are "alive" by the following sweeping generalization:

> With the realization that there is no definite boundary between the living and the non-living it becomes possible to blend the atomic theory, the germ theory, and the cell theory into a unified philosophy, the essence of which is structure or architecture. The chemical, biological and physical properties of matter, whether atoms, molecules, germs, or cells, are directly dependent upon the chemical structure of the matter, and the results of the work with viruses have permitted the conclusion that this structure is fundamentally the same regardless of its occurrence. [1]

Other workers admit that the problem is still open.Salvador Luria, a well-known virologist at the University of Indiana, suggests a re-definition of the word "living" so that it "may be meaningful and useful in this borderline field."[2]

Instead of spending time on Luria's definition, which equates the living with "the possession of an independent, specific, self-replicating pattern of organization,"[3] let us first look at more general definitions of "living" as used by biologists in other fields. Then, we will consider the nature of a virus to determine whether it falls within or outside a generally accepted definition—if we can find one—or whether too little is known about the virus as yet to make a decision. This seems a more satisfactory approach than making an a priori decision that viruses are alive and then adjusting our definition to include them.

In general, the twentieth-century biologists admit their inability to know, by the scientific method, what life is. Claude Villee, professor at Harvard, suggests that our inability to know "the exact chemical composition of a single cell of the human body or of the smallest one-celled plant" is in the same way an explanation of our lack of knowledge of the nature of life.[4] From the Massachusetts Institute of Technology, a scientist of the stature of Norbert Wiener finds "life" a concept "grossly inadequate to precise scientific thinking."[5] Strangely enough, scientists still continue to distinguish between the animate and the inanimate world. The following quotation is an example of the commonsense view generally accepted in practice:

> All plants are alive and, in common with all other living things, possess certain characteristics which differentiate them from non-living things. It is usually easy to distinguish the living from the non-living, although it is rather difficult to establish an absolute set of rules by which they can always be distinguished. [6]

E. Racker, formerly of the Yale University School of Medicine, suggests a single criterion for identifying viruses as living organisms. "They are living in the sense that they contain a genetic apparatus which permits them to struggle for survival—if you wish to call that living," he says.[7]

Continued search reveals a few modern biologists whose method of approach in science is still somewhat rooted in the Aristotelian soil from which it sprang. At least they do not consider themselves unscientific when they pause to examine the problem of life. Garrett Hardin, in his general biology text, after asking what life is, says, "Perhaps not all answers to this question need be nonsense."[8] Unhappily, however, he decides that it is sound strategy to avoid such a question and proceeds to a study of the characteristics of living things. Libbie Hyman discusses the problem, suggesting that living things can only be recognized by certain biological properties such as growth and reproduction. She, too, is hesitant about accepting a definition of life. In her estimation,

"Attempts to define life other than as the sum total of these properties [characteristic of living things] have proved unsatisfactory."[9]

In Aristotle we have both a great biologist and a wise man who made a careful analysis of animals and plants to find out what is common to living beings. He knew there must be some principle or principles from which the operations of living things stem, and attempted to discover what this principle is. This principle, or soul, as he called it, is not mere nature, for, he said, nature does not move in two directions. Plants grow up and down. Growth and decay, as found in plants, are in opposite directions. Nature, however, is determined to one; the apple falls down when it is released by the branch. But the crayfish may move forward or backward; the tree grows, both by pushing its roots deeper into the soil and by reaching out for the heavens with its branches. The soul, Aristotle concluded, is something more than nature. It is the principle of all the qualities and powers attributed to the living.[10] He did not say with Hyman that it is the sum of these powers, but that it is the principle. It is the principle that is present in the bird that is not singing, the hibernating bear that is scarcely metabolizing, the motionless chameleon protectively concealed by its environment, the newborn babe that has not yet taken its first breath.

Further, Aristotle referred to this principle of moving, respiring and sensing as the form, as distinct from the matter, of the organism. For when the soul of a living organism departs, neither the organism nor its parts remain what they were. A dead dog does not bark, nourish himself, grow, run or sense, and hence can only be said to be a dog by using the term in an improper sense. The matter of a dog is still there, but it is no longer organized, or disposed, for the form of a living dog. This principle of life by which an animal performs operations characteristic of the animate can refer either to the matter or to its form, according to Aristotle. Both are principles of life. But the nature or essence of any living thing is constituted more fundamentally by its form than by its matter.[11] It is the cat that purrs, arches its back and rubs against your ankles that exhibits the nature of a cat, not the cold, still, embalmed specimen that the premedical student displays on his dissecting pan. It is the form that gives us an insight into the true nature of catness. The form, however, is only evident to us as the manifestation, actuation, operation of the organized elements, compounds, cells, tissues, organs and systems, as disposed for the form of a cat. In an Aristotelian framework the inquirer into nature would, therefore, be concerned about the matter of the animal as known through such subjects as morphology, anatomy and biochemistry, but more concerned about the form as revealed through psychology, physiology, embryology and ecology.

The soul is the substantial form of the organism, not an accidental form. It is there as a constitutive of the very essence of the being of the animate thing. Matter is only actualized when it is informed. The substantial form constitutes prime matter in being, makes it simply "to be." An accidental form may make the cat to be white or grey, a Persian or an alley cat. The substantial form actualizes this matter in being, simply as cat. Such a form gives catness to the prime matter in potency to be cat, dogness to that in potency to be dog. That it is a substantial form is evidenced by comparing an animal before and after death, the chicken before and after the hatchet has severed its head. The whole life principle, the form, was snuffed out at once. Only a few effects resulting from the form remain, e.g., a few disorganized reflexes.

Aristotle concluded from his inquiry into the nature of the principle by which a living thing takes nourishment, moves, senses and understands, that such a principle must be a form, a substantial form, the first act of a potentially animate body. This provided the major premise for his demonstrative conclusion that the soul is the form or act of the body.[12] His minor premise he derived from the equally valid knowledge of his own internal experience of the unity of the soul as "that by which we primarily live and perceive and move and understand."[13] Thus he used both the observational approach of the modern biologist and the valid but generally unacceptable criterion of personal, internal experience to set up the two premises for a demonstrative definition of the soul.

> The principle by which an organism lives, feels, moves and understands is the form of its body. The soul is the principle by which we live, move, feel and understand. Therefore, the soul is the form of the body.[14]

From his two premises, Aristotle arrived at the conclusion that the soul is the form of a body potentially alive. In other words, the soul is the first act of a body, a physical organic body having life potentially. This act gives being to the organism and allows it to perform operations characteristic of living things. Aristotle explained that there are two ways in which something may be "in act": one may be said to be in act either through having knowledge or through exercising it. The soul is in first act, is that by which the powers of the soul operate. What sight is to the eye, the soul is to the body.[15] Furthermore, just as the eye is for sight, so the body is for the soul. Aristotle summarized the relation of the soul to the body:

> The soul is the cause and principle of the living body. Now these words can be used in many ways. The soul, however, is a cause in three established senses: for it is that whence comes movement; that 'for the sake of which'; and as the essence of living bodies.[16]

First, the soul is the principle or cause of movement in living things. In higher animals, the soul is the principle of local motion and sensation; in plants, it is the principle of such motion as is found in growth, nutrition and reproduction. Second, the soul is that "for the sake of which." We pointed out above that as the eye is for sight, so the body is for the soul. Nature works for an end, structure is for function, matter is for form, the body is for the soul. That the soul is as the essence of living bodies is clear from the fact that it gives existence to the living thing. Prime matter just cannot come into actual existence without an accompanying substantial form. The soul brings the pure potency of prime matter into act as a living being. Aristotle thus denied both mechanism and vitalism. A living being is not just a "natural machine,"[17] as the mechanists claim, nor is it a physical structure with certain added powers or energies, as the vitalist would have it. [18]

If Aristotle's analysis and definition of the soul is accepted, not on authority, but on its sound appeal to reason, we have a basis for continuing our investigation. How shall we recognize that a being has such a form, a soul, the first act of a being having life in potency? Aristotle, like his successors, the modern biologists, knew that living things can only be recognized as such by their operations.

> The animate is distinguished from the inanimate by being alive. To live, however, is predicated in several ways; and even if one only of these is present, we say there is life; as, for example, intellection, sensation, or movement and rest in place; as well as the movement and rest involved in nourishment and growth and decay.
>
> Hence all plants seem to live. They appear to have in themselves a power and principle of this kind, by which they increase or decay in various directions—that is to say, they do not grow up but not down,

but alike either way, and in all their parts they are continually nourished, and they live so long as they can take nourishment.[19]

Both Aristotle and his great commentator, St. Thomas Aquinas, however, knew that the lowest form of life, which is found in plants, is latent and difficult to detect.[20] The ability to take nourishment, which Aristotle suggests as a criterion for life, presents many difficulties. Is the lily plucked from the rest of the plant and put into a vase living? Is the metabolizing "tissue culture" alive? Or are there other and more manifest signs of the plant soul? Aristotle further explained that a motion takes its name from its end, and the end of the vegetative soul is to produce another like itself.[21] If the power of reproduction can be used as a final criterion of the presence of the vegetative soul, then many modern biologists may be right in maintaining that viruses are living organisms. But let us examine the nature of the virus before jumping to any conclusions on its status in our world of richly diversified being.

The viruses are divided into three classes based on the organisms they attack: animals and humans, the flowering plants, and bacteria. They vary in size from that of the smallest bacteria down to that of genes or of protein molecules. The larger, more complex viruses apparently have properties characteristic of pathogenic bacteria, which are usually thought of as being alive. At the lower extreme of size the viruses are composed only of nucleoproteins and may be "merely self-duplicating chemical agents."[22] It is with these at the lower size limit, those which attack bacteria, the so-called bacteriophages, with which we shall be concerned in this paper. The best studied group are the "T" phages active on *Escherichia coli,* strain B. *Escherichia coli* is the colon bacillus, which is a normal inhabitant of the human colon.

There is some inconsistency in the reports of the morphology of the T phages as studied under the electron microscope.[23] As a rule they are reported to be "sperm-shaped entities having roughly spherical heads ranging in diameter from 44A. to 1,000A. and having tails about 1,500A. long and 150A. thick."[24] These are considerably smaller than bacteria, which are measured in microns.[25] The head of the T phages, hexagonal in cross section, and the tail are encased by a protein membrane. Within the membrane of the head is a core of DNA, deoxyribonucleic acid, the basic stuff of all cell nuclei. The internal structure of the head region, the nucleic acid, is more electron-optically opaque than its outer membrane or the tail, which fact is a visible sign of complexity of structure in the virus.

The T2 phage has to a comparatively great extent yielded up the secrets of its "life cycle" to the persistent probing of many workers on bacteriophage in the United States.[26] When the T2 phage particles are introduced into a culture of *Escherichia coli* bacteria, they move about[27] until their tails attach to a susceptible host. Immediately invasion of the host cell begins. The phage nucleic acid, the DNA, is injected through the tail of the virus into the bacterium. The protein shell, emptied from head and tail, remains outside the host and takes no further part in the reproductive cycle. The shells may even be removed without affecting the multiplication of the virus particles. Thus the virus nucleic acid, DNA, is the link between the virus infecting a bacterium and the hundreds of phage particles that are later released.[28] After invasion of the host cell by the nucleic acid core of one or more viruses, there ensues a "latent period" of approximately fifteen to sixty minutes. During this period the infective properties neither of the virus nor of the host are recoverable as separate entities. Besides losing its infective power, the virus loses its identity as a particle. Within the bacteria the phage-specified material is duplicated and assembled from nonphage. The bacteria lyse, or "burst," and hundreds of phage particles are released from each infected cell.

This appears to be a rather normal "life cycle," but let us look more closely at the behavior of the virus before and after infection. It is generally thought that the virus outside of the host cell has no metabolic, respiratory or reproductive activity. In fact, Epstein in reviewing the properties of bacteriophages claims:

> An extracellular phage particle is a nonmetabolizing, nonmultiplying entity; only when it has contacted and merged with a susceptible cell has it the ability to multiply. The evidence to be discussed in this review points strongly to the conclusion that the absorbed phage particle undergoes such a profound alteration shortly after absorption as to render almost meaningless the identification of it with the extracellular particle.[29]

Although the genetic continuity of the phage and its progeny is apparently established,[30] not all agree that its metabolic and reproductive activities are like those of other organisms. The opinion thus arose that viruses, while being nevertheless organisms and in no way inanimate bodies, had no metabolism of their own and thus represented the ultimate stage of parasitism, in which all life activities were borrowed from the host. This opinion still holds at the present time, although there are firm grounds for considering that a virus is in no way a parasite, at least in the ordinary sense of microbiological usage, and consequently the fact that all its life activities are those of the host should no longer be taken as evidence of extreme degeneration or specialization, but rather as evidence that the viruses are of totally different nature and possibly derive their origin from some constituent of the nucleus or cytoplasm that has developed autonomy. [31]

Phages of T2 type lyse infected bacteria shortly after their entry and so are usually considered to be parasitic. However, a virus may be introduced into a bacterium without destroying the bacteria or impeding its metabolic or reproductive activities. After its entry such phage acts like a normal genetic constituent of the bacterium and is transmitted to bacterial offspring as a power to produce bacteriophage. Many generations later, a bacterial progeny of the so-called lysogenic bacteria (bacteria possessing and transmitting the ability to produce virus) may lyse and release hundreds of phage particles. Therefore there is a tendency to look on phage as a parasite by those dealing with the virulent T2 type, but to look on the so-called temperate phages as units liberated from the hereditary constitution of a bacterium. [32]

S. Cohen sees both types of bacteriophage as only different expressions of parasitism:

> It is now possible to describe a gamut of patterns of viral parasitism, from those in which infection leads almost exclusively to the synthesis of virus to those in which infection permits both virus and host cell to multiply together. Such a range may be observed within the group of the bacterial viruses; for these viruses one now speaks of virulent and temperate phages. The virulent phages are best exemplified by the T-even phages, T2, T4, and T6. Following the accumulation of large numbers of virus particles within the infected cell, lysis of the bacterium occurs with the liberation of the virus. The temperate phages are active in lysogenic systems, whose properties have been clarified in large part by Lwoff and his collaborators. [33]

The lysogenic bacterium transmits the bacteriophage in a heritable form, but not as a mature virus particle. If a lysogenic bacterium is artificially lysed, it will not produce virus particles unless it has been already in the process of preparing for such production.[34] Lwoff refers to the bacteriophage during this seemingly inactive stage while carried by the lysogenic bacteria as "prophage." He thinks it should not be called bacteriophage any more than the egg or the pluteus larva of the sea urchin should be called a sea urchin.[35]

The following discussion will highlight the activities characteristic of the virulent type of virus, e.g., T2. The necessity of limiting the scope of this paper requires that the question of the temperate phages, whose life cycles are of more recent discovery and are less well known, be excluded. From present trends of thought among virologists it seems likely that the temperate phages, at least in the provirus stage, will come to be regarded more and more as aberrant bacterial genes or chromosomes that have achieved a certain amount of autonomy.

Why can the phage carry on metabolic activities only within the host? Perhaps an answer to this question will shed some light on whether it is the virus or the bacterium that is metabolizing during the "latent period" when the infective properties of both host and its invader are lost. According to most investigators, the virus possesses no independent enzyme activity and is therefore dependent on the enzymatic constitution of the host. In an infected host cell there is a selective disturbance of the enzymes present according to the type of virus with which it is infected. Also phage infection of the virulent type suppresses specific bacterial synthesis so that an infected bacterium fails to undergo further multiplication.

Is the genetic apparatus controlling the metabolism of the infected host cell that of the virus or that of the host? Luria suggests that the virus introduces not just an additional organizer into the host cell but one that is completely predominant in what could be called "parasitism at the genetic level": the failure of the host cell to continue its normal metabolism of its genetic pattern.[36] The gene pattern of the bacterium is disrupted and replaced by that of the virus, "resulting in viral rather than bacterial specificity of the protoplasm newly synthesized by the available enzymatic machinery."[37] It is interesting that the phages may use either host or medium material in synthesizing new phage.[38]

The problem of the metabolism of the virus-infected bacterium is a leading one, but its solution will not completely answer our question of whether the virus is living or not. Many parasites are dependent on the metabolic processes of the host for their own survival, yet they are man-ifestly alive. It seems that even if the metabolism during the "latent period" could be attributed more to the host than to its invader, or vice versa, this would not be a strict criterion by which to judge of the living or non-living nature of the virus.

In genuine reproduction a living organism, a primary natural unit, from its parts produces another or others like itself. If the infected bacterium rather than the virus is the natural unit, the living organism that produces the phage particles, then this replication is not true reproduction.[41] A much more comprehensive study of viruses is necessary in order to have a general picture of how close virus replication is to genuine reproduction.[42] If such facts as the following are generally true, we might hesitate to think of the bacteriophages as a natural unit. Perhaps we can get closer to the crux of this question by probing into the "latent period" for an insight into the reproduction or replication of the virus. The kind of reproduction common to many lower animals and plants is binary fission. But, as Lwoff points out, binary fission is only the last stage in the growth and preparation for division by a bacterium or ciliate, or the cells of more complex organisms. What goes on at the molecular level? The genes must induce the synthesis of identical structure. The replication of the bacteriophage appears to be comparable to the duplication of cellular constituents rather than of cells, i.e., of reproduction as it operates at the genetic level in all organisms.[39] In fact the name "naked nuclei" has been suggested since the "phages seem to exhibit practically every type of genetic property which has been discovered in higher organisms."[40]

Bacteriophage particles are never produced directly by division of preexisting phage particles but by organization of nonphage material. It appears as though the materials of the phage could not be replicated when in the form of an organized phage particle. [43]

The greater percentage of both the DNA and the protein of the new phage particles is derived from substances assimilated from the sur-rounding medium rather than from the host cell. Only about forty per-cent of the parent virus DNA is conserved and reappears in its descendants. The protein forming the membrane of the head and tail of the virus progeny must come from the host cell and media, as the parent protein does not penetrate the host cell. However, the DNA of the original invading cell appears to be responsible for the reproduction both of the DNA and of the protein for the new phage particles.[44]

In the opinion of some workers this crucial question of replication, unknown in the chemical world, is a reliable criterion for establishing the living nature of the virus.[45] Aristotle might seem to lend assent with his explanation that a motion takes its name from its end, and the end of the vegetative soul is to produce another like itself.[46] But if we are going to settle for just this one criterion, we are faced with other problems. Are the heart cells of the chick embryo, which have been reproducing themselves in tissue culture for the past one-quarter century at Johns Hopkins, alive? Are protoplasmic components, transmissible only by graft, alive?

Today biologists, particularly geneticists, looks more and more to biochemistry for answers to many of their problems, both those dealing with the nature of living organisms and those dealing with their relationships (phylogeny) and their development (ontogeny) as evidenced by material affinities. Serological studies attempting to trace virus specificity during virus reproduction are in progress.[47] So it was not only because some viruses had been crystallized out, bottled away like chemicals and later proved to retain their power of infectivity that the biologist laid the virus problem at the door of the biochemist. The biologist trying to get to the roots of his problems wants to know what is most basic to animate things. The nature of the protoplasmic building blocks and the pathways of biosynthesis are the doors at which he knocks, since he is committed to the dead wood of mechanism not yet raked out of biological circles. The faith of many biochemists in the "unitarian principle underlying the diversity of phenomena in the microbial world" is a useful tool in modern experimental biology.[48] The biochemical and physiological traits of the simplest one-celled animals are giving insights into the chemistry and physiology of the cells of higher animals. But the viruses show that the expectation of finding the key to all infection, duplication and virus liberation by studying molecular transformations is an oversimplification. Chen remarks that with "increasing exploration of animal virus systems, it has become increasingly evident that one may not extrapolate freely from one biological system to another."[49] What is true of the T2 virus may not be an indication at all of the results obtainable from an influenza virus. There is considerable diversity of reaction within the different systems of plant viruses, animal and bacterial. "Infected cells may or may not divide and multiply; they may or may not grossly alter their metabolism, they may or may not lyse as a requisite for virus liberation."[50] The viruses are not a homogeneous group.[51] Even within one viral system, or within the life cycle of one specific virus, there are remarkable differences. Chen gives an example of a phage lambda that multiplies in certain strains of *Escherichia coli*. On entering the host cell, the phage nucleic acid unites with the genetic apparatus of the host, which continues its own life cycle. However, under varying environmental conditions it may cause virus duplication and bacterial cell lysis.[52]

> It is established today the DNA-containing bacteriophages can induce permanent genetic changes in host bacteria without necessarily introducing their own perpetuation, thus indicating the DNA brought in by the virus can intervene in a very intimate way in the duplication, by the host, of its own DNA.[53]

The nucleic acid seems to be the lowest common denominator of three stages of the bacteriophage—the mature virus particle, the prophage and the vegetative stage, and yet how different its activity in these stages.

Perhaps our diversified world of beings will not yield to the faith of the biochemist, who seeks to explain living things from their common biochemical principles whose natures can be predicted if their chemical constituents are known. Matter does not yield its secrets so readily to us. To try to deduce that natures and operations of animate beings from their material constituents would make the scientist guilty of the fault for which he has long pointed an accusing finger at the philosopher. An example of such thinking is found in Stanley's paper:

> Neither the cell nor the atomic theory should be handicapped by a reference to the living state, but should be utilized only to define certain accepted orders of structure...[54]

It is just as serious an intellectual sin against nature to try to reduce her to a world of matter as to reduce her to a world of forms. Long ago Aristotle took the bull by the horns and gave us a solution, a world of composites, one made up of beings composed of matter and form. Living beings have an animating form. The form is manifested to us through the external appearance of an organism, but more through its operations. Recently Lwoff pointed out to us that we are barbarians in our absorption with the external appearances of things.[55]

This paper has attempted to indicate that there is a basis, not entirely arbitrary, for trying to determine whether organisms such as viruses are alive or not. Continued experimentation will doubtless yield more data for rendering a decision. The following table shows the more manifest differences known today between a bacteriophage and a living cell. Most of the differences enumerated by Lwoff can be summarized thus: a bacteriophage differs from a cell in its size; in its function, such as growth and reproduction; and also in its chemical constitution.[58] Yet none of these differences is conclusive enough to assure us that the bacteriophage is or is not living.

Virus:	Cell:
(bacteriophage taken as a type) Phage contains only DNA	Contains both DNA (desoxyribonucleic acid) and RNA (ribonucleic acid)
Reproduced from its nucleic acid from prophage	Reproduced from all its constituents
Produced endogenously	Usually produced exogenously
Can multiply only inside living cells	Can usually be cultured in artificial media
Never produced directly from preexisting phage particles but from organization of nonphage material	Usually produced directly from division of a preexisting cell
Unable to grow or undergo fission[56]	Able to grow and to divide
Contains no enzyme system to provide utilizable energy	Has enzymatic machinery for metabolic activities
Exhibits no metabolic activities outside of a bacterial cell	More commonly functions outside another cell
Less than 200 mu [57]	Usually considerably larger

As both Aristotle and St. Thomas have pointed out, "The universe requires that there should be no gaps in its order, that in nature there should everywhere be a gradual development from the less to the more perfect."[59] Nature usually presents many puzzling cases for us as she apparently grades one species into another; for example, the chimpanzee that can use tools, and the bees that seem to calculate distances and direction, appear to approximate human intellectual nature more than some other animals. The plants that are irritable, e.g., the Venus flytrap that engulfs the unsuspecting fly that alights on its leaves, or the mimosa that recoils when touched, seem to manifest sensitivity, an animal characteristic. It is always difficult to draw fine lines of demarcation when we try to fit nature into a neatly catalogued pattern intelligible to ourselves. Perhaps the virus may be another case like the chimpanzee and the mimosa, where the highest in the lower category resembles the lowest in the higher category.[60] A virus may be only "a specific nucleoprotein which kills the host cell and which multiplies.[61]

It seem that here, as in all attempts at classification, no one criterion is an infallible one. Aristotle told us two thousand years ago "that no single differentia...either by itself or with its antecedents, can possibly express the essence of a species.[62] Aristotle maintained that some groups, such as birds and fishes, are recognized by a "true instinct of mankind."[63] Whether further research will furnish us enough information for such a "true instinct" to enlighten us remains with the future.

Published previously in *The New Scholasticism*, Vol. XXXI No. 3 (July 1957).

8 |

Nature's Law
Competition or Cooperation?

$\mathcal{E}$vidence of struggle in nature, of competition between organisms, of the fact that some animals and plants lived at the expense of others, was noted, of course, long before the time of Charles Darwin. The catch phrases "struggle for existence" and "survival of the fittest," together with his Malthusian "geometrical ratio of increase," were the keynotes of Darwin's theory. Although popularized through his writings and those of his contemporaries, Wallace, Huxley and Spencer, these ideas can be found in the literature from ancient times. Empedocles was so aware of this aspect of nature that he proclaimed strife along with love or friendship as a principle of nature. That the animals most preyed on, such as the hare, produced their young in greater abundance, Herodotus thought worthy of note.[1] Aristotle devoted several chapters of his *History of Animals* to certain animals that war with one another, and to others that are friends.[2] In a letter to Luculius, Seneca pointed out that nature subjects the weak to the strong.[3]

But it was not until after Darwin's five-year voyage on H. M. S. *Beagle,* during which he collected (and later published) such an amazing number of facts in substantiation of the theory of natural selection, that we find conflict in nature, rather then harmony or order, heralded by biologists as the more fundamental principle. Darwin thought of natural selection as nature's way of controlling the tremendous increase in the species of animals and plants by weeding out the less fit. The "survival of the fittest" in natural selection is, of course, a concomitant of the struggle for existence, as he saw it. Spencer did not hesitate to incorporate this theory into his iconoclastic works, whence it filtered into social and political philosophy, giving us "Social Darwinism," the notion of human society itself evolving out of conflict. The seeds of Western individualism and of the Communist warfare of the classes were well planted in the soil of Cartesian mechanism and watered from the spring of the Darwinian struggle for existence.

We are assured by such contemporary biologists as Julian Huxley that "there are no signs that evolutionary biology will not indefinitely remain Darwinian."[4] However, as with many other generalizations about the physical world, e.g., Newtonian mechanics and Mendelian genetics, modifications have been increasingly necessary as the horizons of our knowledge of the facts have become enlarged. The modern evolutionary theory, according to Huxley, is in certain respects "more Darwinian that Darwin was himself."[5] It upholds the principle of natural selection as "omnipresent and virtually the only guiding agency in evolution"[6] and, of course, retains the idea of the prodigality of nature in reproducing the species of animals and plants; but the notion of struggle, by which overpopulation was supposedly controlled, has been considerably altered by an increasing number of biologists. Cooperation, they tell us, rather than conflict, is nature's basic law, the principle on which natural selection operates.

Biology books are still rolling off the press in the old "nature red in tooth and claw" style, but they are much less in vogue now than they were half a century ago. Typical of this struggle-for- existence approach is Asa C. Chandler's *Introduction to Parasitology,* now in its ninth edition:

> One of the most appalling realizations with which every student of nature is brought face to face is the universal and unceasing struggle for existence which goes on during the life of every living organism, from the time of its conception until death. We like to think of nature's beauties, to admire her outward appearance of peacefulness, to set her up as an example for human emulation. Yet under her seeming calm there is going on everywhere in every pool, in every meadow, in every forest—murder, pillage, starvation and suffering.[7]

Arnold J. Toynbee opened his book *An Historian's Approach to Religion* on the note that every creature in the universe is at war with every other creature and even with its Creator.[8] Such views of nature certainly have a Darwinian flavor, but they also bear out Huxley's claim that modern biological theory is in certain respects "more Darwinian than Darwin was himself."[9] In *The Origin of the Species,* for the most part, Darwin ignored nature's cooperative aspects, but he at least adverted to such mutually favorable adaptations as the bee to the flower from which it sips nectar, and vice versa.[10] The dependency of one organism upon another did not escape him, even though he thought this to be true of animals and plants "remote in the scale of nature."[11] More than once he pointed out that natural selection works for the benefit of the individual concerned and does not produce anything exclusively for the good of another.[12] But perhaps Darwin was unconsciously sowing the seed for the present-day emphasis on nature's cooperative character, when he further stated that we are profoundly ignorant of the mutual relationships of all organic beings.[13] He could not have been totally unaware of the view of nature as an ordered whole, an harmonious aggregate, when he said: "Let it also be borne in mind how infinitely complex and close-fitting are the mutual relations of all organic beings to each other and to their physical conditions of life."[14] In closing his chapter on "Struggle for Existence," he sounded a little more optimistic about nature than Chandler and Toynbee above:

> When we reflect on this struggle, we may console ourselves with the full belief, that the war of nature is not incessant, that no fear is felt, that death is generally prompt, and that the vigorous, the healthy, and the happy survive and multiply.[15]

Representative of the new theme in contemporary biological thought is Marston Bates's book *The Nature of Natural History,* one chapter of which is entitled "Partnership and Cooperation." Bates stressed the interdependence of all organisms and claimed that we have gotten into a fallacious habit of seeing the organic world "as a mass of struggling, competing organisms, each trying to best the other for its place in the sun."[16] Such a principle, he warned, is only a superficial one that is superimposed on a more fundamental and essential mutual dependence. "The basic theme in nature is cooperation rather than competition—a cooperation that has become so all-pervasive, so completely integrated, that it is difficult to untwine and follow out the separate strands."[17] Perhaps he is right in suggesting that what science needs today is another Huxley to popularize the theory of cooperation in nature, as Thomas turned his literary genius to serve Darwin's idea of competition. Julian is as prolific a writer as was his grandfather, but his writings, at least on this point, do not seem to have such an influence on contemporary thought. Despite the fact that biologists are stressing nature's tendency to cooperation, rather than her competitive aspects, Bates regretfully noted that the social philosophers have limited themselves to the view of the biological world envisioned by the post-Darwinians and Thomas Huxley.[18]

Let us go back a few years to catch a glimpse of the history of the development of this new theme of harmony and cooperation in nature. Of course, it is not new at all, except to those whose education is limited to the outgrowth of the mechanistic eighteenth- and nineteenth-century evolutionary view of nature. We will begin by trying to discover why cooperation rather than struggle, as the basis for evolution, has gotten a hearing from the modern biologist.

At the close of the nineteenth century, Peter Kropotkin, a Russian prince, published a series of articles that were later collected and reprinted in a book entitled *Mutual Aid a Factor in Evolution*. These essays were provoked by the famous essay of T. H. Huxley, "The Struggle for Existence," which heralded the idea that "from the point of view of the moralist, the animal world is on about the same level as a gladiator's show."[19] Kropotkin, convinced that Huxley had given "a very incorrect representation of the facts of Nature, as one sees them in bush and in the forest," not only upheld the importance of mutual aid in the various classes of animals, but devoted more of these essays to "the importance of the same factor in the evolution of Man."[20]

Contemporary claims for the importance of Kropotkin's contribution to evolutionary thought may be found in the works of Ashley Montagu and the late Warder C. Allee. As a result of a lifetime devoted to the gathering of materials and experimentation, Allee, an ecologist at the University of Chicago, furnished sufficient evidence to satisfy many modern biologists that the fundamental principle in nature is cooperation rather than competition. The extent of Allee's researches, writings, and his many publications over a period of more than thirty years, compares favorably, at least in quantity, with the voluminous writings of

Charles Darwin. Montagu, a contemporary anthropologist, is at home with any of the problems arising between human beings, or between humankind and its environment. The bibliographies in two of his books, *On Being Human* and *Darwin: Competition and Cooperation*, indicate extensive research into the literature of cooperative action in nature. Doubtless the social and political climate is not so well suited to the development of Allee's and Montagu's ideas as was that of the nineteenth century to Darwin's. The 1,250 copies of the first edition of *The Origin of the Species* sold out on the day of publication.

In a historical approach to this question in his book *Cooperation Among Animals,* Allee went back farther than the writings of Kropotkin. A French publication, *Des Societes Animales* by A. V. Espinas, published in 1878, used the behavioristic and ecological approach that Allee himself adopted. Espinas, like Allee, claimed that social life among organisms was not an accident in the animal kingdom, arising fortuitously and capriciously among a few related groups such as beavers, bees and ants. Espinas thought himself in a position to prove that communal life among living creatures was a biological necessity, a universal fact of nature. For Espinas, nature is a homogeneous whole, integrated in all its parts. This integration results from a universal law of cooperation.[21]

William Morton Wheeler, a distinguished American entomologist, furnished Allee with what a materialistic age would categorize as an even more fundamental basis for this law of harmony. "All living things," Wheeler said, "are genetically related as members of one great family, one vast living sumplasm which, though fragmented into individuals in space, is nevertheless absolutely continuous in time."[22] In fact, Allee pushed his analysis back from "unconscious cooperation" or mutual dependence of living things to a "simpler interdependence of antecedent non-living matter."[23] According to his view, nature's harmonious working may be merely the highly specialized biological expression of chemistry's law of mass action.[24] This principle of nature for Allee was not just the result of a family relationship or the fact that two sexes are so commonly needed for cooperation in reproducing the species. The evolution of close-knit societies of animals most likely did arise from such relationship, he thought; but it came about more readily because of the "existence of an underlying pervasive element of unconscious proto-cooperation, or automatic tendency toward mutual aid among animals."[25]

Allee did innumerable experiments to demonstrate this automatic cooperative tendency among animals. He found among groups of goldfish a higher tolerance for collodial silver than single fish had, when exposed to the same concentration of this toxic substance. An aggregation of planaria in ultraviolet light disintegrated less rapidly than isolated specimens did. Dilute suspensions of sperm of Arbacia, the common sea urchin, lost their fertilizing power much more readily than concentrated suspensions. More crowded cultures of Arbacia larvae were more precocious in their development than were sparser populations.[26] From further laboratory experiments with goldfish, Allee thought he had demonstrated a device of nature by which more aggressive fish would regurgitate enough food to be of real nutritional value to their less fortunate comrades. This, he concluded, was a sort of automatic sharing.[27] Another significant fact, he pointed out, is the inability of some species when reduced below a certain threshold number to reestablish themselves. The heath hen was last seen in 1932, even though it had been protected by law and by enthusiastic nature lovers since 1907. At that time there were an estimated seventy-seven, but this number increased to two thousand by 1916. Nevertheless, the heath hen became extinct.[28] Even behavioral studies furnished evidence of the effects of numbers. Allee did not claim increased survival in all cases for increasing numbers, but warned us of the fallacy of deciding there is no such value because it is not evident.[29]

Allee acknowledged that the harmful effects of large aggregations of nonsocial animals [30] was experimentally established in the 1850s by the work of Hogg on water snails,[31] but he saw the many exceptions to Hogg's conclusion as evidence of another principle at work. The most notable of these exceptions are the large aggregations of nonsocial species of animals at breeding time, during migrations and hibernations, but aside from such obviously mutually beneficial aggregations, Allee cited numerous other examples, such as the layer of euglena causing the green "bloom" over many stagnant ponds,[32] the colonial forms of various invertebrates,[33] overnight aggregations of certain insects collecting around lights and sleeping together,[34] and stag parties of Scottish deer.[35] Such aggregations may not always be to the best interests of the animal, yet in the long run, Allee pointed out, animal behavior must be beneficial or the species would be exterminated.[36] Evolution, and perhaps the development of sex, Allee thought, resulted from the beneficial aspects of aggregations.[37]

From a wide variety of animal phyla, Allee collected an impressive amount of evidence for a world of order, mutual aid and harmony, which he extended to humans. He thought this automatic cooperation sufficiently widespread among animals to warrant its adoption as a fundamental property of animal protoplasm, and probably of all protoplasm.[38] The acceptance of this biological principle in social theory and as a basis for human behavior, he prophesied, would chart a new course in human history.[39]

In his book *On Being Human,* Montagu attempted to reconcile positions as diverse as the rank materialism of our scientific age, which reduces humans to pi mesons and neutrinos with the rest of matter,[40] and the ineffable idealism of that love given us by Christ Himself which can transform and transfigure a human being into a creature, somehow divine.[41] As Darwin, in proclaiming nature's struggle-for-existence law, supplied a scientific basis for the social and political theory of his time, so Montagu now envisions biology as underwriting Christ's doctrine of love for one's neighbor. Montagu did not discount materialistic evolution, but thought it bore more valid testimony to an opposite law of love, rather than to Darwin's theory of struggle and strife. Nature tells us not to compete, he reechoed from Kropotkin's *Mutual Aid:*[42]

> Today, contrary to the "nature, red in tooth and claw" school of natural selectionists, the evidence does not act principally to favor variations which through a ruthless kind of competition better adjust the organism to its environment. Adjustment is, of course, necessary, but the important point is that natural selection favors the co-operative, as opposed to the disoperative, struggle for life. To "struggle for life" is to be cooperative, for life is of its nature social and all activities calculated to maintain it in the individual and in the species are co-operative.[43]

Insofar as humans are concerned, Montagu says, competition has no adaptive value in the modern world, he stated.[44] That "man is born for co-operation, not for competition and conflict...is a basic discovery of modern science."[45] The sense of mutuality and cooperativeness may be suppressed, but it will eventually assert itself again, for it is of the essence of human protoplasm, Montagu insisted.[46] "Man can retain his health and flourish only in love of, and co-operation with his fellow man."[47] He attributed many of the evils of our Western world, such as mental disorders, fears, anxiety and insecurity, to the competitive attitude humans take toward one another. The basic need of humankind is security, which love alone can satisfy. In fact, Montagu identified love with security.[48] Such a love, which is fundamentally a property of protoplasm[49] and develops under the aegis of the organism's "ever-present urge to feel secure,"[50] lacks, of course, the transforming properties of the theological virtue of charity. But for one who knows that grace perfects nature, even a naturally enriched substrate for charity, a scientific promise for a world whose hope rests in science, is "good news."

Both Allee and Montagu gave extensive references in verification of this principle of harmony in nature. Neither of them, however, attempted such a universal substantiation of their views as did Herbert Spencer in establishing his principles of nature. Whereas Allee laid his foundation primarily in protoplasm, in which he found an inherent automatic cooperation, an unconscious kind of mutualism,[51] and Montagu suggested that the fundamental social nature of all things stems from the physiological relationship between parent and offspring,[52] Spencer dug deeply into the inanimate and found his universal principle in evidence at the level of the mineral, the inanimate.[53] If the principle that is to stand is the one that can best be substantiated from the facts of nature, it seems necessary to call to the witness stand any related fields that can give testimony.

Our concepts of the material universe as explained by the contemporary chemist and physicist are based on statistical laws throughout. Probability and laws of chance applied to statistical aggregates account for the rate of disintegration of uranium and of the pressure of a gas in its container. The action or nature of one atom of uranium cannot be known, but laws for the disintegration of large aggregates of such atoms can be established. Such order arises from the very tendency of large aggregates to randomness—our faith in which has been established by the second law of thermodynamics, entropy. Biologists quickly fell in line, marching to the same tune. Today geneticists tell us of a comparable randomness among genetic entities. Only large numbers of genes, statistical aggregates, provide foundation blocks for Mendelian genetics.

George Gaylord Simpson pointed out that "the shuffling of existing stocks of genes in sexual reproduction is, in the main, random."[54] Evolution is an interplay between "the largely random operation of the whole mechanism of heredity" and the orienting effect of adaptation.[55]

Does this basic arbitrariness, randomness in nature, which physics and chemistry report to us indicate a lack of order, a sort of chaos as the bedrock of our material universe? Perhaps such "laws" are really only an acknowledgement of our ignorance. At least at the time that he wrote *The Origin of the Species,* Darwin thought so:

> I have hitherto sometimes spoken as if the variations—so common and multiform with organic beings under domestication, and in a lesser degree with those under nature—were due to chance. This, of course, is a wholly incorrect expression, but it serves to acknowledge plainly our ignorance of the cause of each particular variation.[56]

In *Creative Evolution,* Henri Bergson pointed out that the appearance of chance, disorder, randomness in nature is only a negative finding disguised in a positive expression. Because one does not find the order in nature that one expected (which is only one out of a number of possible orders that nature could display for an inquiring mind) nature is said to be based on disorder or randomness.[57]

Is this so-called disorder, randomness in nature, which becomes intelligible for many today only in the light of laws of chance, somehow akin to Darwin's principle of struggle, to Empedocles' principle of strife? The modern biologist supports the idea of mutual aid, of cooperation in the biotic world, but sees no contradiction in stating that this order stems from chance, from randomness. There seem to be only two ways of explaining the world: either it arose out of design or from chance. If we admit it is a product of design, of a Divine Creator, then a basic principle of harmony in nature, its fundamental tendency to order, would be a sign of His handiwork. If the apparent order in nature, which none can deny, has come to be by chance, if humankind itself is only a fortuitous accident, could strife and struggle be nature's foundation stones? Darwin's idea of struggle has not been without supporters among sociologists, economists, biologists, philosophers and even would-be theologians. Allee and Montagu, representing biology and anthropology, found spokesmen from as many fields represented among the advocates of cooperation.[58] Which yields a more fruitful approach to nature, a truer conception of the real world?

Simpson, a geneticist, rejected the Darwinian concept of struggle, which he thought to be a cause of serious misunderstanding of the work of natural selection,[59] but he regarded this process of selection as a blind force, not as an harmonious principle established by design.[60] We become suspicious of Simpson's tenets when we examine some of his conclusions. Seemingly this is another case of a little error in the beginning becoming a big error in the conclusion.

> It has also been shown that purpose and plan are not characteristic of organic evolution and are not a key to any of its operations.... Man was certainly not the goal of evolution, which evidently had no goal. He was not planned, in an operation wholly planless.[61]

Or let us listen to the creed of another contemporary biologist:

> Most basically, natural selection converts accident into apparent design, randomness into organized pattern. Mutation merely provides the raw material of evolution; it is a random affair, and takes place in all directions. [62]

Is there no way out of the dilemma? It is plainly evident that there is competition for life going on in nature. When we sit down to table we are enjoying nourishment at the expense of other forms of life. Yet when we behold with Shelley "nature's unchanging harmony,"[66] we are convinced with Tennyson that "the whole wood-world is one full peal of praise."[67] Here is order, here is harmony, here is peace, here is God. The scientist stands back in awe and lets the poet speak: There is a clue to the Christian, when he reads the blasphemous conclusions with regard to God that some modern biologists are making,[63] that either their principles are wrong or their logic is faulty. However, it may be confusing to see the same principle used as evidence in support of, or against, religious beliefs and a moral code. Montagu claimed a confirmation of religious truths in his principle of love in nature.[64] Allee was ready to drop any ideas in conflict with the whims of modern science. In his book, *Cooperation Among Animals,* he suggested in an offhand way that most of the genetic ill effects of a population badly shattered by war could be prevented, if monogamy were "less of an ingrained human practice."[65]

Flower in the crannied wall,
I pluck you out of the crannies,
I hold you here, root and all, in my hand,
Little flower—but *if* I could understand
What you are, root and all, and all in all,
I should know what God and man is.[68]

But is no one qualified to speak out with certitude in favor of one principle as being the more fundamental? Must we despair of arriving at the truth through human reason? Is Allee correct in thinking that metaphysics as a unifying discipline is powerless today,[69] especially as it appears on the stage as a subordinate character to modern science, which certainly has the lead? Perhaps the following, from Alfred N. Whitehead's *Science and the Modern World,* may give us a valuable clue:

The men of the Middle Ages were in pursuit of an excellency of which we have nearly forgotten the existence. They set before themselves the ideal of the attainment of a harmony of the understanding. We are contents with superficial ordering from diverse arbitrary starting points.[70]

Whence did the scholars of the Middle Ages acquire a hope of such an excellent type of knowledge, whereby truth could be harmonized and ordered, so that some truths could be established and held with certainty, others with more or less probability? They did not have to wait to see how many facts from sensible experience future generations could muster, to get their starting points. They eagerly welcomed all the facts nature reluctantly yields to questing minds to give the correct overtones and amplifications to the principles they understood, accepted and defended through their reason.[71]

Metaphysics served as a handmaid to their theology, and directed and regulated human science. It was the guardian of the principles of all less noble sciences—the study of mobile being, mathematics and moral science. In defending the principles of the other sciences in the light of their highest causes, metaphysics is at once a science and a wisdom. As a science, it provides certain conclusions; as a wisdom, it puts order in all knowledge. What was the origin of such a rational system? Like so much in Western thought, it came from the fruitful period of Greek thought when humans had confidence in their power to reason. In the mind of a great scientific genius, Aristotle, the Greeks brought forth a whole schema of human learning and established the order and relation-ship of all the natural disciplines. In book three, chapter four, of his *Metaphysics,* Aristotle pointed out the mistake that Empedocles made in making strife a principle and a cause. How many blind alleys modern science might have avoided if metaphysics had continued to light up its way. Then came the thirteenth century. It captured the crown from the Greeks when it brought forth its great intellectual light, Thomas Aquinas, and through him brought theology into this beautiful synthe-sis of the sciences as its queen.

Without this synthesis, at least without metaphysics, we have no reg-ulative science, no guide through human reason, no criteria for accept-ing one explanation in favor of another. Rather, we then have to depend on the larger and more compelling number of experiments performed, in the hope that nature will thereby confirm some particular principle. Wisdom becomes only an empty dream with which not even a poet would want to consort. In *Cooperation Among Animals,* Allee pointed out that there is at least one major attempt being made today to unify all knowledge around metaphysics. He concluded: "Such efforts, while furnishing an excellent corrective for overconfident scientists, seem mis-chievously naïve as a serious, present-day movement."[72] But if such naïveté can get us out of our present dilemma, then let us be naïve. By what standard did Toynbee decide that all creatures are at war with all other creatures and even with their Creator? If we can during our life count more experiences in favor of Darwin's struggle, shall we take his starting point? Or, if we can muster more actual cases on the side of cooperation, will we then side with Allee and Montagu? Should we wait until the end of our lives to get our starting point, or shall we continue to be satisfied with "diverse arbitrary starting points"?

In 1948, Schrödinger delivered a series of lectures at University Col-lege, London, on "Nature and the Greeks."[73] He proposed and devel-oped the idea that a return to ancient thought would be productive of greater fertility for science and philosophy. Had the Greeks' "highly flexible and open-minded spirit" been retained with the fruits of their thought, many supposed laws of modern science would have been pruned of error sooner.[74] In fact, the modern crisis in theoretical phys-ics, with Newton's absolute space and time yielding to relativity, and the latter with quantum mechanics perhaps yielding to Heisenberg's new field theory, has shown the necessity of reexamining the foundation stones of modern physical theory[75] Marston Bates indicated a similar need in biology:

> We still, I think, have managed little improvement of Darwin's theory. The woods are full of neo-Darwinians, anti-Darwinians, Lamarckians, Bergsonians, orthogenicists, and goodness knows what else, all with theories to sell, mostly wrapped in almost impenetrable layers of verbiage. The core, when finally arrived at, usually looks to me like metaphysics— an *elan vital,* an innate tendency of some kind beyond the reach of the experimental method. Such theories then belong to the province of the philosophers, and ought to be examined there.[76]

In the spirit of Schrödinger's and Bates's suggestions, let us ask Aristotle what nature's fundamental working principle is. Is it order, harmony, cooperation, based on design, or struggle, strife, competition, based on pure chance? Aristotle did not wait for biology to settle this principle of nature, but found the answer in the more general natural science, physics. In the second book of his *Physics,* he asked nature whether her operations are from design or by chance. Again, does nature operate for the sake of something or just from necessity? Does it rain to make corn grow, or just from the necessity of the water vapor that has condensed and has become a burden to the sky? Are teeth differentiated into incisors, canines, molars from a necessity of nature or in order to perform diverse functions better, such as cutting, tearing and chewing?

Aristotle thought it impossible that nature acted only because of chance or from the necessity of matter. Things are not said to be by chance when they happen regularly. If we touch a hot stove we do not say that it is by chance we were burned, or that is by chance that a chicken hatches from a chicken egg. Obviously, what happens regularly, or for the most part, is not by chance. But that which we say is from nature happens regularly or for the most part, and therefore is not by chance.

When a series has an end or completion, all the steps in the series are for the end. When an artist paints a picture, all the steps are for the end, the landscape to be portrayed. In the same way, the steps nature takes are for a determinate end and so are ordered to it. The bird constructs its nest in a certain way, characteristic of the species, in order to hold and to protect the eggs and the young birds. Leaves on a tree are arranged to give maximum surface exposure for absorption of sunlight and also to protect the fruit. Water seeks its own level and thus provides innumerable benefits for all organic life. The fact that nature does not deliberate presented no problem to Aristotle. Neither does art deliberate; if it did, the wood could make itself into a bed. Just as intelligent action is for an end, so nature is for an end. To say nature acts haphazardly because we cannot see the deliberation in the Mind of a Divine Artist is like saying that an arrow is not directed to the target by the mind of the archer, but only by a necessity of his hormones, sinews, arms, fingers, the bow, the medium through which it travels and so on.

After establishing dialectically the opinion that nature operates for an end,[77] Aristotle used it in all his subsequent investigations of the natural world—his chemistry, astronomy, psychology and biology. He then scrutinized it from the heights of metaphysics.[78] He found no fundamental inconsistency, so for him this is an established and sure starting point for further advance in knowledge of the physical world.

St. Thomas did not stop at Aristotle's elevation of natural wisdom. Trained rigorously in the disciplines of the ancients, under the shadow of divine revelation, he was able to use, to clarify, often to correct and amplify, if need be, the principles, and certainly the development, of Aristotle's natural wisdom—that it might be transformed and touch on the divine. He regarded the whole rhythm and movement of the universe, down to its tiniest atom as in the all-true and pure light of the Trinity. He considered all things in the order and the harmony with which they proceed from God.

As he commented on the *Physics,* St. Thomas reasoned with Aristotle that nature works for an end. In the *Summa* he observed repeatedly that things tend more to the common good than to their own individual good.[79] St. Thomas used another argument from Aristotle when he pointed out that the good of the universe resembles the good of an army, in that the good of an army is both in the order of its parts and in its leader, but more in the leader, for the order is dependent on him, and not vice versa.[80] Aristotle had already pointed out that all things in the universe are somehow ordered.[81] Therefore, said St. Thomas, the order of the universe must have been properly intended by God and is not the result of a succession of agents, as some thought. If the order of the whole depended on Him, then He must have an idea of each of the parts, as a builder could not conceive the whole building without having an idea of each of its parts.[82]

Modern science would readily yield testimony in favor of this intellectually satisfying approach to our problem. Never before have we been so aware of the delicate balance of materials and forces here on earth as we are at present. As we contemplate rocketing into the hostile environment of outer space, we are making very careful examinations of our "womb-like utopia"[83]—the earth.

If we are able to take Laika's place in a Sputnik or any other spaceship, we must capture a small bit of mother earth and take her with us. Again art must imitate nature, for we must build our little earth, our artificial external environment, so as to reproduce and maintain a close approximation to the conditions found on earth. Our foods must conform to the standards set by nature when she produces carbohydrates, fats and proteins for us, and enriches them with minerals and vitamins. We must have the bulk mother earth provides, for, according to rocket expert Willy Ley, a meal in a pill will not work.[84]

We will have trouble pulling ourselves and our little earth away from our natural home. An astronaut weighing 180 pounds on earth will weigh over half a ton during take-off into space. Normally we are accustomed to the gravitation stress of one g at sea level. At seven g our blood becomes like liquid iron.[85] In launching a rocket, peaks of up to nine g may be experienced.[86] Then, as the speed in the spaceship counterbalances the so-called pull of gravity, our astronaut must adjust to the ordeal of weightlessness. Dr. Siegfried J. Gerathewohl of the Army Ballistic Missile Agency at Redstone Arsenal, Alabama, has investigated the digestive difficulties to be faced. About one third of those subjected to virtual weightless conditions, he found, suffered from minor to severe gastrointestinal complaints.[87] The psychological effects of weightlessness on humans may indeed by even more drastic. In fact, Colonel J. P. Henry predicted that an astronaut might suffer a mental breakdown after only a few hours of weightlessness, if proper stimuli were not provided.[88]

All in all the new field of space medicine makes us more aware that we are "at home" on earth for a great variety of reasons. As humans become the center of the evolutionary stage, the evidence for an Antichance Cause becomes ever more compelling. If humanity is the end or goal of nature, our existence on this earth sheds light on the whole unfolding of the universe during the ages it was being prepared for our advent. To decide arbitrarily that chance, or competition based on chance, can explain this mysterious universe is one approach, but one that can scarcely satisfy open minds that have not been dulled by the biased answers cluttering the minds of many of our modern scientists. Here, obviously, is a case of carefully laid and executed plans, the blueprint for a fitting home for humans to become co-creators of the earth. It seems equally obvious that only the most detailed cooperative efforts on our part will permit us to explore the realms of space. Cooperation, not competition, is the price of survival.

First published in *The New Scholasticism* Vol. XXXIII No. 4 (October 1959)

9.

The Cell and the Organism
A Re-Examination

Current Attitudes Toward Cell and Organism

                *I*n this biological era of absorption in DNA synthesis, of genetic code breakthrough, of analyses of all organisms and pieces of organisms into subcellular components and into macromolecules, interest in cells and organisms may seem an outmoded area of investigation for biologists. For many, biology has become molecular biology, and its proponents are as often as not drawn from other fields. *Life* magazine, in an article on the mysterious DNA molecule, reported that the pioneers of "molecule biology" are a new breed, of whom many began their careers as mathematicians, physicists, and chemists.[1] The biochemist Edward Tatum is an example. In his Nobel Prize address in Stockholm he referred to himself not only as a biochemist but also as a biologist and a geneticist.[2]

The large sums of money available for biochemical research, the extravagant claims of conceptual breakthroughs of modern molecular biology are attracting more and more scientists into this field. *Newsweek* on May 13, 1963 in an article entitled "Exploring the Secret of Life," exalted the triumphs of molecular biology and quoted a Nobel Prize winner as saying that scientists are now "playing God for real." The "brave new world" seems to be in process of realization, as reports appear that scientists are closing in on the secret of life by decoding "the atom of life," DNA, and that research in biochemistry is leading inexorably toward the control of human inheritance.[3] Students looking for the shortest road to success in the biological sciences are flocking to these expanding and exciting new frontiers in biology.

Nobel prizes to Beadle and Tatum in 1958 for their experiments in relating genes and enzymes, to Ochoa and Kornberg in 1959 for synthesizing DNA from a purified enzyme preparation acting *in vitro*, and to Watson and Crick in 1962 for working out a plausible explanation of the structure of the DNA molecule highlight the main areas of interest in so-called biology laboratories of the mid-twentieth century.

Traditionalists Survive

Looking for another side to this story in current biological literature, biology lecture rooms and some research laboratories, we find that there are still many biologists who have resisted the attractions of the above-mentioned more popular avenues of biological investigation. In cases where they are using the tools and techniques of modern biology, they have refused to resort to oversimplified molecular explanations of complex biological phenomena. Their critical examination of their own work in its relation to that of the molecular biologist promises new and healthy growth in biological ideas and makes a periodic re-examination a profitable endeavor.

Evidence from Literature

Paul Weiss, eminent embryologist at Rockefeller Institute, is typical of this group of scientists who are not overawed by the dramatic evolution of molecular biology. In one of the papers he presented at the study program in biophysical science conducted by the National Institute of Health at Boulder, Colorado in 1958, Weiss reminded scientists present that "the level of the organism is reached from the level of molecular biology not in one single jump over the conceptual gap customarily bridged by the word 'organization,'" but only when "one learns to think in terms of a hierarchy of ordered systems, each one with some degree of identity and stability even on supramolecular levels." Because there have been such "phenomenal advances made in the study of the partial and isolated system, in contrast to the dearth of information on the *organized interactions of such systems in the living cell and organism,*" Weiss pleaded for a more balanced effort and more extensive occupation with higher level problems.[4]

In support of the same position, Francis Schmitt's paper for the same study program, "Molecular Biology and the Physical Basis of Life," was a masterful critique of molecular biology set in a historical framework of the controversies and achievements that helped mold its embryonic development and that must be taken into account if molecular biology is to have healthy and vigorous growth in the future. The spectacular discoveries in the biophysical sciences are certainly the sequel to the analytical approach of molecular biology, but Schmitt suggested the following limitations to this approach:

> Actually, the tendency of physicists who have become biologists or biophysicists has been to search for simplified models of complex biological processes and, by a sophisticated study of such models, to discover fundamental new principles in biology. In this approach the numerous complexities and vast areas of ignorance that lie between the simplified model system and the end biological process under study are characteristically and purposely avoided or neglected. It is recognized that there is a formidable "black box" between the molecular effectors, as studied in the model system, and the final behavior of the cells or organisms under study.[5]

It is to cast light in the direction of this black box, to lessen the chasm between the model system of the biophysicist and the cell and the organism, that Schmitt directed himself in his paper. Schmitt expressed the hope that his historical sketch would not only provide a much needed perspective of the organismic properties of living things, but also might stimulate some to consider the vast opportunities opening up in theoretical biology, a field he considered to be almost non-existent at the time of the study program in 1959. Such a theoretical biology, Schmitt elucidated, would of necessity deal not only with the properties of subcellular elements but also with the properties of the organism as a whole.[6]

It is of interest to note that, perhaps in answer to Schmitt's challenge, the *Journal of Theoretical Biology* came into existence just three years later. The eminent physiologist Albert Szent-Gyorgyi, one of the first contributors to this journal, in a paper entitled "The Supra- and Sub-molecular in Biology," echoed Schmitt's concern and the growing concern of many about the overemphasis on molecular biology. He acknowledged the tremendous advances made in the field of biochemistry in such areas as intermediary metabolism, in the isolation and the chemical identification of hormones, enzymes, vitamins, and nucleic acids, but followed it by warning that "in spite of these achievements, biochemistry has failed to bring us closer to the understanding of the more complex and subtle biological phenomena, like motion, nervous activity, [and] secretion." All of these more complex and peculiarly biological functions are somehow "linked to the cellular structures which biochemists, interested in extracts, discard as the 'residue.' " The DNA and RNA that the protein chemists have been trying to decode come mainly from these soluble protein extracts. Szent-Gyorgyi has no doubt that "the molecular concept has greatly helped to clarify the structure and function of extractable substances"; yet he emphasized "that it breaks down in the realm of biological structures, and its rigorous application actually retards progress."[7]

Barry Commoner, chairman of the Committee on Molecular Biology at Washington University, St. Louis, in an address as retiring vice president of the American Association for the Advancement of Science, was not being facetious when he asked if the "DNA story" was not really an attack on biology.[8] Even the eminent and very serious scientist Jean Brachet did not take very seriously his own attempt to explain the phenomenon of differentiation of cells in terms of molecular biology. He concluded with the statement that it was amusing to attempt such an explanation even though his theorizing was highly speculative and might well prove to be entirely wrong.[9] The February 1964 issue of *Bio-Science,* the newly named publication of the American Institute of Biological Sciences, carries an article by Robert Zuck entitled "Molecular Botany—a New Anti-Intellectualism?"[10]

There are certainly dead ends that result when one area of a science expands drastically at the expense of all of the others. There is also another ambush to which biologists are being alerted by critical thinkers in their midst. When those in one field of science begin making extrapolations into another without consideration of the necessary and appropriate conversions, more error than truth may be generated. Photoelectric cells resemble sense organs only in an analogous way.[11] An organism is not just "a collection of substances organized according to a dynamic programme which keeps it going and enables it to reproduce itself," "a self-perpetuating programme."[12] "Much of homeostasis can be understood in terms of mechanistic models, such as relatively straightforward feedback cycles, but it is by no means certain that homeostasis can be entirely comprehended in these terms."[13] The switching on and off of metabolic syntheses at particular genetic sites does not completely account for the differentiation of cells and tissues.[14] In the opinion of a growing number of biologists, appropriate mathematical and physical models have not yet been evolved that are specifically tailored to biological phenomena.[15]

Physicists, too, are concerned about these careless extrapolations from one field to another. J. R. Platt observed that "men of the greatest experience and insight cannot be perfectly certain of their approximations when they extend their results from one field to another." There is, as he said, no absolute standard by which to judge the validity of their intuitions and approximations. Only by empirical evidence can this be established. "This means," according to Platt, "that every science that is a science will always have to develop its own peculiar and powerful methods of inference and methods of organizing and structuring its field." He concluded that the rules of any science and "its own 'new properties of matter' are the best theoretical guides in making appropriate approximations and inferences."[16] The mathematics, physics, chemistry and engineering needed to advance and accelerate biological knowledge will have to be developed within the framework of biological principles. In this field the "matter" under investigation is that of living things. It is formally alive.

But despite the many difficulties attendant on the merging of diverse disciplines, the biological community has grown and has been strengthened and enriched as the result of extending the range of tools, techniques and interests in biology and of the recruitments from other fields. Recent publications of outstanding biologists and their biochemist confreres reveal a kind of wholesome ecumenism at work among them. Biologists refer to "molecular ecology,"[17] "complex biomolecules,"[18] "topographical chemistry,"[19] and "super-macromolecular aggregates"[20] as an admission that organisms are made up of molecules. But the discussion of molecules in terms of super-macromolecular aggregates suggests that organisms can be explained not in terms of isolated molecular units but only as systems of interacting molecules which are structured into more complex units such as cells or organisms.

On the part of biochemists, there seems to be a growing awareness of and an enhanced respect for the enormous complexity of the problem they assumed when they accepted the challenge to probe the nature of life with their analytical techniques for studying metabolic pathways and biosynthetic reactions. It has become increasingly apparent that an understanding of individual reactions involves complex cycles and chains of analyses and syntheses. An understanding of the complexities existing at any one level, it is now realized, may be dependent on examination by appropriate techniques of the interrelationships existing between the level under study and the higher and lower levels. Horizontal isolation of problems may be a necessary but often misleading occupation for biochemical biologists, whose tendency now is to put their molecules back into their environing conditions, thus considering larger and larger aggregates. F. J. Bollum of Oak Ridge National Laboratories at a Symposium on "Macromolecular Aspects of the Cell Cycle" held at Gatlinburg in April 1963 pointed out that the size of the biochemist's nucleic acid molecule has jumped from 1,000–2,000 g/mole, in a popular textbook of the 1930s, to a recent proposal of a molecular weight of four billion for the DNA molecule of *Escherichia coli*. At this point, Bollum declared the "molecular biologists have gone too far" for the realm of chemistry is exceeded when the molecule reaches the range of microscopic observation.[21]

It is particularly refreshing to know that so many biologists are suggesting that completely new approaches are necessary, that new techniques must be developed if biological problems are to be solved. "Multifactorial investigations will naturally demand entirely new conceptual and experimental methods." Rene Dubos, with his characteristic daring, claimed that these investigations will be "very different from those involving only one variable, which have been the stock in trade of experimental science during the past three hundred years and to which there is an increasing tendency to limit biological research."[22] Revolutionary proposals of this kind from eminent scientists prepare biologists for a return to biological investigations and to theoretical considerations of cells and organisms.

The Cell Theory

The most basic powers of living things—growth, nutrition and reproduction—are certainly evident at the cellular and organismal levels. For the majority of biologists, excepting those who have the title by reason of having transferred to the biology department from the mathematics, physics, or chemistry department, the fundamental reproducing unit is the cell; for, as Harold Blum pointed out, "It has not been unequivocally shown that any smaller unit is capable of truly independent reproduction."[23]

Lack of evidence for true reproduction of subcellular units, and the growing skeptical attitude of a group of scientists (such as those quoted above) concerning the ability of molecular biology to give satisfactory answers to biological questions, makes this a favorable time for a re-examination of the cell versus the organism as the unit of life and therefore as the principal subject of biological investigations. The organismal theory has the longest history in biology, but the cell theory has had great heuristic value, and biology on the whole has advanced and prospered since its formulations.

These basic theories in science, like the perennial problems in philosophy, need re-examination in every age, for, like organisms, they must have continuity lest they perish and become extinct. Sometimes the old arguments only need restatement, but more often the arguments that convince one generation of thinkers must be reassessed and replaced by those with more appeal to a new generation. In this "age of analysis," the experimentalist is the only authority whose voice will be sympathetically heard, and, in fact, this is the healthy frame of mind that has been the foundation stone for the edifice of science in the Western world. Aristotle himself criticized those physicists whose "explanation of the observation is not consistent with the observations[24] His advice is as pertinent today as it was two thousand years ago when he wrote:

> Lack of experience diminishes our power of taking a comprehensive view of the admitted facts. Hence those who dwell in intimate association with nature and its phenomena grow more and more able to formulate, as foundations of their theories, principles such as to admit of a wide and coherent development; while those whom devotion to abstract discussions has rendered unobservant of the facts are too ready to dogmatize on the basis of a few observations.[25]

It is an encouraging sign of the growth in mid-twentieth-century biology that it is not a rarity to find scientists whose experiments are designed to answer basic theoretical problems and whose publications discuss their results in the light of these fundamental ideas.

Before I turn to these experiments, I shall first formulate some of the questions pertinent to the problem of the cell or the organism as the primary natural unit of biology. These may be stated: Is the power of life resident in the cell, as Schwann claimed,[26] or is it rather in the organism as a whole? In other words, is the cell the unit of life? Does the cell make other cells like itself and, ultimately, does a conglomeration or an organized pattern of closely and loosely bound cells determine the organism? Does the cell send only those signals that are established in its own nucleus and thus determine the emergence of the specializations and new powers of the developing embryo?

Or is the cell not the sole director of its own fate and that of the environing cells? Do the cells receive directives from a higher level? Do they in some way play a subordinate part to some more autonomous level or levels of organization above?

Whence comes the power that directs the developing embryo through its marvelous series of forms into the adult fly or human? Does the organism have some kind of mysterious power of directing the whole? Is there a uniqueness to the organism, to the cell, or are all levels of organization equally unique?[27]

In his paper "Microscopical Researches," Schwann's argument in favor of the cell theory rested heavily on the fact that cells, such as eggs, spores and individual cells of simpler plants, can grow and develop apart from the organism. From this, Schwann argued that "every elementary part possesses a power of its own, an independent life, by means of which it would be enabled to develop itself independently, if the relations which it bore to external parts were but similar to those in which it stands in the organism." Schwann argued that the cause of growth should be the same in all cells and that, since some are capable of independent growth and development, all must have this capacity. The cause of growth should not lie at one time in the cell and another in the whole organism.[28]

There are several important problems posed by Schwann's thesis. His proposal that some cells, such as fertilized eggs and spores, can develop independently is based on the assumption that an egg is only a cell. In fact, it is a very special kind of cell, a cell that is a potential organism, a potential whole. There are evident difficulties that arise when the same term, "cell," is used for an egg, a potential organism; for a liver cell, a part of an organism; and for a ciliate, a whole organism.[29] In this paper, reference to the cell will be to that entity which is a part of the organism, the cell *sensu stricto*. One-celled or acellular animals or plants will be regarded as organisms, not as cells. The problem of the egg as a potential organism is too complex for inclusion in this paper.

Another problem proposed by Schwann that seems premature for his time but is of considerable interest today is the consideration that growth and differentiation of cells in tissue culture does seem to depend to a great extent on the provision of a suitable environment.[30] There are investigators today who think that the cell, when cultured in nutritionally adequate media, can produce the full symphony of structures and functions of a living organism. But the complexities of the homeostatic regulatory processes within an organism provoke the question whether any situation less than that of the internal media of an organism itself can provide such an environment.

Let us look at the record. That cells grow and proliferate in tissue culture has been known since the latter part of the nineteenth century. In 1887 Arnold observed cell division in artificial culture. He soaked thin slices of pith from an elder twig in the aqueous humor from a frog's eye and planted them in the peritoneal cavity of another frog. Subsequently he removed them for examination under the microscope. The leukocytes that had collected in the pith crept out and could be observed moving and dividing.[31] Methods for culturing cells in vitro are now far more varied, more carefully controlled, and more precise. It is well known that cell or tissues planted in suitable culture media can grow, but what is the evidence that these cells growing in artificial culture can differentiate into tissues or organs?

Generalizations in a field such as tissue culture are likely to be short-lived, for new techniques are rendering the experiments of a few months earlier obsolete. If a whole or a part of an embryonic rudiment is explanted in a so-called organ culture, the tissues will retain their specialized characteristics and may become progressively differentiated. Literature of the second quarter of the twentieth century, when organ and tissue culture was more popular, emphasized the stability of cell types of differentiated tissue. But for the last ten or fifteen years cell culture has largely replaced tissue culture. In 1959 Clifford Grobstein, a well-known experimental embryologist at Stanford University, noted:

"The growing literature of cell culture emphasized departure from properties in vivo, variation, and the difficulty of establishing differentiated cell type."[32] Cells cultured without the stabilizing influence of other cells and tissues of the organ or the organism from which they came lose overt differentiation rather rapidly. Until quite recently there were no recorded exceptions to the generalization that individual cells can grow but cannot differentiate in tissue culture.[33]

This tendency of cells grown in culture to de-differentiate, to revert to a common cell type, some attributed to a return to the embryonic state, but in the cases where redifferentiation of the cell has been induced, the characteristic pattern expressed by the cell is that of its place of origin.[37] Dedifferentiated skin cells redifferentiate into epithelial tissue, keratin, and feathers. The "blueprint" for its specialized features is in some way in the cell itself. This leads us to the question of whether the specificity of the cell is genetically determined. If a cell differentiates, must it do so according to the pattern or code dictated to it by the genes in its nucleus? After extensive studies on the functions of artificially cultured mammalian cells, Harry Eagle, chairman of the Department of Cell Biology of the Albert Einstein College of Medicine, concluded that "with only a few exceptions ... the highly diversified functions of differentiated cells in the intact animal have not been reproduced in serially propagated cultures."[34] The cell in culture seems incapable of pursuing the course it would have followed in vivo. With regard to the failure of these cells to carry out the functions of the organs from which they originated, Eagle questioned whether the specifically active cell has in fact not been propagated, or whether instead the active cell has been propagated but fails to exert its functional capacity in serial culture.[35] It has been shown that the first cells migrating out of a liver explant lacked enzymes proper to liver tissue in vivo. Either they were already functionally inadequate or they were cells of a type other than the liver gland cells.[36]

Genetic or Functional Determination of the Cell?

There is considerable evidence accumulating that the genetic makeup of the cell is not of great significance to cells growing in culture media. Eagle observed that "the development of polyploidy, heteroploidy, and of gross chromosomal aberrations has not been regularly accompanied by demonstrable changes in the nutritional requirements or metabolic activity of the cells."[38] He has found that almost all serially propagated lines of cultured cells are heteroploid and that they have wide variations in chromosome number within any one culture. The similarity of their metabolic requirements and functions stands out in sharp contrast to the chromosomal variation. He has even been unable to discern metabolic differences between cancer and normal tissue grown in vitro.[39]

Walter Tulecke, in reviewing some of the recent experimental work on plant cell cultures, found that the same holds true for plants. Plant cells in artificial culture are heteroploid for the most part; but, like animal cells, they too converge to a common cell type. In cell culture their range of enzymes is restricted, their metabolic activities are simplified and their characteristic functions are lost.[40]

Daniel Mazia, referring to experiments in which chromosomes have been removed from the cells prior to division, concluded that not even cell division is dependent on the chromosome; in other words, cell division is not genetically determined.[41]

Experiments by A. A. Moscona also lend support to the conclusion that cells grown in artificial culture are determined more by the function or form of the organ from which they originated than by the genetic endowment of the cells. Moscona has worked out a technique for dissociating cells of mammalian and avian embryonic tissues by treating them with low concentrations of tryptic enzymes. In the last few years he has been able to standardize a technique for reaggregating these cells in a highly consistent and diagnostically reliable way by mechanical means. Under constant conditions of temperature, of volume and kind of media, and of number and kind of cells, cells of like tissues come together in characteristic patterns based on the type of tissue employed in the experiment. The cell population from any one tissue Moscona found to be quite distinctive, e.g., cells from a seven-day embryonic chick liver coalesced consistently in a single mass, whereas those of neuro-retinal cells under the same conditions formed a number of characteristic, irregularly shaped clusters.

At first the cells of like tissues simply reaggregate, but within hours the aggregated cells begin to construct characteristic, histologically identifiable structures that closely reproduce the essential architectural features of their tissue of origin;[42] for example, aggregated liver cells form the liver parenchyma and bile ducts. Since this restoration of histotypic structure occurs within the first twenty-four hours of aggregation and before significant mitotic division is resumed, Moscona assumed that it is due to reshuffling and resorting of cells. The mechanical means of preparing these aggregations assures that all cells are brought toward the center of a rotating flask and thus arbitrarily into contact with one another. Those cells of like origin "recognize" one another and cohere. The architecture of the tissue and the organ is in some way ingrained in the cell, yet, strangely enough, Moscona found that the cells are not species-specific. Homologous cells of comparable age from mouse or chick will cohere in the same characteristic patterns irrespective of the species. Liver cells from mouse and chick will cohere in one mass, as though from one animal, and will form chimeric liver structure. Moscona concluded that homologous functional traits, rather than genetic traits, are being expressed in these characteristic patterns of embryonic cell populations. Properties transcending the differences between species or the genetic determinants of the cells are at work.[43]

Paul Weiss obtained similar results with in vivo experiments. He stated that cells can "locate" their proper destinations in a host embryo even if they are deprived of their customary way of getting there. Weiss and G. Andres in 1952 introduced precursor cells of pigmented skin of the embryo of a black chicken into the vascular system of a host embryo of a nonpigmented white chicken. They chose the precursors of pigmented cells for the obvious reason that these would be identifiable if they differentiated further in the host embryo.

About eight per cent of the chicks that had received the precursor cells had patches of black in their skin and feathers. In no case was a pigmented cell seen in a place where pigmentation did not normally occur. This indicated that the cells in vivo also "'recognize" their kind or cohere to cells of the same functional types and only continue differentiation when established in a colony of such cells.[44] This "homing" instinct in cells again points up function as a more important determinant to the cell than its genetic makeup. Although the cell retained its ability to express itself ultimately as a black version of skin epithelium and feathers, still, only those cells survived and differentiated that located a familiar colony of skin cells.

The interaction of diverse tissues in the differentiation of the parts of an embryo might be surmised by anyone who has watched the successive formation of embryonic organs in vivo, as in a chick egg or a fish egg. In recent years the necessity of including diverse types of tissue in one culture for the successful induction of differentiation has been established by a number of carefully designed experiments.

If somite tissue that is ready to form cartilage is explanted in nutrient media that has been prepared only for growing cells, not for causing differentiation, it will not differentiate. But if a bit of embryonic spinal cord is included in intimate association with the somite tissue, cartilage is formed. Clifford Grobstein and Golosow explanted the embryonic rudiment of the mouse pancreas with its surrounding mesenchyme into nutrient media. Reasonably normal development of acinar cells, duct cells and islet cells ensued. If they removed the mesenchyme before making the explant, little or no growth took place and no acinar cells were formed. When the mesenchyme was added to the embryonic pancreas, growth and development were initiated and progressed just as if the mesenchyme and pancreas had been explanted together.[45]

The interaction of diverse tissues may affect growth and differentiation directly or indirectly. That it may be indirect is shown experimentally by placing cellophane between two interacting masses of tissue. Cellophane allows the passage of only very small particles and may effectively inhibit the interaction of one tissue on the other. If the filter used permits the passage of large molecules, as an agar block does, the interaction of the tissues is not impeded.[46]

In some cases, a media conditioned by the growth of cells is all that is needed as an effective substrate for differentiation of other tissue. Just recently, muscle tissues have been obtained from single cells growing in such a conditioned media. An investigator at Oak Ridge National Laboratories has caused pieces of prospective ectoderm to differentiate into mesoderm by growing it in a protein extracted from guinea pig bone marrow.[47]

All this evidence indicates that the interaction of tissues and of their secretions is an important factor in their differentiation. The evidence that the tissues are the end result of the signals the cell is sending is not compelling. However, even Paul Weiss is willing to consider whether the specific architectural plan of the tissues lies in the ground substance secreted by the cells. His attempt to explain how the substances secreted by the cells could then orientate themselves into characteristic tissues is, according to his own statement, "sheer conjecture," with no facts to support or contradict it. Yet the very uncertainty of such conjectures, he explained, "point up the immensity of our ignorance in matters of supracellular organization." Weiss is unconvinced that the organization of tissues can be explained in terms of cellular dynamics. He suggested that one who thinks otherwise should raise his sights from cells to the level of interaction where such differentiation can be achieved. His long years of study of experimental embryology have given him a tremendous respect for the orderliness of the assembly of tissues within the organism in contrast to "the relative disorder and simplicity of the shattered fragments" of tissues and cells on which so many prefer to concentrate.[48]

The Cell vs. the Organismal Theory

In line with this suggestion of Weiss, we turn now to the role of the organism in this interesting and dynamic interplay of its parts. Alan Haber of Oak Ridge National Laboratories, in a series of fine papers published in the *American Journal of Botany* in the last few years, reported on very interesting experiments with irradiated wheat seedlings. His experiments cast considerable light on the problem with which we are concerned: the relationship of the cell and the organism in growth and differentiation. By irradiating wheat seeds before germination, Haber can inhibit cell division. Subsequently, the seeds will germinate and grow into plants of a limited size, which he refers to as gamma plantlets. He found that growth in these gamma plantlets is not immediately and causally related to cell division. The plantlets grow without division and multiplication of the cells in their leaves.

The shape of the leaves also proved to be independent of cell division. Leaves of irradiated gamma plantlets and those of nonirradiated controls of the same length have the same shape, even though comparable cells in these leaves are quite different. Haber concluded that genetic information specifies the leaf form and growth independently of any influence it may have on the cell. He did not question the popular dogma of the day that the characteristics of a plant are genetically determined, but he did show that if genes determine the leaf shape and growth and the cell shape and growth, they do so independently in the two cases. It is always possible, he pointed out, to describe the leaf form in terms of its constituent cells, their sizes, shapes, numbers and orientation; but the leaf form is not determined by the constituent cells. That genetic information does not specify organ form by means of cell form, Haber considers one of the most crucial aspects of the cell theory. His conclusion is that "since the development of an organ can proceed with little relation to the manner in which it is partitioned into cells, the cell theory 'may be a misleading point of view.'"[49] He also seriously questioned "whether the individual cells are in fact units of function in growth and morphogenesis."[50]

Haber is not alone in his attempt to solve fundamental biological problems by presenting his questions to living things. Ernest Ball, of North Carolina State University, with the aid of the German ultrapak microscope and much of his own improvised equipment, has developed a method of marking meristematic cells, following the marked cells as they develop and grow in the living shoot tip, and identifying them in mature tissue. In 1946, Ball showed that such stem tips in a small amount of basal media can grow in vitro and produce normal shoots.[51]

Like Haber, Ball questioned the assumptions made concerning the determination of growth through cell division. Contrary to the ideas of many investigators, who for the most part have drawn their conclusions from killed, embedded and sectional material, Ball is unable to locate any special cells or group of cells within the short apex that initiate or otherwise determine growth. From long years of careful study of growing shoot apices, he concluded that "we must consider the shoot apex to be, from the point of view of its growth, a protoplasmic system that produces cells."

As Ball points out, this conclusion supports the ideas of the German botanist, Hofmeister, who, in 1867 held "that the formation of new cells in the shoot apex is a function of the general growth, not its cause."[52] All cells in the apical meristem are of equal importance in furthering the growth processes in the production of tissues and organs.

Using microsurgical technique in a series of operations, Ball has changed the relative positions of cells in the apical meristem. He found that the cells function according to their new position rather than to their original one; every cell in the shoot apex has the same potential for growth and division. There is no quiescent region in the shoot apex. There are no special cells that initiate growth. According to Ball, the actual forces that control cell division in the apical meristem are unknown, but "It is obvious," he concluded, "that these divisions are determined in an organismal manner so that the characteristic form and structure of the shoot apex are maintained."[53]

More definite evidence of the role of the organism in adapting and regulating the normal processes of cell division, metabolism, growth and differentiation will follow when more investigators observe individual cells intact in their normal environment as Ball has done.

Conclusion

The experimental data gathered for this paper indicate that cells do have certain independent operations that they readily carry out in vitro, but their independence appears to be greatly restricted. They cannot, according to evidence currently available, proceed far toward morphological or functional specialization without the interaction of other tissues of a similar or of a dissimilar kind.

From the standpoint of the organism, has our data yielded evidence that the organism does direct the specializations of its individual parts, its organs and cells? Are there properties, functions of the whole organism, that are not the cumulative properties or functions of the parts? If the solution is to carry weight for the modern mind, questions such as these will have to be settled in the court of experimental evidence.

Individual cells, grown in cell culture, do manifest fundamental characteristics of living things: metabolism, growth and reproduction. But living things are capable of more than these basic functions. They usually have characteristic shapes and sizes, and they proceed in a unified manner toward some goal. Cells do manifest an ability to "recognize" their kind, to differentiate to some degree when grown in "conditioned" media or when diverse tissues are allowed to interact with them. Shape, pattern and other morphological characteristics of cells grown in culture are dependent on the conditions of the media. To obtain differentiation in culture consistently, organ explants must be used for the most part. Within the developing embryo some cells must receive instruction to become differentiated from other cells and tissues to form structures such as limb buds and "these in turn must cause the orderly development not merely of the skeleton and muscles of the limb but also the appropriate innervation from the developing nervous system as well as the various secondary patterns of organization of the limb such as the color and pattern of feathers, hair and so on."[54]

The complex and time-consuming problems of providing tissues or cells grown in culture with the right substrate so that some semblance of morphological and functional differentiation may follow should remind biologists of an important aspect of biology. The ability of an organism to provide under normal conditions a suitable substrate, the enzymes, the hormones at a particular place and at the right time for a specific reaction to proceed, needs more investigation and thought. In our present state of knowledge one may well wonder if anything less than an embryo or organism is capable of providing in a sustained manner this rich interplay of substances to the cells. The power by which an organism takes care of orderly development, regulation, maintenance and repair is not explained by cellular activity, nor even by the coding of DNA.[55]

If we accept Schwann's assumption that life, or the cause of growth, resides either in the whole organism or in each elementary part, each cell, which alternative shall we accept? Schwann, like most modern scientists, thought that the law of parsimony demands that we choose between these alternatives. If life is one, indivisible; if it is an elementary fact not deducible from the internal events of the cell or of the organism; if it is to biology what the quantum of action is to physics as the great physicist Niels Bohr has insisted;[56] it can only reside properly in the cell or in the organism. If it resides in the cell, then the organism is to be regarded as a society of cells rather than a functional unit itself.

But the oneness of the organism is manifested in so many ways. Since one of the most popular witnesses in biology today is the bacterium, I shall bring it to the stand. The use of microorganisms in many industrial processes, in innumerable biochemical and pharmacological tests, provides examples of the dependable and unified performance of organisms. One of these tests that is receiving considerable attention at present is the "bacterial inhibition assay" developed by Robert Guthrie, of the University of Buffalo.[57] He discovered that the bacterium *Bacillus subtilis* offers a more sensitive and a more reliable test for early routine screening of babies with phenylketonuria than the chemical test presently in use. The rare disease phenylketonuria, which causes severe brain damage and mental retardation, may be controlled by diet if detected at an early age. The test consists in culturing Bacillus subtilis in media that inhibits its growth and then adding a disk impregnated with the blood of the person to be tested. If the person has phenylketonuria, the amino acid phenylalanine, present in the blood of such persons, will remove the inhibition and the bacteria will grow. The microorganism reacts to the low level of phenylalanine found in babies' blood in the first four or five days after birth, whereas the chemical test with ferric chloride does not give reliable results until several weeks later.

Other uses of microorganisms, such as the making of wines, tanning of leather, restoring nitrates to the soil and decomposing wastes have long been known. Microorganisms can often function in a way that no cell or subcellular fraction can, which is a persuasive argument for their functional unity. But it may take many more discoveries like that of the bacteriological assay just mentioned to focus the attention of scientists on the unified action of organisms. Only then perhaps will we rediscover our own unity and thus prepare our minds for the argument the Greeks wisely proposed in support of a scientific biology that is based on the unity of the organism. If the organism regains its place of preeminence as the primary natural unit of biology, the unit of life, biologists need have no fears that their field will be resolved finally into physics and chemistry.

First published in *Philosophical Problems in Biology: St. John's University Studies Philosophical Series 1964.*

10.

The New Biology
Barbara McClintock and
an Emerging Holistic Science

*D*uring my quarter century of teaching biology, I searched for renewal of the life sciences, which were deeply mired in the Cartesian Newtonian mindset of Western culture—as they still are today. Each announcement of a "new biology" inspired me with the hope of finding an alternative to the sterile, mechanistic worldview we inherited from Isaac Newton and Rene Descartes.

Not until the 1980s did the "pearl of great price" loom on the horizon with the award of the 1983 Nobel Prize to Barbara McClintock for her revolutionary work in genetics. More than thirty years after publishing this phase of her research in corn cytogenetics and at eighty-one years of age this remarkable woman saw her long-overlooked ideas become accessible to searchers like me. At the same time, a superb, in-depth biography by Evelyn Fox Keller became available. Its title, *A Feeling for the Organism*, indicates how personal McClintock's relationship with her corn plants was and how radical was her break with our current vested conceptualization of nature as a machine rather than as a living organism.

It seems appropriate to explore Dr. McClintock's innovative life work, which I am calling a "new biology," as a Teilhard de Chardin Lecture. Her solitary years of pioneering a frontier of genetics and biology without recognition from the academic community are reminiscent of the isolation that Teilhard endured during the decades of paleontological field work spent mostly in China. He was not permitted to publish his philosophical and theological writing by a conservative church hierarchy. Barbara published but was labelled "obscure" or "mad" by a scientific community locked in thought patterns that could not understand the subtlety of her research. The real reason, I believe, was the underlying, perhaps unconscious fear that her work would destroy the bulging edifice of genetic dogma that dominates medical and biological science to this day. Doubtless the misunderstanding of their peers contributed to the maturation of these two profoundly humanistic scientists as they deepened and expanded their insights beyond the confines of their own disciplines.

Before embarking on an exploration of Barbara McClintock's philosophy and methodology as a model for a "new biology," I wish to give some background of my own quest for renewal of the life sciences. I found the resources available to biology teachers to be miserably inadequate, and a pervasive bias controlling the kind of biological research that was funded. My hope lies in the scientists today who are dissatisfied with Newtonian biology and medicine, and in others who themselves have offered creative alternatives to prepare the way for an emerging holistic science such as Barbara McClintock's. Her understanding of the parts, the genes, chromosomes and cells in their dynamic *relationship* to the whole organism in its environment could replace the reductionistic science of the manipulation and control of the bits and pieces of a mindless and meaningless mechanical world.

The "New" Science of Aristotle

My own efforts to find a "new biology" began in the 1950s and 1960s while I was teaching and researching with college science students. At that time I was deeply influenced by Robert Hutchins, President of the University of Chicago, and Mortimer Adler at St. John's College Annapolis, who developed the *Great Books of the Western World* Program as a basis for a true liberal arts education. Convinced that science is "thinking about the world in the Greek way,"[1] I searched for the kind of science initiated in Greece as a pursuit of wonder and wisdom rather than a means to power over and manipulation of the natural world. I knew that a biology integral to sound philosophy and theology can expand and deepen the meaning of one's life and world and challenge students to be creative in their approach to nature rather than limiting themselves to be transmuters or transmitters of the works of others.

The one biology textbook I found to invite students to undertake this alternative way was a beautiful book, entitled *Biology*, by Karl Von Frisch. Most of the available texts were compilations of data to be memorized or manuals for asking inane mechanical questions of nature. But despite such dead-end limitations, serious science students were willing to supplement the tedium of their texts with the writings of Hippocrates, Aristotle, Galen, Harvey, Pasteur, Bernard, Darwin and other such scientists.

In Aristotle's *Physics* and *Posterior Analytics*, students could discover the general principles of scientific knowing. His was a commonsense approach to nature not dependent on instruments or experiments, a logical and experiential but pre-mathematical way to knowledge.[2] Critical students grasped the importance of beginning with a general science of nature based on their own experience of the natural world before they were swamped with the endless details of their textbooks.

Students who accepted William Harvey's counsel of "one road to science, that to wit, in which we proceed from things more known to things less known, from matters more manifest to matters more obscure"[3] found a more sensible learning procedure than beginning with sophisticated formulas that they did not understand, but could only memorize. (Physics students who begin their study with the formula f=ma, without any background in the depth of knowledge that brought Newton to such a conclusion, end as technicians rather than as scientists who, like an Einstein, can see reality in a completely new way.) They realized that their own ability to be creative depended on working in areas where they understood the foundational philosophy that led to a certain conclusion or hypothesis. In so doing they could rise above an educational system that rewarded those who conformed and memorized. The texts they were given, replete with excessive charts and graphs, convinced students that Aristotle was right also in rejecting a monolithic Pythagorean and Platonic mathematical approach to nature.

Science for Aristotle was knowledge of things in terms of their proper causes. His famous four causes were comprehensive ways of answering the "why" of something. The material cause is "that out of which a thing comes to be and which persists, e.g. the bronze of the statue.... In another sense the form or archetype is a cause," that is, the organizing principle that accounts for a flea rather than an elephant—the formal cause. The efficient cause of a thing is its primary source of change or coming to rest, or the agent moving something to become what it is, as the mother is the cause of the child. The final cause is the purpose for which a thing exists or " 'that for the sake of which' a thing is done, e.g. health is the cause of walking."[4]

Aristotle taught that in the study of physics one must know all four causes.[5] Ignorant of this truth, modern scientists have omitted and self-righteously spurned knowledge of the formal and final causes and thus have spawned a twentieth-century biological science that finds a fragmented world devoid of mind and meaning where the search for wisdom has been neglected or forgotten. My purpose in this paper is to bring to our attention an exemplary scientist, Barbara McClintock, who was not mired in the absurdities and fraudulence of such a worldview but rather challenges biologists to deepen their understanding of the reality of a vibrant natural realm.

The Modern Scientific Establishment

Before I turn to Barbara's contribution and leave the topic of my pursuit of better teaching methods and texts, I want to include my delight at finally in the 1960s finding two research laboratories that challenged staff and students to become humanistic scientists like Barbara McClintock and Pierre Teilhard de Chardin. The excitement of such research was for me a treasure provided by scientists who were grounded in the liberal arts and thus could grow beyond the boundaries of mechanics and data.

With Dr. Harold Bold in the Botany Department at the University of Texas, I was fascinated to observe the growth and behavior of algae that would later reveal to my students the healthy or polluted conditions of the Mississippi River. I came to know one green alga very well and was delighted that under the microscope it would produce zoospores at three p.m. each day. I was eager to make a long-term commitment to know it better and to reveal its secrets to others.

Working with Dr. Hans Selye at the Institute of Experimental Medicine at the University of Montreal provided an opportunity to understand the cause and effect of the stress that people suffer in today's industrial world. Our studies with white rats and mice in stressful situations helped us to find avenues to relieve or treat the effects of such pressures on people. Results were read in terms of the behavior and state of health of the animals, very much like the way our own health records reveal the deleterious effects of our hectic urban lifestyle. Even here, working with whole organisms, we were not free from the grumbling of staff members who wanted to grind up the animals and read the results in chemical and mathematical terms.

Hopefully, scientists today are increasingly awakening to the fact that they more often than not serve as handmaidens to the military industrial complex. They are beginning to take responsibility for the impoverishment of our lives and the assault on our planet by the mechanistic forces dominating the study of science. Physicists as well as some biologists are deeply worried that the so-called life sciences manifest so little concern for the critical state of our ravaged planet and its inhabitants. It has been over half a century since Einstein's relativity theory, Bohr's quantum revolution and Heisenberg's uncertainty principle superseded the Newtonian paradigm and forged a new holistic world vision Yet many biologists remain caught in the old machine model.

Lynn Margulis, Distinguished Professor of Botany of the University of Massachusetts at Amherst, in an article in the 1988 book *Doing Science*, boldly describes the stranglehold on biologists imprisoned in outmoded research and dogmatic reporting:

> More and more, like the monasteries of the Middle Ages, today's universities and professional societies guard their knowledge. Collusively, the university biology curriculum, the textbook publishers, the National Science Foundation, review committees, the graduate record examiners, and the various microbiological, evolutionary and zoological societies map out domains of the known and the knowable; they distinguish required from forbidden knowledge, subtly punishing the trespassers with rejection and oblivion; they award the faithful liturgists by granting degrees and dispersing funds and fellowships. Universities and academies, well within the boundaries of given disciplines…, determine who is permitted to know and just what it is that he or she may know. Biology, botany, zoology, biochemistry, and microbiology departments within the U.S. universi-

ties determine access to knowledge about life, dispensing it at high prices in peculiar parcels called credit hours.[6]

The effect of such control on graduate students and on scientists is apparent to anyone who has worked in typical university departments of science. My own last year of graduate work at the University of Notre Dame when a chemist was hired to head the biology department is a case in point. In short order he let the faculty know that chemical analysis was the prevailing methodology, the only way to get financial support, and that their interpretation of what constituted science was no longer acceptable.

The scientists who obtain research funds, as Lynn Margulis pointed out, are those who dutifully apply for grants from government, corporations or other such guardians of our militaristic society. They must play by rules set up by a consumer mentality. The gifted writer and physician Lewis Thomas, in his insightful book *The Lives of a Cell*, finds the way science is practiced to be quite mysterious and is fascinated by the way scientists hover around the central mystery of science—"that we do it all, and that we do it under such compulsion." He knows of no other human occupation "in which the people engaged in it are so caught up, so totally preoccupied, so driven beyond their strength and resources."[7] I am reminded of an article I read years ago by the psychologist Lawrence Kubie of Yale University, who claimed that the pressures in science laboratories on young immature scientists is making Frankensteins of them. It seems to me that messages such as those from Lewis Thomas and Lawrence Kubie about the assault of modern science on our humanity are needed to stir us from our apathy in a way that the plight of planet earth has been unable to do.

Another critic of science laboratories and of academia in general, James Lovelock, the author of the Gaia hypothesis, writes that "what people call, or think of as, science is, in fact, technology." For him science is something "to be done at home, like writing, painting, or composing music."[8] This description of science enjoyed at home aptly describes Barbara McClintock patiently tending her corn fields for some twenty years at Cornell University and for fifty years at Cold Spring Harbor Laboratory on Long Island. I feel it would also apply to Aristotle's biological studies, which achieved such a comprehensive account of the generation, the habits, the anatomy, the physiology and life cycles of a wide variety of animals.

Let us hope that the growing criticisms of their colleagues will awaken biologists from their mechanistic dreams before our technology kills off the myriad species of animals and plants crucial to the habitability of the biosphere and to human psychic and spiritual wholeness. As the earth continues to lose its life support systems one wonders if our present technology has brought us only "new levels of ignorance," as John Briggs and F. David Peat claim in their fascinating book, *Looking Glass Universe: The Emerging Science of Wholeness.*[9] The pollution of the air, water and land; corruption of our family and community life; and the alienation of persons from one another is a sure and sad consequence of a materialistic establishment. I believe there is a desperate need for a "new biology," a radical global mind change toward a profound appreciation of the grandeur of our living planet.

The Emergence of a New Biology

The vision of a novel, holistic and systems biology, one in which Teilhard could be at home, have been present ever since physicists, earlier in the century, revealed the interconnected, dynamic nature of reality. The hope of those seeking an Einstein for the life sciences was to awaken biologists from their contentment with the evolving Darwinian world of natural selection and the survival of the fittest, a world bereft of any direction and purpose.

William Beck of Harvard used the term "new biology" in a paper he gave at St. John's University in 1964 and characterized its major trends as a growing interest among biologists in cybernetics, in the nature and function of the gene and in psycho-physiological advances. He expressed appreciation for molecular biologists' grandiose expectations to explain all of life's mysteries in mechanistic terms, but saw their discipline as a product of the physics of the nineteenth century. Referring to the changes that physics has since undergone and the many neglected areas of biology during its quantitative heyday he ends on the note that "further progress may demand from us a deeper analysis of the scientific method itself."[10]

Watson and Crick's much heralded discovery of the structure of DNA was accepted by some as a new biology, in accordance with Crick's claims. However revolutionary this breakthrough may have been at the time of its discovery in 1953, it only served to mire biologists, chemists and or physicists that jumped on the DNA band wagon, deeper into the same old Newtonian Cartesian frame of reference.

A more hopeful prospect of a new biology is found in William Irwin Thompson's book, *Gaia A Way of Knowing: Political Implications of the New Biology*. This collection of talks given in a Zen Buddhist monastery was the result of Thompson's dream that at this Lindisfarne gathering they would "for the first time since Newton... have the chance to create a new ecology of consciousness, the basis for a new political and economic order which, because it arises out of the study of life, is life-enhancing and life-embracing."[11]

In his introductory talk, "The Cultural Implications of the New Biology" Thompson admitted his title was an oversimplification, as there is "not one new biology but several competing ones."[12] He depicts two of them, one from the right and another from the left. From the right, he quotes from a typical but extreme mechanistic approach of E.O. Wilson, a sociobiologist from Harvard University:

> The transition from purely phenomenological to fundamental theory in sociology must await a full, neuronal explanation of the human brain. Only when the machinery can be torn down on paper at the level of the cell and put together again, will the properties of emotion and ethical judgement come clear.[13]

To characterize the left, a new cognitive biology, Thompson includes a long quotation from Humberto Maturana, a neurobiologist at the University of Chile at Santiago. He explains that neurons are anatomical but not structural units of the functioning nervous system. The structural units have not been defined, and when they are, he thinks, they will be found in relational activities between neurons embodied in interconnections, not as separate anatomical units. He says that the relations of the parts appear so obvious that the observer is deluded into believing that the structure of the functioning system is attributable to a part. "Accordingly," he concludes, "the full explanation of the organization of the nervous system (and of the organism) will not arise from any particular observation or detailed description and enumeration of its parts, but rather like any explanation, from the synthesis, conceptual or concrete, of a system that does what the nervous system (or the organism) does."[14]

Maturana is suggesting that the various components of the nervous system can only be known and its activity accounted for by a systems approach, a communion of the observer and the observed nervous system. This sounds like an entrée to and renewed appreciation of the world of the medieval alchemist[15] or the brilliant insights into the "patterns that connect" of Gregory Bateson, whose contribution to this volume was prepared less than a month before his untimely death in 1980.

Such a strange and unfolding universe in which the observer is a participant in what is observed obliges one to enter more deeply into the essence of what it is to know. A purely rational approach to nature is no longer adequate when the quantum realities call for a systemic communion with, and a participatory consciousness of, the wider world in which we live. This way of knowing is familiar to primitive peoples, to the medieval alchemists, to Buddhists and mystics. As we will find, Barbara McClintock was not locked into the tacit assumptions that held most scientists in a Newtonian mindset. She could hear the organism speak for itself, respected her own "feel for the organism," and thus profoundly personified a dawning new biological vision. What is this systems approach, this cognitive biology that Maturana and FranciscoVarela describe and to which Gregory Bateson dedicated so much of the last years of his life? They, together with other scientists and philosophers involved in consciousness and perception studies such as Arthur Zajonc, Piet Hut and Evan Thompson, are inviting biologists to a new evolutionary paradigm distinguished by a emergent sentience. An entrée into this school of thought is the *Journal of Consciousness Studies*. Drawing upon the twentieth-century insights of Einstein, Bohr, Schrödinger and Heisenberg in relativity and quantum physics along with more recent contributions from David Bohm, Ilya Prigogine and others, they no longer see an organic, perceptive entity as an isolated object but more as an integral participant.[16] By these lights, a person, in acts of inquiry and observation, becomes an empathic subject within an encompassing nature, as exemplified by Barbara McClintock.

The Mind of Gregory Bateson

In preparation for understanding Barbara McClintock, I wish to further consider the thought of Gregory Bateson, another "new biology" pioneer and a formidable foe of the obsolete Cartesian dualism that had excised any notion of mind from its atomistic paradigm. Covering an awesome depth of scholarship in the fields of anthropology, biology and psychology, Bateson's revolutionary book, *Mind and Nature: A Necessary Unity,* is a challenging exercise in putting mind and cognition back into the impoverished scientific world of twentieth-century life, which he saw as afflicted by "greed, monstrous over-growth, war, tyranny and pollution."[17] In his sagacious ability to integrate and relate human knowing "with the wider knowing which is the glue holding together the starfishes, and sea anemones and redwood forests and human committees,"[18] he built on the work of his father, William Bateson, who in the 1890s was similarly engaged in the task of understanding the function of mind in nature. He concluded that his father would agree with him that mental process is analogous to the laws of biological variation, that evolution is best understood as a cognitive process. For Gregory, "Thinking is mental variation."[19] I began to comprehend his appreciation of creative thought and the creativity of evolution as analogous processes of nature as I think of the gestation period needed to write this paper. It was for me like letting my life work come to term, or, as Kabir writes, "If you want the truth, I'll tell you the truth: Listen to the secret sound, the real sound, which is inside you."[20]

The key concept is to see with Bateson that mind fits "with very little modification into the general scene of biological explanation," which "would indeed alter the basis of biology from the very ground up and would alter our ideas about our relationship to mind, our relationship to each other, our relationship to free will, and so on. In a word, our complete epistemology."[21] Such an immanent mind is for me indispensable for a new biology, along with the admission of the innate patterns and systemic dynamics of nature.

Bateson insisted that he was not referring to the mind of God or any mind that had a religious or supernatural component, but this did not exclude for him the presence of the sacred in nature. In his book *Angels Fear: Towards an Epistemology of the Sacred,* completed by his daughter Mary Catherine Bateson and published seven years after his death, he clarified his position. Here, like Thomas Aquinas, whose scientific rigor he appreciated, he was intent on bringing the secular into harmony with the sacred. Mary Catherine Bateson suggests that her father "attributes a certain sacredness to the organization of the biological world,"[22] which is reminiscent of St. Thomas's claim that there is a trace of the divinity in all things. For even though Bateson decried much that passed under the banner of religion, he was a deeply spiritual person. As his daughter explains, he wanted to state that fact clearly in their book: "He had become aware gradually that the unity of nature he had affirmed in *Mind and Nature* might only be comprehensible through the kind of metaphors familiar from religion, that, in fact, he was approaching that integrative dimension of experience he called the *sacred*."[23] Like his father, he recognized the sacred in nature and referred to one form of learning as "the awakening to ecstasy."[24]

The notion of such an awakening is quite characteristic of Barbara McClintock who modestly claimed to enjoy the ecstasy of science and was "proud to call herself a 'mystic.' "[25] Even as a child she knew the oneness of all things and said, "There is no way in which you draw a line between things. What we do is to make these subdivisions, but they're not real. Our educational system is full of subdivisions that are artificial, that shouldn't be there. I think maybe poets...have some understanding of this."[26] She knew and respected a knowledge beyond that of natural science and states: "Things are much more marvelous than the scientific method allows us to conceive."[27]

Barbara McClintock was in many ways a kindred spirit to Gregory Bateson's father, William. As a humanist, a classicist, he recognized the inadequacy of reason or the scientific method to arrive at the full truth about nature and was himself attempting to develop a science of feeling. Feeling for him was a way of knowing and was a necessary element in an "intuitive grasp of essential relations."[28] After the rediscovery of Mendel's work with peas at the turn of the century, William Bateson gave his attention to problems of heredity and, in 1905, coined the term "genetics." As an ardent opponent of the developing mechanical, materialistic gene-chromosome theory of inheritance, and in his understanding of the primacy of form and relationships among plants and animals, he prepared the way for scientist like his son, Gregory, and for Barbara McClintock. If Bateson's views of inheritance had prevailed in the 1920s, as Morris Berman writes in his book, *The Reenchantment of the World*, then "the potential horrors of gene manipulation and recombinant DNA...might have been avoided."[29] Such threats would at least have been modified if the seminal contribution of Barbara McClintock in the field of genetics had been understood and accepted in the 1950s when first published.

I will conclude my survey of some hopeful signs of a new biology on the horizon with a listing of the requirements for such a Teilhardian mind change. Certainly it cannot dismiss the extraordinary achievements of our high-tech computer age, which allows me to write this paper with much less effort than I have written in the past. It must resonate with the wisdom of the classical scientist while it reaches into the cosmic insights flowing from quantum theory and a new ecology of consciousness. The emergent view needs to describe inheritance within the framework of the major problems of developing forms still mystifying embryology and evolutionary thought. It must awaken in us a deep ecological concern for our critically endangered planet and its inhabitants and call us to a new way of being earthlings.

It seems to me that Barbara McClintock is the scientist who has modeled just such an approach to biology. She has lately won the acclaim of the scientific community for her revolutionary genetic insights, which were published in contemporary reductionist language many years before their genius was recognized. But the question remains: how long will it take for geneticists and biologists to accept her greater challenge, a methodology and philosophy that reconnect with classical Greek science and opens a frontier to a new cognitive science of form, pattern and interrelation?

Barbara McClintock's New Biology

Barbara McClintock's genius—and my claim that she exemplifies a "new biology"—is based on her extraordinary fluency in the many languages of science. My first point is her approach to scientific knowledge, clearly in agreement with Aristotle, whence we begin with "things that are more knowable and obvious to us and proceeds toward those which are clearer and more knowable by nature...[but he explains that] what is to us plain and obvious at first is rather confused masses, the elements and principles of which become known to us later by analysis."[31] Second, she reported her carefully designed and executed experiments in the rigorous technical and mathematical language demanded by the reductionistic standards of the field of genetics. Third, her genius is apparent in a passion for ferreting out the truth no matter how costly in time and energy, in her ability to question and even set aside assumptions taken for granted by her confreres, and in a strong commitment to defend and hold onto results too radical and subtle for them to accept.

Fourth, a love of and openness to what nature has to teach, coupled with a remarkable skill in the laboratory and a capacity to see more than her colleagues, brought insights beyond the popular genetic dogma that a gene, a molecule of matter, could be identified and even isolated as the causal agent of a character in a living organism.

As my fifth point I cite McClintock's ability to keep the whole organism and its environment at the center of her attention. This meant that she was never out of touch with the major unsolved problems in biology, particularly those in embryology, evolution and ecology. Sixth and finally, like an artist, a primitive or a child, she was able to enter into communion with what she saw in the chromosome, the cell and the whole corn plant. This is the epitome of the new participative consciousness called for by biologists like Gregory Bateson, historians of science like Morris Berman and Thomas Berry, and frontier physicists such as David Bohm and Fritjof Capra. And here, of course, is the noetic vision we find so presciently in Teilhard.

I will now expand on these six points to help us appreciate Barbara McClintock's contribution. She indeed deserves to be ranked among the truly first-rate scientists by virtue of her organismal or holistic sensibility. It was obvious for her to follow the same procedure in science that Aristotle outlined, which is to begin with a general knowledge of that which is already known. She planted the corn seeds, tended the seedlings, kept them watered during hot weather and drought, and knew each plant intimately before she made the crosses that would open up to her new pathways in genetics. She saw and carefully tabulated the variations in the leaves and kernels before linking them with changes in the structure of the chromosomes.

Seeing parts of organisms in their relationship to the whole, a fundamental requisite of classical science, was only natural to McClintock. She thus never lost touch with the development of organic form, a central problem of biology for Aristotle. Her penchant for understanding the entire organism, "that for the sake of which" the parts came to be, attends to Aristotle's final cause.[32] Because of this focus on the whole organism, she avoided the small errors in the beginning that Aristotle warned would be multiplied a thousandfold later.[33] It is the absence of a holistic view that creates danger in genetic engineering when biologists are unable to see the wider effects of their experiments. A familiarity with McClintock's methodology reveals that she, like the sages of ancient Greece and the alchemists of the Middle Ages, was in pursuit of nature's wisdom rather than attempting to control, manipulate and deplete her resources.

My second claim, that McClintock's careful planning of and conduct of her research satisfied the demands of the most exacting experimental scientist, is attested to by her election at forty-two years of age to the National Academy of Science. She consistently published her results with more than adequate supporting evidence in familiar technical and quantitative language, providing colleagues ample opportunity to follow the development of her thought. Why biologists have not yet responded to the revolution in their field implicit in her research is fairly and beautifully told by Evelyn Fox Keller in *A Feeling for the Organism*.

McClintock's breakthrough in genetics followed years of tracking a noticeable change in the rate of mutation in the green streaks in the leaves and stalk tissues, which differed from the rate of mutation in the corn plant as a whole. She noticed that these changes often occurred in pairs, the rate of change being speeded up in some husks and kernels and slowed down in others. Such changes she concluded resulted from two cells, twins, in which "one cell lost what the other cell gained." It was her excitement over this last-mentioned clue and a passion to know the reason behind it that kept her at the tedious but absorbing quest. With some trepidation she finally presented these radical results to her colleagues at the 1951 Cold Spring Harbor Symposium. She knew the intricacy of her work made it more difficult for them to accept her challenge to the prevailing dogmatic belief in genes as fixed unchanging units of heredity. The genes in the corn plants moved about, effected changes in other genes and were themselves influenced by the cell, the organism and the environment. Keller poignantly describes this event: "She had unveiled her creation, a beautiful explanatory model with full supporting evidence, the object of six years of loving attention and grueling hard work, and her colleagues had turned their backs."[34]

And that brings me to my third point. McClintock's genius is manifest in a commitment to the truth her research unearthed even when it was spurned by her colleagues. Their indifference to and non-acceptance of her creative insights was no doubt a bitter disappointment to this already distinguished cytogeneticist. It is an example of the subtle control that a tacit or generally accepted paradigm can have on the subliminal state of mind, so as to block the recognition of any evidence that does not agree.

She had offered them a radically new perception of the nature of the gene. Such a breakthrough Einstein referred to as "rather like climbing a mountain, gaining new and wider views, discovering unexpected connections between our starting point and its rich environment."[35] Her colleagues for whatever reason were not ready to make that climb to view the fertile landscape she had prepared for rooting and nourishing a "new biology." Her concern with the organism as a whole, an "inner knowledge" that she was on the "right track," opened up a new vista that had to wait thirty years for its vindication with the award of the Nobel Prize.

My fourth point gets at the heart of the matter. Because McClintock was taught in nature's own school an intimate sense of the organism, its development and growth, its variations and its interrelatedness with its environment, she was saved from the dangerous limitations of a narrow, quantitative and purely analytical method. For her the gene was "merely a symbol." Her experiments directly challenged the established belief that a unit of matter, a gene, was a sole carrier of a hereditary trait. She was and is "duly skeptical" of wasteful projects like the $3 billion federal subsidy for identifying and cataloging the 50,000–100,000 genes of the human body. She was free of the DNA "thought collective" that would attribute afflictions such as muscular dystrophy, Huntington's disease, cancer or even alcoholism solely to the effect of a single isolated gene.

Sixth and finally, McClintock's breadth of knowledge opened her to many of the same insights that Einstein, Bohr, Heisenberg and Schrödinger brought to early twentieth-century physics, and that Bell, Bohm, Capra and Prigogne are bringing to physics today.[39] These later physicists, who are now attempting to advise the life sciences of the interconnected holographic nature of the world, where the observer and the observed are one, will find in Barbara McClintock a biologist who has come to similar truth through her longtime intimate studies of corn plants. She told her friend Marcus Rhoades, in answer to his query as to how she could see so much, "Well, you know, when I look at a cell, I get down there in that cell and look around."[40] Gregory Bateson stated it as, "The observer must be included within the focus of observation, and what can be studied is always a relationship or an infinite regress of relationships. Never a 'thing'."[41] Keller describes how McClintock could enter into the mysteries of genetics while her peers were restricted by a molecular emphasis. "Over and over again she tells us that we must have the time to look, the patience to hear what the material has to say to you: 'the openness to let it come to you.' Above all one must have 'a feeling for the organism.'"[42] Fifth, despite her commitment to the field of genetics and cytology, Barbara McClintock was able to uncover connections to other areas of biology. Her 1934 paper "The Relation of a Particular Chromosomal Element to the Development of the Nucleoli in Zea Mays" is a classic paper on the Nucleolar Organizer Region (NOR). Again this contribution to the organization of the nucleoli did not penetrate the field of cell biology: "I feel that it was a only a relatively few people...who really got the point of the organization—of why I called it an organizer."[37] In her 1951 presentation she stated that it was not the gene per se that accounted for inheritance but "organized systems that function as units at any one time in development."[38] Here is the salient concept, for it is not the DNA alone but the entire genetic system that is involved in the growth and life of an organism. Because of McClintock's concern with the whole organism she was able to move beyond her specialty to make significant contributions to developmental problems and remain faithful to a methodology with roots in the original Greek tradition.

I believe the life and work of Barbara McClintock can exemplify a new biology that no longer sees us as spectators alienated from the natural world but as integral participants in communion with a living planet in all its magnificent array of life forms. There is a mystical quality in her total dedication to the wisdom the corn plants revealed to her. She presents an ideal model for science students who wish to take up her insightful journey into the mysteries of nature. With Thomas Aquinas, Thomas Berry and Gregory Bateson, she calls us to return to the sacred dimensions of a self-organizing universe with a new story that can save our earth home and its manifold inhabitants from destruction and challenge us to reclaim the meaning in our life pilgrimage. Indeed, we find in Barbara McClintock a continuity with Teilhard's life and approach, and in an emerging holistic science a verification of his organic and numinous vision.

Published in *Teilhard Studies,* no. 26 (Spring 1992)

Dedicated to the memory of my friend and mentor, Dr. Vincent Edward Smith

11.

Universe Coding, Not Genetic Coding

*T*hroughout the last three hundred years a mechanistic philosophy has prevailed in science. This scientific worldview has left us disenchanted, in a machine world stripped of wonder, myth, meaning and spirit, on a polluted, crime-ridden and war-torn planet, amidst an endangered earth community. The pivotal role of science in forming such a worldview moves me to this critique of the mechanical paradigm underlying our way of life and to offer signs of a nascent holistic vision of nature.

The mechanistic view as evident in the neo-Darwinian gene chromosome theory and its followers' latest extravaganza, the Human Genome Project, reductive and manipulative in the extreme, is the focus of my critique. At the same time, like ships passing, an alternative approach to nature as a dynamic organism is transforming physics and beginning to inform biological thought. My intention is to explore the premises of the gene theory so as to identify the philosophical grounding needed for a holistic approach to inheritance.

A minority of biologists, adhering to a traditional or commonsense philosophy, refuse the reduction of their field to chemistry and physics and insist on the organism itself as biology's primary unit. I propose the organic thought of Aristotle and Goethe as a historical base for their position as well as for the new sciences of complexity and the genetics revolution implicit in the research of Barbara McClintock. These frontier sciences may reveal the presence and activity of universal formative fields in nature to replace one fragmented into atoms and molecules. A society informed by such a holistic science would conceivably engender a healthier biosphere, a kinder world and a promise for its survival.

The prevailing neodarwinian orthodoxy in biology began in the 1950s and 1960s, when physicists and mathematicians jumped on the DNA bandwagon to become molecular biologists. Relativity theory and quantum mechanics had little effect on the Mendelian/Darwinian mechanistic bent as Nobel Prizes spurred on enthusiasm for a particulate theory of genes and inheritance. The genetic triumphs of these decades affected education, medicine, the media, language and popular thinking. Evidence abounds in the media: i.e., in the January 18, 1993 article in *U.S. News and World Report;* "Molecular TickTock. A complex array of genes and proteins controls the rhythms of our lives" or "Clock Watching: Nestled in the green leaves of a plant is a genetic clue to the identity of the mysterious inner clock that runs us all" in *Discover* in May 1990.

The hold this theory has on scientists is demonstrated by the October 6, 1992 *New York Times* full page display of a linkage map of twenty-three human chromosomes under the title "Blueprint For a Human," crediting the Human Genome Project of the National Institutes of Health as its source. In the center of the page under a picture of a human fetus is the misleading claim: "The genetic instructions to specify a human are contained in some three billion units of DNA, arranged over twenty-three pairs of chromosomes and carrying 100,000 genes.... Shown here is the most comprehensive genetic linkage map yet constructed."

This exercise in megascience is costing taxpayers some three billion dollars. Yet many argue that the molecular obsession of deciphering 50,000 to 100,000 human "genes" may turn out to be a pointless enterprise. During the fifteen-year tenure of this federal grant, the scientists involved are not likely to have or take time to consider the tacit philosophical assumptions underlying such a questionable endeavor. This project, like the equally myopic Superconducting Supercollider, diverts attention from the many unsolved biological, economic and social problems on our deteriorating planet.

One biologist who has sounded the alarm is Lynn Margulis, Distinguished Professor of Microbiology at the University of Massachusetts at Amherst. She has written extensively about the stranglehold that academia, funding sources, elder statesmen in the field, etc., have on biologists to keep them subservient to the mainstream orthodoxy. As a radical opponent to such subservience, Margulis calls for dismissal of neo-Darwinism as "a minor twentieth-century religious sect within the sprawling religious persuasion of Anglo-Saxon biology."[1] She also cites Abner Shimony's exposure of natural selection as a "null theory." The blind adherence of scientists and society to implausible facts, Margulis documents from the experiences of Ludwik Fleck. In his book *Genesis and Development of a Scientific Fact*, Fleck describes the way ideas invented from inadequate data are exalted to the status of fact and then socialized into the body politic as universal truth. Tribalism within the scientific community and an uncritical society at large assures their propagation.[2]

It is important to note that objection to a particulate theory of inheritance is not just of recent vintage. At the turn of the century when Mendelian genetics had just been rediscovered, William Bateson, who in 1906 coined the term genetics, was already a formidable foe of such a molecular theory. As a classicist he knew that the form of an organism cannot be explained by its chemical elements. Another senior scientist of the same era, J.S. Haldane, likewise exposed this anti-intellectual bias in biology and medicine:

> In whatever way mechanistic theories of reproduction may twist and turn they never make anything else than sheer nonsense. Yet biologists are constantly returning to them like moths to a candle, because they think that there must be some physico-chemical explanation. At the same time they refuse to consider what philosophy has had to say on the subject, since they argue that biology has to do with facts of observation, and not with "metaphysics." They never realize that they are themselves in the grip of metaphysics, and bad metaphysics, when they endeavor to twist biological observation into the form of physical and chemical interpretation. The manner in which, since the time of Galileo, Descartes and Newton, European culture got into the grip of bad metaphysics when men supposed that they were freeing themselves from metaphysics and going back to facts is something which future generations will laugh over; and particularly over ideas at present current as to what science or "exact science" is. [3]

During the period that DNA was capturing the headlines, organismal biologists continued to protest the analytical tide. One of them, a beacon of scientific common sense, was the eminent researcher and exquisite artist of detail Libbie Hyman, who in the first volume of *The Invertebrates* stated that "it is impossible that the genes alone can be responsible for morphological differentiation since all body cell contain the same set of genes. The role of the gene in morphogenesis remains a total mystery." For her, particulate theories are "intellectually unsatisfactory since the very matters for which explanation is sought are attributed without explanation to imaginary particles." She saw the gene chromosome theory as a return to the preformation idea that was laid to rest by earlier biologists as well as by Aristotle's refutation of the pangenesis of Hippocrates. She explained:

> The whole is not to be understood by an analysis of its parts any more than an architectural masterpiece can be comprehended by chemical and physical analysis of the stones of which it is built. The conception of the organism as a physicochemical machine encounters the insuperable difficulties of explaining a machine which runs itself, repairs itself, alters itself to meet the exigencies of surrounding conditions and reproduces itself, and what is still worse, attains its final form by developing from a simple beginning through an orderly sequence of forms and evolves through time into a succession of machines of ever-increasing complexity of construction.[4]

Objection to the neo-Darwinian gene chromosome theory is increasing today among creative scientists. In 1987 Gail Fleisschaker, a philosopher of science at Boston University and MIT, wrote in her doctoral thesis that to claim genes are the ordering agents of an organism is "altogether unwarranted." She is well aware of a correlation between changes in the organism and in the structure of its chromosome, but she also knows that there is no experimental basis for claiming that the chromosomal changes are the cause of changes in the organism. The English biologist Rupert Sheldrake agrees:

> The idea of DNA shaping the organism or programming its behavior is a quite illegitimate extrapolation from anything we know about what DNA does.... Everything to do with heredity and properties of living organisms is being projected on to DNA with the mechanistic model—all the unsolved problems of biology are being attributed to DNA.[5]

The Nobel laureate Frances Crick, a discoverer of the structure of DNA, admits the inadequacy of molecular biology to deal with the development, embryology and differentiation of multicellular organisms—an area he finds mysterious.[6] His colleague Sydney Brenner likewise concludes that the genetic and molecular work of the last sixty years has now come full circle with the explanation of development left unresolved. Brenner calls for a new language for biologists and thinks a theory of elaborate systems is needed for solving fundamental problems.[7] Another senior geneticist, Gunther Stent of the University of California, claimed in a 1968 issue of *Science* that molecular biologists have no important intellectual challenges left. He suggests their last frontier, the "study of the nervous system is bringing us to the limits of human understanding."[8]

My expectation that science is now moving from a Newtonian, Cartesian paradigm to a holistic conception of nature is based on the increasing numbers of researchers who propose alternatives to mainstream orthodoxy. John Briggs and F. David Peat celebrate the work of these frontier scientists in their book, *Looking Glass Universe.* They are recapturing a holistic and organic view of nature that was the basic philosophy of Western science from the time of Aristotle until the last three hundred years, when it was replaced by the mechanical, Newtonian worldview.

The "looking glass" scientist and Nobel laureate Ilya Prigogne, in his and Isabelle Stengers's book *Order Out of Chaos*, provides exciting new ways of dialoguing with nature. Deeply rooted in philosophy and the humanities, Prigogne and Stenger deeply oppose the current scientism, realize the inadequacy of the prevailing science of nature, and give an account of their own search for a more holistic science. They claim:

> In the last one hundred fifty years, science has been downgraded from a source of integration for Western culture to a threat. Not only does it threaten man's material existence, but also, more subtly, it threatens to destroy the traditions and experiences that are most deeply rooted in our cultural life. It is not just the technological fallout of one or another scientific breakthrough that is being accused, but 'the spirit of science' itself."[9]

Prigogne and Stenger find that traditional biologists like Paul Weiss and Conrad Waddington "have rightly criticized" the very language of modern science and the way it "attributes to individual molecules the power to produce the global order biology aims to understand and, by so doing, mistakes the formulation of the problem for its solution."[10] They find a holistic approach to nature in Greek science, explaining, "One of the main sources of Aristotle's thinking was the observation of embryonic growth, a highly organized process in which interlocking, although apparently independent, events participate in a process that seems to be part of some global plan. Like the developing embryo, the whole of Aristotelian nature is organized according to final causes." Aristotle's four causes, they explain, probe the essence of living creatures and are "the key to understanding nature."[11] They regret with the poet John Donne the passing of the Aristotelian cosmos:

> And new Philosophy calls all in doubt,
> The Element of fire is quite put out.
> The Sun is lost, and th'earth, and no man's wit
> Can well direct him where to look for it.
> And freely men confess that this world's spent
> When in the Planets and the Firmament.
> They seek so many new, then they see that this
> Is crumbled out again to his Atomies
> "Tis all in Pieces, all coherence gone.[12]

In his foreword, Alvin Toffler hails *Order Out of Chaos* as "a lever for changing science itself, for compelling us to reexamine its goals, its methods, its epistemology—its worldview. Indeed, this book can serve as a symbol of today's historic transformation in sciences—one that no informed person can afford to ignore."[13]

The 1990s' new sciences of complexity offer biologists another revolutionary perspective for research on the neglected problems of embryonic development and differentiation. A pioneer in this field, Brian Goodwin, a theoretical biologist at Sussex University and former colleague of the geneticist C. H. Waddington, is committed to the study of the whole organism and to the genesis of form. He and the biologist Stuart Kaufman of the Santa Fe Institute agree that the theories of natural selection and genetic coding cannot account for evolving organisms. Their collaboration in seeking a deeper order in biology and their long engagement with the complexity of embryonic development is personally recounted in Roger Lewin's book *Complexity: Life at the Edge of Chaos*.[14] Lewin describes the struggle of Goodwin and Kaufman to justify their commitment to a science of complexity that could explain both biological form and order within a proposed new physics of biology.

My own work with problems in the genesis of organisms was grounded in Aristotelian science available in the philosophy department during my graduate studies at Notre Dame. I have discovered two other sources of a holistic philosophy of biology in the writings of Johann Wolfgang von Goethe (1749–1832) and Gregory Bateson (1904–1980).

Gregory Bateson dedicated much of the last years of his career to restoring mind to a mechanistic science from which it was completely expunged. He understood mind not as a mechanical or supernatural entity but as the key to "the pattern that connects all living things." He knew that understanding the relational nature of reality was of "very great and deep importance…important to the survival of the whole biosphere."[17] In confronting the obsolescence of Cartesian science, Bateson found in Goethe a kindred spirit who "had a great ability in recognizing the nontrivial (i.e., in recognizing the pattern that connects)." Bateson also quotes Goethe as an ally in his own demand for the use of relational language:Goethe's visionary scientific work is now receiving growing recognition by modern scientists. In his introduction to *The Metamorphosis of Plants*, Goethe writes, "If, however, we observe the organic forms, we find nowhere something continuing, something at rest, but, on the contrary, that all is in continuous fluctuating movement."[15] His research for a generative principle in plants producing a series of transformations of form doubtless contributed to the theory of morphogenetic fields of Rupert Sheldrake, who studied Goethe while on sabbatical at Harvard. Brian Goodwin and Stuart Kauffman view their quest for the qualitative rather than the quantitative aspect of reality as essential Goethean science. According to Goodwin they, like Goethe, view "nature as essentially intelligible" and believe that "the "creative principle of emergence is a deep mystery in many ways…a property of complex dynamical systems."[16]

"A stem is that which bears leaves."
"A leaf is that which has a bud in its angle."
"A stem is what was once a bud in that position."[18]

A brilliant geneticist who surely epitomizes the Goethean approach to the archetypal nature of plants is the Nobel laureate Barbara McClintock. Her intimate knowledge of each corn plant, which she grew from seed, watered as a seedling, tended and observed throughout its growth before cross fertilizing the mature plant to study its chromosomal structure, reminds one of Goethe's long persistence in searching for the generative principle of the plant, for that which made it plant. His botanizing afforded him "quiet inexpressible joy," while McClintock found "a great pleasure" in her intimate knowledge of each plant.[19]

McClintock's research revolutionizes our perception of genes and chromosomes. No longer static and autonomous units, they have become complex dynamic structures, acting on and being acted on by other "jumping genes," the cell, the organism and its environment. The unit of inheritance is now a complex system of all the dynamic interacting parts. The isolated gene for McClintock was "merely a symbol" and an inadequate concept for use by population geneticists as the cornerstone of neo-Darwinism. And as for the human genome project, McClintock "was duly skeptical of those 'who thought they were going to solve the genome.' "[20]

McClintock's methodology calls for rethinking the very nature of science. In a commitment to the whole organism and an ability to keep its form at the center of her attention, she is an exemplar of Aristotelian science. She was also faithful to Aristotle's simple prescription that scientific conclusions be based on premises that are better known. McClintock prided herself on knowing each corn plant and usually could tell by looking at the plant what her microscope would reveal about changes in its chromosomal structure. Her conviction that "everything affects everything else" and that the gene per se is not the unit of heredity but "it is organized systems that operate as units,"[21] alerts us to the need for a new language and a new way of thinking about inheritance. Her work is celebrated in a recent Festschrift where several scientists advocated a systems approach to genetics, which likely indicates added skeptics of the atomistic Human Genome Project for the future.[22]

Mindful of Francis Thompson's insight that to pluck a flower is to disturb a star, is it not closer to reality to attribute the coding of organisms to the integral nature of the universe than to molecular genes? In the light of the connectedness of all nature and the need for a new language in science, I propose the use of *universe* coding rather than *genetic* coding to refer to inheritance. Universe coding would remind us of our place as integral participants in a multiconnected web of cosmic unity.

This is an opportune moment for biologists to reconceptualize the earth in all its "patterns that connect," to reclaim organisms as primary units of investigation, to return to the fields, rivers, mountains, ponds and oceans as laboratories of life. A new holistic language would enable biologists to emphasize the whole as a determinant of its interacting parts rather than being determined by them. Thus universe coding would become more appropriate than genetic coding as an explanation of the marvelous array of nature's diversity. Such a revision in our language and conceptualization of science could contribute to the healing of the earth community and to the restoration of the organic beauty and the ecological harmony that formerly graced this planet.

ACKNOWLEDGEMENT: I want to express gratitude to Arthur Fabel, editor of *Teilhard Studies*, for his editing and generous contribution of ideas.

This chapter was requested for *Frontier Sciences* at Temple University, 1994.

12.

A Rudolf Steiner
Sustainable Community

*A*fter attending the Earth Summit in Louisville on May 25–28, 1993, Laura Miller, an Associate in my Dominican community, and I began thinking about sustainable development or how to ensure a future for humans as well as other endangered species on this evolving planet.

What does sustainable development mean for religious communities? In our search we visited a variety of new communities. The Rudolf Steiner Fellowship Community in the beautiful hill country of Spring Valley, New York, impressed us as a model of a creative and sustainable lifestyle for its members, young and old, those in good health and those in need of care. In preparation for this article, we returned to talk to residents, to walk at leisure around the beautiful spacious grounds and to observe the manifold activities underway there.

Fellowship Community is primarily a retirement and care home, but the ages of residents ranges from three years old to 103. The seniors, co-workers and volunteers live together like our extended families of the past. Seniors who live independently, as well as those in need of care, share in the rich and varied opportunities available there. Hilltop House, where those in need of care reside, was designed to make this living space a hub around which all community life revolves. It contains the common dining room and the Goetheanum room for cultural, educational and recreational events. Even the laundry is an important part of the social life of this building, as it attracts the children and the infirm to lend a hand in routine community chores.

The campus gives evidence of lots of youthful energy in the community. The sandbox for small children; the nearby Green Meadow Waldorf School for kindergarten through twelfth grade; the Waldorf Institute, providing college courses in the arts and sciences; the Weleda Industries, begun in Switzerland, producing natural cosmetics and healing remedies; the Hand and Hoe Shop for sharing the fruits of one's labors with others; the abundance of flowers surrounding the buildings—all indicate a thriving community life. A greenhouse, a herb garden, an apple orchard, twenty acres of biodynamic gardens, compost piles, sheep, chickens, a bake shop all call for lots of hands at work. A variety of skills are developed in the eurythmy and drama schools, in the greenhouse and the printshop, in candle making, pottery, and weaving arts.

In this community we were especially interested in learning about the caretakers for the elderly, for the biodynamic garden, the farm animals. Who does the baking; who plans, prepares and cooks the meals? Who plants, cares for and harvests the vegetables in the garden and brings them to the kitchen? Who cans the vegetables and prepares the produce for the root cellar for the winter? Who preserves the foods from the gardens, bakes the bread and sells their extra produce in the Hand and Hoe Shop? Who sees that this community is maintained?

I referred above to coworkers and volunteers who live in this community and provide the youthful energy needed to sustain such a vital community life. In return, they share in the cultural, educational and spiritual opportunities afforded by this thirty-year-old experiment in community living, in this "blueprint for a new culture." Many of the coworkers live on campus with their families. Housing and a rich, meaningful life of service are certainly drawing cards. An excellent education for children from kindergarten through the twelfth grade in the adjoining Waldorf school is an inducement for families.

Coworkers come from nearly all the professions: three are doctors, several are nurses; contractors and bankers are here associated with artists, scientists and the less skilled. No one has a title, but all take part in the care of the elderly and the children, and all, with the help of volunteers and seniors, take responsibility for planning and administering daily life.

Volunteers are not paid for their services. All income for medical services, for the produce from the farm, for art and science classes, for the lovely pottery or woven materials made by co-workers, volunteers and the seniors goes into a community fund. Each co-worker gets a small stipend according to his or her need. Volunteers are invited to participate in the the arts and sciences programs available on campus, and to attend concerts and plays. Do these benefits explain the fact that there were thirty people on the waiting list to become co-workers when we visited Fellowship Community last summer?

I felt that I came closer to answering this puzzle when co-worker Miriam Karnow, whose husband is one of the doctors, explained their returning to Fellowship after his internship in Chicago. Both have a deep commitment to Anthroposophy, the philosophy of Rudolf Steiner, which gives focus to this creative sustainable way of life.

My own excitement has grown as I learn more of the pioneering work of Rudolf Steiner, whose Catholic background prepared him to move beyond the materialistic science of his day into a deeper spiritual approach to the natural world. His contributions in the fields of science, education, art and medicine are amazing. There are now fifteen hundred biodynamic farms in many countries, three hundred Waldorf schools ("the second largest independent school system in the world"), over two hundred facilities for the mentally retarded in twenty countries, and the Weleda Industries producing popular pharmaceutical remedies in several countries.

The twenty-five thousand members of the Anthroposophical Society add to the reason that Rudolf Steiner is beginning to interest scientists, as well as artists, physicians and educators today. I have become intrigued with Steiner's approach to the intellectual, natural and spiritual world.

Previously published in *Dominican News,* September 1993

13.

Is This the Time?

*E*cclesiastes reminds us, "There is a time for every matter under heaven." Could this be the time for psychodramatists to study in depth J. L. Moreno's dream for a creative revolution, a new social order?

Moreno found it curious that his innovative techniques in support of such a revolution had been universally accepted but the underlying philosophy of his life work was "misunderstood" and "relegated to the dark corners of library shelves or entirely pushed aside."

What prompts me to suggest this as the time? I and other religious women experienced a creative revolution in our lives following the 1960 Vatican II Decree on Renewal of Religious Life. We were challenged by this decree to simplify our lives, return to the spirit of our founders and the Gospel message. Within fifteen or twenty years religious women dropped outmoded customs and rituals accumulated over the centuries, discarded the habit, left ministries we had staffed in schools, hospitals and other institutions. With a newfound freedom we searched and continue to search for creative ways to respond to the pressing needs of a deteriorating American culture that has to change if it is to survive.

What if Moreno's prophetic and creative vision became the basic orientation of our psychodrama sessions? Using our own imagination how could we contribute creatively to the growth of the seeds he planted? Could our psychodrama sessions make a greater contribution to a creative revolution, to the new social order he envisioned? The distressing condition of American culture certainly makes it worth a try.

In 1969 Moreno wrote that a creative revolution needed an appraisal of our system of values with special emphasis on the human as a creative agent. He referred to the need for instruments and institutions by which "his dream of a romantic new universe" could be realized. Science and technology, according to Moreno, had distorted our institutions. The robots, the machines that humans produced, had become agents of destruction, in conflict with the creative act itself. The title of his book *Who Shall Survive?* expressed his deep concern over the battle between machines and the creative potentiality of all humans. He expected that those who developed their God-given creativity and spontaneity would do battle with the machines, the robots and cultural conserves that control so much of our institutions and our lives.

No doubt the problems of our technological world are an overwhelming challenge—a failing school system, a polluted environment that threatens all life on planet earth, a capitalistic system that puts profits ahead of persons, an economy driven by corporations that make the rich richer while further impoverishing the poor. Moreno provided encouragement for us to believe in the part each of us can play toward a better world. Considering himself a lone prophet, he courageously planted the seeds for a desperately needed revolution, a new social order that he said might take a hundred years to bear fruit. He had faith "that the apparently impossible can be achieved, even if it should take a thousand years."

Basic to Moreno's vision of a new social order was "an investment in spontaneity-creativity as a propelling force in human progress." As a child Moreno began producing and taking the part of God in plays with other children. This God playing stayed with him throughout his life and brought him the realization that it was in God he could find the source of infinite creativity and spontaneity. It was his concentration on the God of the first day of creation, he said, that provided the genesis of psychodrama and the guide for all his future work.

In this age of disbelief when so many are disillusioned by dogmas and religion, Moreno's claim that all his inspiration for his methods and techniques came directly or indirectly from his idea of the Godhead and from the principle of his genesis may be an obstacle. But Moreno did not have a monolithic idea of God. For him, the loss of faith in a supreme being was one of the greatest dilemmas facing humans. Moreno granted that there might not be a personal God but was confident that each of us is called to embody the divine in our own lives. The infinitely creative and spontaneous supreme being, he concluded, had shared a measure of creativity and spontaneity with each creature.

Moreno's search "for a new vision of God for a universal religion of the future" extended to primitive religions and foreshadowed the movement of many Christians and Jews who are now finding enrichment in Native American, Buddhist, Zen and Sufi spiritualities. He found great delight in a human Jesus, who embodied the Divine for us to emulate. For Moreno God was not dead as long as there are millions of us to embody the Divine as Jesus did.

Frequently Moreno referred to Jesus, Buddha, Socrates and Gandhi as the real healers. Healers he thought were creative-spontaneous protagonists in the midst of their societies. These great leaders not only reached out compassionately to individuals but were motivated by a desire for a new order in their respective societies. They each embodied the truth of what they taught and left this challenge to those they inspired to follow their example. Likewise, Moreno expected that the seeds he planted would be nourished into further growth by those who took up his commitment to bring forth a new social order.

For Moreno there was no division between God and nature. Nature was "the master model for creativity." How insightful was his belief that "the secrets and inventions" of the mind of a creative genius are attained "in a miraculous way" by "communicating with the mysteries of nature." He was thus a forerunner to those ecologists who are awakening us to the necessity to learn from nature if we are to turn from the suicidal path now destroying the life support systems on this planet.

Recognizing the desperate need for community apparent today, we can appreciate Moreno's search for "a technique of balancing the spontaneous social forces to the greatest possible harmony and unity of all." His basic hypothesis was "love and mutual sharing as powerful, indispensable working principles in group life." These elements for him are principles needed for superdynamic communities that could be antidotes to the violence, alienation and despair of our disintegrating culture. Could such a vision enrich psychodrama by helping protagonists to face personal problems of adjusting to the insanity of our society but within the context of being co-creators of a more human order?

We have nothing to lose and lots to gain by setting our psychodrama session within a more profound context—the commitment to a new social order as envisioned by our founding father, J. L. Moreno.

April, 2001

14.

Women Scientists
Ancient Wisdom and Modern Science

The ancient wisdom of the West is the seedbed from which modern science originated. If rerooted in the Greek and Medieval soil, modern science could become an integral part of the rich wisdom tradition of the West. My thesis is that women scientists, in their critique of the male-dominated and exclusionary approach of modern science, are in reality in search of a methodology to be found in the wisdom of Greek and medieval science. As women scientists continue in their demand for equality, they could enrich science with a renewed common-sense approach to nature's wisdom.

Modern science is in crisis. Its foundations and assumptions are challenged, new paradigms are in process, the very nature of science and its future are in dispute. Quantum mechanics and relativity theory toppled the reductive materialistic physics of Newton and Descartes in the early part of this century. Three decades ago Thomas Kuhn's book *The Structure of Scientific Revolutions* brought the whole scientific enterprise into question, especially as to its sociopolitical character.[1] In the last twenty years women scientists have significantly added to the questioning as they unmask the political and social nature of a science that has kept men dominating the field while excluding women and their social experience. Women scientists call for radical transformation with profound social and political consequences. The focus of this paper is on those aspects of women's critique of modern science and their search for an alternative, which I claim validates the scientific methodology of the ancient wisdom of the West, the seedbed from which science germinated. I include women philosophers and theologians, as science, philosophy and religion were not distinct intellectual enterprises in the wisdom traditions of ancient cultures.

Women and Science

Developments in the feminist movement of the last twenty years bear significantly on women's relationship to science. Having painstakingly broken through the barriers that kept them from education in this field, women have now produced a wealth of literature exposing the masculine bias in and domination of modern science and culture. Even though they have only a "toehold" in this "male preserve," women boldly and confidently expose the "traditions in philosophy and in science that are deeply hostile to women."[2] In so doing they are advancing at least in theory toward a transformation of the prevailing "religion of advanced patriarchy,"[3] which perpetuates masculine control of and power over a capitalistic system that is industrializing and militarizing the world.

My personal experience of the control of industry over modern science came while I was engaged in postdoctoral study at the Institute of Experimental Medicine at the University of Montreal. Much nonsensical research was done to use up funds provided by pharmaceutical corporations, to insure the continual flow of such cash. When my research interests with white rats changed to the study of algae in the Botany Department at the University of Texas, I was made acutely aware of the depth of male discrimination in the sciences. When I questioned the absence of women on the faculty of that department, the chairman without apology responded, "There are not any, and what's more, there will not be. We had too much trouble getting rid of the one we had." Ruth Hubbard, one of the first women to secure tenure as a professor at Harvard, explains this mindset: "As long as the overwhelming majority of scientists are men who are rooted in the ruling class, socially or intellectually (or both), science will supply the 'objective' support and technical innovations needed to sustain patriarchal ruling-class power."[4]

The ecological crisis, the deterioration of our social and political institutions and our quality of life, impacts everyone, especially the poor. All this contributes to women's loss of faith in modern science and technology. The publication of Rachel Carson's *Silent Spring* and Betty Friedan's *Feminine Mystique* in the 1960s stirred women to a new awareness of their latent power to make a difference in a culture that is ravaging and poisoning the earth, impoverishing and threatening the lives of its inhabitants. Recent Sierra Club books include works of men who have joined women to become ecofeminists, ecotheologians and ecopsychologists.[5] They would support Betty Roszak's claim that "our compulsively masculine science and technology... lies at the root of our environmental disconnection."[6] Scientist Brian Swimme proposes that a "holistic poetic vision alive in ecofeminism" is needed as a corrective to a world that is the product of a patriarchal, "fragmented scientific" mindset.[7]

Understanding these political and social realities, women scientists identify them as the cause of our hierarchically structured exploitative society, which "reflects the interests of a ruling capitalist class."[8] Science and technology have produced a consumer culture geared to profit making, "tied to militarism, capitalism, colonialism, and male supremacy... in the interests of unfettered power."[9] Ruth Hubbard left her tenured position at Harvard to join women scientists in exposing this male-biased science that has affected our whole scientifically based way of life. She explains:

> The pretense that science is objective, apolitical and value-neutral is instead profoundly political because it obscures the political role that science and technology play in underwriting the existing distribution of power in society. Science and technology always operate in somebody's interest and serve someone or some group of people. To the extent that scientists are "neutral" that merely means that they support the existing distribution of interests and power.[10]

She further comments that "scientists work not so much because they believe that the knowledge they produce is relevant to human needs or values but often in order to generate publications, jobs, research funds and prizes."[11]

Women realize that they too are part of the squandered resources of the earth and are determined to document the connection between the exploitation of nature and their subjugation. Among the targets of this concern are the writings of one of the fathers of modern science, Francis

Bacon. His brazen imagery identifying the mastery of nature with the denigration of women is another example in the long history of according women an inferior status. Bacon presents nature as female and then claims "the task of science is the exercise of the right kind of male domination over her."[12] The influence of the witchcraft trials underway in the England of his day apparently colors Bacon's speaking of science as "leading to you nature with all her children to bind her to your service and make her your slave."[13]

Women also target the "medicalization of childbirth" as a masculine "redesign and appropriation of reproduction" so as to "create new profit-making technologies for capitalism" and thus give men control of what were "heretofore natural processes mediated by women."[14] Scientist and political activist Ruth Bleier warns that this "patriarchal social, political and economic system... gains much in power, privileges and profits for itself and for individual men from the subordinate position of women" but "now finds itself faced with the first serious historic threat to its dominance."[15]

A Feminist Science

As women advance against the androcentrism of modern science they search for a feminist science that is inclusive of their experience and contribution. But is there a distinctive feminist method of inquiry? Women scientists do not see the possibility of such a science within our present male-dominated culture.[16] But this has not brought them to an impasse in their struggle to visualize the intellectual structures needed for a better world we do not yet have. Harvard theologian Elizabeth Schussler Fiorenza explains, "A shift from an androcentric to a feminist interpretation of the world implies a revolutionary shift in scientific paradigm, a shift with far-reaching ramifications not only for the interpretation of the world but also for its change."[17] In its full implication it calls women "to reinvent both science and theorizing itself to make sense of women's social experience"[18] and to demand respect for nature.

Women scientists envision creating a "science with a human face, science which aims more at co-operating with than at conquering Nature, which learns more by conversing or conducting a dialogue with Nature than by putting it on the rack, to force it to reveal its secrets."[19] They want a science "that works for rather than against life," one that is not harnessed to making money and waging war. Such scientific knowledge would have to be "constructed by an interactive dialogic community," one "characterized by equality of intellectual authority." "For knowledge to count as genuine," according to Helen Longino, "the community must be adequately diverse."[20]

Such an inclusive and cooperative science would call for non-invasive ways of understanding nature. This demands respect for animals in laboratories with safeguards for their use and against their abuse in test studies. It advocates industries with concern for people and the environment rather than just for profit. It would appreciate the creative work of women's "craft labor" rather than just mechanical "industrialized labor."

Many women realize there has been a gynocentric science all along. Their traditional work in home, garden and sickroom has contributed much to the understanding of nature, but has not been accorded the honorific title of "Science." Women's knowledge is often labeled art. The "art" of midwifery becomes the science of obstetrics, and the "art" of cooking becomes food science when taken over by men. To find a feminist science with a base in woman's experience women have to "look outside of the histories, conceptual frameworks, literature, and possibly even the language that has been generated by men."[21]

Barbara McClintock's Empathic Science

When Barbara McClintock's exceptional scientific study of corn cytogenetics was finally acknowledged with a Nobel Prize in 1983, women scientists rejoiced in this legitimation of a woman's alternative to the traditional view of science. Evelyn Fox Keller's excellent biography of McClintock, *The Feeling for the Organism,* was an inspiration and an encouragement for many women scientists. Keller claims McClintock as a model, "perhaps the most striking exemplar of dynamic objectivity in present-day science," [22] and an example of what a gender-free science might look like. Among the key elements that Keller identifies to distinguish McClintock's vision and practice of science are: respect for the differences she observed in her corn plants as "the cornerstone of her distinctive philosophy of science,"[23] exposing the critical flaw in the accepted central dogma of genetics and providing "evidence that genetic organization is necessarily more complex, and in fact more globally interdependent than such a model assumes." [24]

McClintock's award was for me the validation of a commonsense approach to an understanding of the natural world. Her long, patient and intimate relationship with corn plants, their genes and chromosomes, unveiled secrets unknown to her colleagues. I have elsewhere described her work as the epitome of the commonsense scientific methodology of Aristotle.[25] The debate among women scientists as to whether Barbara McClintock "might be regarded as an exemplar of a 'feminist science' " provided me the opportunity to argue in this paper that a feminine and more human alternative to our androcentric science is already at hand in Aristotle's general science of nature.[26]

The Search for a New Paradigm

When did my quest for a new scientific paradigm begin? I was fortunate to be in graduate school in the 1950s when Notre Dame was one of the few universities where one could study ancient science. In Aristotle's philosophy of nature I found an approach to science that helped me envision an alternative to the inane and boring memory work prescribed for a doctorate in biology. My disappointment with the biology department was compensated by the fine lectures of the philosophy faculty with whom I studied Aristotle's *Physics, Posterior* and *Prior Analytics* along with the *Commentaries* on them by Thomas Aquinas. Aquinas integrated Aristotle's philosophy of science into a meaningful world view that enabled me during my years in the classroom to introduce students to the extraordinary genius of Aristotle's methodology. I also recommended other scientists from the *Great Books of the Western World* who were being popularized through the insights and giftedness of Robert Hutchins and Mortimer Adler at the University of Chicago. My students could thus compare the ancients' approach to the study of nature to the hodgepodge of data collected into textbooks to train students as anti-intellectual technicians instead of scientists.

It is understandable that Aristotle's antifeminism has been a barrier to the consideration of his scientific methodology by women scientists. In fact, Andrea Nye claims that the perceptual identification of the relation between misogyny and traditional philosophy has been "a defining characteristic of feminist philosophy" and caused women to suspect the writings of those philosophers "guilty of deeply rooted male 'bias.'"[27] But despite Aristotle's bias toward women and the debunking accorded him by philosophers over the last four hundred years, there are women whose scholarship provides a new respect for his genius. This gives me hope that some women scientists will be open to my argument for the validity of Aristotle's philosophy of science.

Historian of science Donna Haraway optimistically asks if there is "a specifically feminine theory of knowledge growing today which is analogous in its implications to theories which are the heritage of Greek science?"[28] Sandra Harding reminds us that "controlled experimentation is not a modern invention as "Aristotle was an experimentalist."[29] Could she be referring to ancient culture when she asks if there is "another world invisible to science and to which science is indifferent or perhaps even hostile?"[30] Evelyn Fox Keller seems to appreciate the Greek world view when she quotes from Theodore Gomperz:

> You need not know of the doctrines and writings of the great masters of antiquity: of Plato and Aristotle, you need never have heard their name, none the less you are under the spell of their authority.... Our entire thinking, the logical categories in which it moves, the linguistic patterns it uses... is, in the main, the product of the great thinkers of antiquity.[31]

Several feminist philosophers are indeed removing the barriers to the rich heritage of ancient science. Charlotte Witt, a member of a "tiny world of Aristotelians," thinks it unlikely that students of Aristotle and feminists will in the near future "see any relationship between their respective philosophical concerns." Yet she concludes that "feminist reflections concerning what it is to be human" are continuous with the philosophical tradition of Aristotle.[32] Despite Aristotle's reputation as an antifeminist, Marcia Homiak finds that his ideal of the rational life is neither inherently masculine or exploitative. She concludes then that his image of what it is to be human is "worthy of emulation by women and men."[33] Surprisingly Andrea Nye names Aristotle "the canonical authority" for feminist philosophers who "were forced to a deeper level of social and political critique" and then suggests that he "might be taken as describing the aims of a new, deeply critical feminist social and political philosophy."[34] Genevieve Lloyd similarly approves Aristotle's rapprochement of form and matter as necessary to provide "the possibility for changeable material things to be the proper object of genuine knowledge."[35]

But the woman scholar who most strongly commits her writing and teaching to the experiential philosophy of Aristotle with a moving defense of his rational ideal is Martha C. Nussbaum, one of the Greek revivalists of the 1970s. Her magnificent book about Greek tragedy and philosophy, *The Fragility of Goodness,* gives a scholarly and detailed explanation of Aristotle's science of nature, to which I will return later.

These women scientists who have unearthed value in our Greek heritage have credible allies among the founding fathers of quantum mechanics. Nobel laureate Erwin Schrödinger in his Sherman Lectures on "Nature and the Greeks" called for "an assiduous study of Greek thought," not only in "the hope of unearthing obliterated wisdom, but also of discovering inveterate error at the source, where it is easier to recognize."[36] He quoted from John Burnett's *Early Greek Philosophy*: "that science is a Greek invention: that science has never existed except among peoples who came under Greek influence."[37] Werner Heisenberg claimed that Aristotle "actually created the basis for the scientific language" and "contributed immensely to the clarification, to the establishment of order in our methods of thought."[38]

Barbara McClintock and Martha Nussbaum

What is the nature of Barbara McClintock's research that wins her such universal acclaim among women scientists? And what is the significance of Martha Nussbaum's reinterpretation of Aristotle's organic philosophy of science to disclose its real meaning? By bringing together the commonsense scholarship of these two remarkable women I hope to provide insight into the nature of Barbara McClintock's research as an example of the methodology Martha Nussbaum reveals as the science of Aristotle.

Nussbaum's invaluable description of Aristotle's experiential methodology refutes its long history of scorn as "deductive" science. She explains that "his principles of science in the *Analytics* have been thought by centuries of commentators... to be *a priori* truths grasped by special acts of intellectual intuition, apart from all experience."[39] Instead, Nussbaum explains at length that Aristotle demands that data "be drawn from aspects of the natural world" and that he "promises to work within and to defend a method that is thoroughly committed to the data of human experience."[40] Aristotle was convinced, according to Nussbaum, that "we have no access to any truth beyond the deepest and most pervasive appearances."[41] He insists on returning to the actual phenomena to check the consistency of any conclusion. "At every step, Aristotle is concerned to show how his norm arises out of the appearances and embodies their requirements."[42] He is disdainful of Plato's talk of nonphysical forms as "insufficiently rooted in experience even to be coherent talk."[43]

The centrality of the sensible in nature in all its phenomenal aspects for Aristotle likewise distinguishes McClintock's patient decades of nurturing her corn plants, from which she concludes:

No two plants are exactly alike. They're all different, and as a consequence, you have to know that difference.... I start with the seedling, and I don't want to leave it. I don't really feel I know the story if I don't watch the plant all the way along. So I know every plant in the field. I know them intimately, and I find it a great pleasure to know them.[44]

Keller explains that McClintock's "fidelity to her own experience" may account for her being "more open than most other scientists" to unconventional ideas.[45] Seemingly it was the unwillingness of her colleagues to respect her carefully documented findings that caused them to dismiss her common sense but unorthodox approach to the study of genetics. Had they been disciples of Aristotle they would have been open to "any radical or new view"[46] that she brought to their attention as an effective way to explain the differences she observed in her corn plants. Aristotle appealed to "our broadly shared belief that natural beings are 'things that have within themselves a principle of change,' (Ph.II.I)" which "implies a commitment to abide by the results of scientific investigation into these inner structures."[47] Never a defender of the status quo, Aristotle asked for "the cultivation of imagination and responsiveness to all...alternatives."[48] In fact, Nussbaum claims Aristotle himself, true to his own principles, would likely have been open to reasoned persuasion to change his views on the inferior status of women.[49]

Like other women scientists, Barbara McClintock was aware of the limitations in the scientific method. From "what we label scientific knowledge," she acknowledged, "You get lots of correlations, but you don't get the truth.... Things are much more marvelous than the scientific method allows us to conceive." With regard to her inability to communicate this holistic, empathic method to her colleagues she explained: "I couldn't tell other people at the time because it was against the 'scientific method.' "[50] She often questioned her colleagues mechanistic modelling of DNA. For her, "models, when they first begin to be promulgated, are so bothersome." She added, "Trying to make everything fit into a set dogma won't work." Scientists "don't know they are bound to a dogma and you couldn't show them...even if you made an effort."[51] Similarly, Aristotle cautioned, "The moment we begin to theorize, we are...in acute danger of oversimplying" and in danger of "mechanism in scientific explanation." He warned many times that "oversimplification and reduction will be deep and ever-present dangers."[52]

McClintock's passion was to understand each individual part in its relationship to the whole organism: "The important thing is to develop the capacity to see one kernel that is different, and make that understandable." She explains that when something "doesn't fit, there's a reason, and you find out what it is." Researchers who overlook and label differences "an exception, an aberration, a contaminant" miss, to their and our cost, "what is going on."[53] Martha Nussbaum says Aristotle likewise committed to the truth of ordinary experience, saw the flaws in the work of many scientists of his day because they did not return to the phenomena to account for the appearances.[54] For him natural philosophy needed to "show us the way back to the ordinary and.make it an object of interest and pleasure, rather than contempt and evasion."[55] Nussbaum concludes that Aristotle saw "philosophical issues more clearly than his reductionist opponents both ancient and contemporary."[56]

"To capture the full power" of Aristotle's revolutionary philosophy, Nussbaum explains that one needs to grasp the depth of meaning in his insight that "all human beings by nature reach out for understanding." She continues:

> The discussion that follows these famous words traces the development of philosophy back to a natural inclination, on the part of all human beings, to sort out and interpret the world for themselves,

making distinctions, clarifying, finding explanations for that which seems strange or wonderful. He concludes: "Our natural desires will not be satisfied so long as something apparently arbitrary eludes us."[57]

According to Keller, "Understanding was the cornerstone of Barbara McClintock's whole approach to science." In fact, what she consistently pursued was nothing less than an understanding of the entire organism."[58] "Because of her commitment to the whole organism," she "never lost her interest in developmental problems," to which she contributed significantly.[59] Aristotle too was committed to a deep understanding of the whole organism, as apparent in "the immense mass of new material" he left in four surviving works on animals.[60] In Nussbaum's articulation of Aristotle's ethics, she finds that his inquiry into human action is carried out as a part of a larger inquiry into the movements of animals. Human action is very little singled out; instead we find a discussion of sweeping generality that ranges over the entire animal kingdom. It is this generality that we must seek to understand if we are to understand the distinctive contribution this account makes to ethics.[61]

Aristotle claimed, "It is because of wonder that human beings undertake philosophy, both now and at its origins....The person who is at a loss and in a state of wonder thinks he fails to grasp something; this is why the lover of stories is in a sense a philosopher, for stories are composed out of wonders."[62] McClintock found the stories her corn plants revealed were fantastic "beyond our wildest expectations."[63] No one doubts Barbara McClintock's sense of wonder in her intense and devoted "feeling for the organism," which sustained her through the years of virtual isolation without the recognition of colleagues and with little funding. It is her "feeling for the organism," her participative knowledge of nature and its relational reality that identifies her science with the integral organic vision of the ancients.

Closing

In closing I want to reaffirm science as an essential element of ancient wisdom. Both the Greek sages and the medieval scholastics integrated their natural philosophy, their search for the virtuous human life in their primary pursuit of wisdom. It is this perennial wisdom that provides an affirmative answer to Sandra Harding's insightful question: "Is there then another world, invisible to science and to which science is indifferent or even hostile?" In his recovery of ancient teachings, Thomas Aquinas unearthed the depth of meaning in the works of Aristotle. Richard Tarnas explains, "The essential impact Aquinas had on Western thought lay especially in his conviction that the judicious exercise of man's {sic} empirical and rational intelligence, which had been developed and empowered by the Greeks, could now marvelously serve the Christian cause." He continues, "Aquinas converted medieval Christianity to Aristotle and to the values Aristotle represented."[64] Thus Aquinas, "in his relatively short life," forged "a world view that dramatically epitomized the high Middle Ages turning of Western thought on its axis, to a new dimension of which the modern mind would be the heir and trustee."[65] As heirs and trustees of this ageless tradition, women scientists, while progressing toward their own equality, could enrich modern science by reconnecting it with its nutrient roots in ancient wisdom.

15.

A Call to Dominican
Religious Women

$\mathcal{F}$or several years theologian Sandra Schneider has reminded religious women of the serious crisis in faith threatening the very nature of religious life. In a 1997 keynote address to the Leadership Conference of Women Religious, Sandra described the struggle that many religious women are having with the Church and Catholic religion. She challenged the leaders to open discussions concerning this crisis in their respective communities. The response of religious women to Vatican II, heightened by the incredible developments in the feminist movement, according to Sandra, caused many "to seriously question a Catholic Christianity which they found inadequate, much less a preferable, access to Holy Mystery or compelling motivation for ministry." In her view, many religious women find "the God of Christianity...too small, too violent, and too male; the focus of Jesus Christ... narrow and exclusive, the Resurrection...mythological, if not incredible and, in any case, irrelevant to a world in anguish."[1]

It is understandable that religious leaders have been reluctant to initiate dialogue in their respective communities concerning the developments in the faith choices of members. Individual religious hesitate to discuss disturbing changes or lack of change in the prayer practices among their companions for fear of being labeled out of date or reactionary in some cases and heretical in others. As a result there is little exposure in the media of this radical development in the faith lives of religious women. My immediate concern in writing this article is the deep division in religious communities resulting from adverse feelings about and criticism of sisters who have elected to participate in other forms of prayer, meditation and rituals rather than those in male-dominated institutionalized liturgies in Catholic parishes.

Role of Dominican Religious Women

I believe that Dominican religious women could play a unique role in bringing understanding to an important aspect of this issue—that of many religious women's interest in and practice of Eastern religions. My insight resulted from an article by Bede Griffiths that it was our Dominican brothers Thomas Aquinas and Meister Eckhart who brought the great advance in consciousness of the Axial Period of history into the Catholic tradition.[2] It was in the Axial Period (800–200 BCE) that Buddhism, Confucianism, Hinduism, the Hebrew Prophets and Greek philosophy arose independently in China, India, and Europe. If Dominicans realized that the spiritualities from the Axial Period were integral to their Dominican theology and spirituality, it seems that we would find in Buddhism and other Eastern religions not a threat, but a source of nourishment for women whose spiritual lives have been impoverished in a patriarchal Catholic Church.

The above claims call for fuller explanations: first, what was the advance in consciousness in the Axial Period; second, how was this new consciousness brought into the Catholic tradition through Thomas Aquinas and Meister Eckhart and how does this bring Dominican theology into relationship with Axial Period spiritualities; and third, how would these insights if realized by Dominican women help us to confront at least one aspect of the faith crisis we now face?

Axial Period Consciousness

First, the radically new consciousness of the Axial Period arose independently in diverse regions of the earth with Confucius and Lao-tse in China, with the Upanishads and Buddha in India, the prophets Isaiah and Jeremiah in Palestine and Homer, Socrates, Plato and Aristotle in Greece. Through these new beginnings of world religions, humans were moved from a tribal mentality into an individualistic, moral and spiritual consciousness that is the basis of the way we think today. The historian Karl Jaspers named the time of "this awakening of the specifically

human spirit" an Axial Period of history because it "gave birth to everything which, since then, man [sic] has been able to be, the point most
overwhelmingly fruitful in fashioning humanity." Jaspers claimed the
history of Christianity was incomplete without acknowledgement of the
advance in human consciousness attributable to the other great religions
of the world.[3]

My second point: how did Thomas Aquinas and Meister Eckhart
bring the new consciousness and spirituality of the Axial Period into the
Catholic tradition and how could their theology bring us into closer
relationship with these traditions? Through their study of the Christian
teaching of Dionysius the Aeropagite, a fifth-century Syrian monk,
thought mistakenly to be a disciple of St. Paul, St. Albert and St. Thomas gave him the legitimacy of a doctor of the Church. Thomas was
first introduced to the riches of this Neoplatonic mystic when as a student of Albert in Cologne he recorded the class notes on Dionysius's
work, *The Divine Names*. Thomas later came to consider Dionysius a
witness to the truth as he did Augustine and Aristotle, and so adapted
the negative theology of Dionysius into his own treatises on the Mystery
of God. After any positive statement of knowledge of God, Thomas balanced it with the negative statement, a Dionysian contention: "Complete ignorance is the way to know him who is above all that is
known."[4]

The presence of the Dionysian negative theology of knowing and
unknowing of God as a cornerstone in the works of Albert the Great,
Thomas Aquinas and Meister Eckhart assured its preservation for the
Christian West and its significance to us Dominicans. However, more
study is needed to reveal the relationship of the neglected Christian negative theology to these ancient religions. According to Bede Griffiths
these early religions were initially introduced into the Catholic tradition
by Thomas Aquinas and Meister Eckhart. Griffiths, after thirty-five
years of monastic sharing and living the Eastern religion practices and
prayers in his Christian ashram in India, left us this insight:

> One of the greatest needs of humanity today, is to transcend the cul-
> tural limitations of the great religions and to find a wisdom, a philos-
> ophy, which can reconcile their differences and reveal the unity
> which underlies all their diversities. This has been called the "peren-
> nial philosophy," which has been revealed in a different way in each
> religion.[5]

New Perspective for Struggles with Faith

The need to transcend the cultural limitations of the great religions and find a wisdom to reconcile their differences offers a unique opportunity for Dominican women to see our faith difficulties from a completely new perspective, which is the subject of my third point. A contributing insight is the development of the mystical spirituality of Albert the Great, Thomas Aquinas, and the uniquely gifted preacher and teacher of this Dionysian negative theology, Meister Eckhart, and his disciples, Henry Suso, John Tauler and Dominican women mystics. Richard Woods, in *Mysticism and Prophecy*, writes: "For some time large numbers of Beguines had been flocking to Dominican convents. What attracted them and large numbers of other well-educated women to the Dominicans in the late thirteenth and early fourteenth centuries was, it appears, the emphasis on study in the order together with the mystical character of its spirituality. The encounter between dynamic preachers and these God-centered women produced one of the most spectacular upsurges of mystical spirituality in the history of Europe."[6] The contribution of women to this mystical spirituality, only recently getting the acknowledgment that it so richly deserves, could be an inspiration for us today in resolving our differences with a church so much in need.

How then could the integration of insights from the Axial Period into the Catholic tradition help religious women confront the faith crisis in religious life? This crisis needs to be understood in the context of the radical transformation of religious communities after Vatican II when the feminist and environmental movements awakened many women to the general oppression they have suffered through the ages. As women religious entered the main stream of civil society in new avenues now opened to women, the Leadership Conference of Women Religious provided a collective voice to take on the male preserve of the Catholic Church by demanding full participation for women in its life and ministry.

Remaining committed to full equality in the Church, but realizing that this change in women's status could not be accomplished overnight, many women religious joined with others in search of a more liberating spirituality than the institutionalized prayer practices of the male-dominated Catholic Church. Native American, Feminist and Creation spiritualities all had participants from among the different congregations of women religious. Similarly, the human potential movement awakened women to the value of feelings in a spirituality free of a dogmatic and legalistic approach to religion. Many discovered new life in the increasingly popular and more experiential Eastern religious traditions—Zen, Buddhist, Hindu, and others. But these fresh currents were threatening to those who were committed to the prayer practices to which they had long been accustomed.

Negative Neoplatonic Theology

That Eastern religious traditions are filling a spiritual void in the lives of some of our companions could be the wake up call needed for Dominican women to recapture that part of our heritage that has been neglected in our study of theology. It is in the negative Neoplatonic theology of Thomas, Albert and Meister Eckhart that we find a kinship of Dominican theology to Eastern religions. If these ancient traditions from the Axial Period prepared the consciousness of humans for the coming of Christ, then they could well be the grounding now needed for a renewal of Christianity. If it was in the soil of this period that the Gospels were so fruitfully planted by Christ, then Christianity could find in the convergence of its truth with that of the truths of these traditions the universal wisdom that underlies all their diversities. The increasing interest in and practice of these ancient traditions by women religious is an encouraging movement toward a more universal church for the future. Women could be thus promoting the new epoch that Karl Rahner predicted would follow the post-Vatican II church coming to the "the discovery and official recognition of itself as world-Church."[7]

As we Dominican women deepen our study of a Neoplatonic negative theology, a Dominican heritage, it can open up creative mind-stretching pathways to us. Simon Tugwell pointed out that taking Dionysian negative theology seriously "frees us from the various tyrannies that narrow our religious language and practice."[8] In this regard I was shocked at first by a sister friend who said she no longer had a personal God. But on recalling St. Thomas's statement that God is not 'a' being, but supremely Being, I could begin to let go of my image of God. If God is not 'a' being, then it can equally be true that one does not have a personal God. God is not an object to be named, but rather a presence to be experienced. The Mystery of the Divine is beyond naming, yet in some sense all creatures are said to be 'names' of God. Lao-Tse, the Taoist sage, pointed out that a name that can be named is not the eternal name. I am comfortable with the naming of a nameless God who is Truth. My faithful guide has been "Know the Truth and the Truth shall set you free." It was by the discovery of Truth that the Buddha became enlightened.

Eastern Spiritualities

Among ancient spiritualities attracting many religious today are Mystery Schools that originated in Greece, Egypt, Italy and Afghanistan, among indigenous peoples and among the druids of Old Europe. In these Mystery Schools many religious learn the beauty of new and liberating rituals that include dancing, theater, communal sharing of life stories, the study of mystics from different traditions, and walking and sitting meditations. Through dream and faith sharing sessions we deepen our ability to listen to one another, a skill most often lacking in our earlier regimented religious communities. In learning to listen to one another we grow in self knowledge, which can be a means of growing into God. Such creative communal forms of ritual are a welcome substitute for assembly line dispensing of sacraments by male priests in our factory-like churches. Many religious find Zen sitting sesshins and retreats of immense support for disciplined reflection and Christian centering prayer. By these new practices religious women can help each other understand that the various spiritualities attracting our companions are enriching and are a potential offering for the renewal of a Church in dire need of relationship with a world in crisis. As I come to the realization that I am enriched by knowing many approaches to the Divine, I become more accepting of the views of others. Eckhart reminds us that when one seeks God in a special way one gets the way and misses God.

Conclusion

What I have tried to point out is that Dominican women through study and appreciation of Dionysian negative theology could bring new understanding of the riches of ancient religions, as well as a deeper appreciation of our own Dominican heritage. Both of these sources would cause us to relax and even rejoice in the courage of sisters who experiment with new avenues to the Divine. When Eckhart said, "I pray God to rid me of God," he was saying that our images of God may be a stumbling block to the experience of the Divine for which we all long. If Axial Period religions arose independently in three areas of the world and brought humans there to a new preparedness for the coming of Christ's Word, they could help us overcome negative and limiting attitudes toward other religions and toward our community members who are now enjoying a variety of new forms of prayer and relationships. As we enter into creative dialogue with those of different religious traditions we may be, like Bede Griffiths, "finding the other part of our soul" and thus make our contribution toward an enriched World Church in which women would be equal members. We could bring new life to a church whose dwindling vitality is apparent in its aging parishioners and could stimulate outreach to a younger generation attracted to Eastern traditions. The Neoplatonic theology that bore such fruit in the lives of the Beguines and the Dominican nuns in the Middle Ages thus challenges us to search for new and creative rituals and spiritualities that benefit from the convergence of perennial truth and wisdom from all the great religious traditions.

Epilogue

The chapters for this book, entitled *Earth-friendly: Re-Visioning Science and Spirituality*, seem disproportionately concentrated on science. My hope is that the complementarity of science and spirituality as they are envisioned in their interdependence on the living processes of nature has now become more apparent. An organismally alive science with respect for the sacredness of nature surely impacts a life-giving spirituality. Evidence for a new paradigm in science, rooted in the wisdom of the past, is now receiving support from ecological and nature-loving scientists, as well as from those in academia, making the spiritual treasure of Steiner's life and work better known. Steiner prophetically foresaw the limitations of a mechanistic modern science that separated humans from the world of nature, as an important stage in the whole evolution of human consciousness. That evolution which Steiner committed himself to advance through his spiritual science would reestablish humans in a new and freely chosen relationship with the earth. This is happening today and is an important base for a revised spirituality. Those interested in the heritage of St. Thomas could further Steiner's hopes that Aquinas's thought when enkindled by that of Goethe would become a creative amalgam with Steiner's thought for a spiritual science of the twenty-first century. Owen Barfield proposed in an offhand way that spiritual science and a revisioned spirituality are complementary: "There will be a revival of Christianity when it becomes impossible to write a popular manual of science without referring to the incarnation of the Word."[1]

The revisioning of spirituality and the revival of Christianity suggested by Barfield have become imperative in the light of the rapid decline in church attendance and in the astonishing growth of Eastern religions in the United States. Steiner early recognized the dependence of a renewal of Christianity on the recovery of the ancient traditions that prepared the way for Christ's coming, which I will return to later. The present-day disillusionment with the lifeless liturgies in too many of the churches is not unlike the experience of Rudolf Steiner with the Catholic Church in his youth. Steiner's long resistance to any freedom-limiting, dogmatic approach to the spiritual was rewarded at the end of the nineteenth century with an illumination that he recounts in his autobiography: "A conscious knowledge of true Christianity began to develop within me. Around the turn of the century, this knowledge grew deeper. The inner test occurred shortly before the turn of the century. This experience culminated in my standing in the spiritual presence of the mystery of Golgotha in a most profound and solemn festival of knowledge."[2]

The experience of a true Christianity awakened in Steiner a deep belief in and reliance on the promises of Jesus. "For Christ stands before us not like one fully dead, but fully alive, and what He has to give us can be experienced always anew by those whose spiritual eyes are opened."[3] Much of Steiner's life work was to open the spiritual eyes of those who read his books, heard his lectures, adopted the practices he proposed and joined the Anthroposophical Society, which he founded. He realized that "with the Mystery of Golgotha something *objective* had happened: the incarnation, death and resurrection of the Logos, the Word, had changed the spiritual-physical condition of the earth and of all men [sic], irrespective of their religious beliefs or lack of them."[4]

After his Golgotha experience, Steiner began writing and lecturing about this key event in the evolution of the earth. His book *Christianity as Mystical Fact* is a revelation of the part the mystery religions played in preparing the earth, especially humans, for the incarnation of the Word of God. The recent study of this book with my Dominican community provided an opportunity for me to acknowledge another great mentor and friend, Sr. Aquinata Martin, a Kentucky Dominican, my History of Civilization teacher in undergraduate school at Siena College in Memphis before I entered her Dominican community. Sr. Aquinata saw Christ, the Incarnation of the Word of God, as "a culminating point of the history of the earth, a turning point of time to which all at first led down and from which all thereafter was to lead upward."[5] She taught from all the great religions of the world and was ahead of the

Church's Second Vatican Council in giving us a deep respect for and love of the traditions that prepared the way for Christianity. She recognized the mystery religions as forerunners for a Christianity in which the life, death and resurrection of Jesus has parallels in many ancient traditions.

I believe that Sr. Aquinata qualifies as an initiate of Rudolf Steiner's thought and practice even though she never knew him. She, like Steiner, was a free spirit who knew that real love frees us from law. A conference I will call in her memory at our motherhouse in Kentucky will include a preparatory study of Georg Kühlewind's *Becoming Aware of the Logos*, a fruit of his thirty years of study and meditating on the Prologue to St. John's Gospel. Similar to Kühlewind's study of the Prologue, Sr. Aquinata meditated, spoke, wrote and lived the words of St. Paul: "He is the image of the invisible God, the first-born of all creation, for in him all things were created, in heaven and on earth, visible and invisible... all things were created through him and for him. He is before all things, and in him all things hold together."[6] This conference to honor Sr. Aquinata will be an invitation to the Dominican community she loved so well to become better acquainted with her deep intellectual and spiritual life by appreciating her ministry in the light of the knowledge and practices of Rudolf Steiner and his commentators. Sr. Aquinata's students and friends will remember her as an ardent promoter of scholarship in pursuit of the truth that sets a person free. This pursuit of truth as a means to becoming free is surely a trademark of Steiner's deeply spiritual and mystical life.

Sr. Aquinata's understanding that ancient spiritual traditions were a necessary preparation of humans for the coming of Christ was unique, as it has been so utterly neglected in the Catholic tradition in the West, even among religious men and women, including those of her Dominican community. Within the last generation Thomas Merton (1915–1968) initiated a change as he popularized the exploration and practice of Eastern spirituality. Steiner's hopes for a return to the thought of St. Thomas will certainly be explored at this conference, as St. Thomas, like Steiner, saw the value of the ancient traditions for Christianity—a fact too little known. His writing, teaching and preaching and that of his mentor St. Albert included the mystical insights and the dark knowledge of God of Dionysius the Aeropagite, a Hindu monk of the sixth century, assuring its inclusion in the Catholic tradition. In the decades after these spiritual giants, Meister Eckhart, John Tauler and Henry Susso would "provide Germany, and the world, with some of the greatest preachers and mystics of the Middle Ages.... Much would pivot on the influence in German mysticism of the dark knowledge of God inherited from the ancient Church, Albert's lasting legacy."[7] Dominicans will be amazed to find how frequent are Steiner's references to these Dominican mystics in support of a spirituality that sets a person free.

St. Albert's legacy of the dark knowledge of God provided a nutrient soil for the extraordinary flowering of mysticism among Dominican women in the late thirteenth and early fourteenth centuries, recently becoming known through the prolific publications of Bernard McGinn at the University of Chicago and his colleagues. This new interest in and scholarship about German women mystics, including Marguerite Porete, is revealing their likely influence on Meister Eckhart and other preachers and confessors. "The encounter between dynamic preachers and these God-centered women produced one of the most spectacular upsurges of mystical spirituality in the history of Europe."[8] Significant also in the fourteenth century is the attempt at equality between Dominican nuns and their spiritual advisors that Debra Stoudt found in analyzing their letters. She noted "insights into the divergent attempts religious women made at asserting their own spiritual identity and offering their male confessors some advice and guidance of their own."[9] The attraction of large numbers of Beguines and other well educated women to Dominican convents during these centuries, Richard Woods explains, "was, it appears, the emphasis placed on study in the order together with the mystical character of its spirituality."[10] This offers a challenge to Dominican women today, when the thirst for a deeper spiritual life is becoming so prevalent.

As the history of the contribution of women mystics of the thirteenth and fourteenth centuries to a flourishing mystical tradition in the church finally becomes better known, it may presage a breakthrough in the current patriarchal preserve of the Catholic Church. My expectation is that religious women who are now finding new spiritual life in the practice of eastern religions are making a distinct contribution to a future, more inclusive Christian religion promoting life-giving spiritualities. Such a renewal of spirituality within the Christian community would be a special invitation to the many who have left their Christian tradition in search of a deeper spiritual life in Eastern meditation practices.

That the present time is ready for such new Christian life is witnessed in the rapid growth of the meditation centers opened by Benedictine and Trappist monks within the last thirty years. Three Trappist monks in a monastery in Spencer, Massachusetts in the mid-1970s, after "intense, sustained dialogues" with ecumenically oriented theologians and practitioners of Eastern meditation, offer a way into contemplative experience with roots in ancient forms of prayer for those in all walks of life. Their centering prayer has become amazingly popular throughout the United States and abroad, and is now linking individuals and small faith communities through its headquarters, known as Contemplative Outreach, in Butler, New Jersey (www.centeringprayer.com). A Benedictine monk, John Main (1926–1982) began his ministry for Christian Meditation groups in England in 1975. He had discovered the use of the mantra, an ancient meditation practice, which a fourth-century monk, John Cassian had learned in Egypt as the prayer of the heart. Main added this prayer of the heart to the meditation practice he had learned from an Indian monk years earlier while he was in China. These insights into eastern meditation were the basis of the prayer practice he offered, not intended for monks and nuns but to anyone or groups interested in personal or communal meditation. His emphasis on community building was initiated by a first Christian Meditation Community at a Benedictine priory in Montreal in 1977. Now his charismatic ministry has an outreach around the world headquartered in London as World Community for Christian Meditation (wccm.org) Computer networking has, of course, been of immense help in spreading these meditation ministries, both of them having an important focus on community building.

The popularity of such new forms of ancient prayer is certainly an invitation to Dominicans to rethink their own rich heritage of prayer and study. The Steiner approach to a deeper spiritual life, which I propose to lovers of the thought of St. Thomas, like the other forms of prayer being popularized today requires disciplined practice and lifestyle. Steiner's insistence that St. Thomas's thought enkindled by that of Goethe become a spiritual science for today is of special appeal to me, as I think it would be for all nature lovers, writers, artists, scientists and others wanting to enrich their lives. Realizing that Goethe's experience of the living processes of nature unleashed his great powers as a scientist and poet, Steiner uniquely explored the type of "living thinking" characteristic of such great artists and thinkers—"the power to think life into the world"—such as Dante, Shakespeare, the ancient Greeks and Goethe. Living thinking or intuition, "fresh, creative thinking, the power to create fresh forms out of life itself, that is to say, out of the part of Nature which is still coming into being,"[11] would certainly be a radical reform of our impoverished modern scientific way of thinking. Those willing to prepare themselves for such a transformation could be channels for the release of the gifts of the Spirit into a world in need.

The spirituality Steiner proposes for practitioners is an invitation to reclaim a relationship with the natural world, and one with which St. Albert and St. Thomas were both familiar. Both were, like Goethe, aware of the spiritual-psychic content of nature. Steiner reports:

> Now, both Albertus and Thomas Aquinas had knowledge of the fact of the working of the psychic-spiritual upon the physical body, and how, when its work on the body is fully complete, the soul becomes a mirror to itself. They also had an idea of how man {sic} grows in his own individual life, how he develops from year to year and from decade to decade, entirely through the impressions he receives in his soul from the external world and through the activity with which he responds to those impressions. And so the thought arose in them, that the world which lies manifestly around us is in fact itself a revelation of a super-world, a spiritual world.... If then, they felt, we observe the world of nature with logical analysis, with every capacity of our soul, and with all our power of thought, we shall become aware of those realities which the spiritual world has implanted in the world of nature.[12]

According to Steiner, St. Thomas spoke of the spiritual world "as though it were the most normal thing for human concepts to rise from sense perception to spirit perception."[13] St. Thomas claimed, says Steiner, that "the spiritual-psychic element has an actual effect on every activity of the human organism."[14] Both Albertus and Thomas knew that others before them "could see beyond them into the spiritual world, the world of thought which Aquinas himself speaks of as the real world, in which he perceives the immaterial, intellectual beings which he calls angels. These are not abstractions but real beings, but without material bodies."[15] But because of the times in which they lived and the pressing need for St. Albert and St. Thomas to defend and bring into harmony the one truth of the content of faith and that of reason they did not turn their attention to the spiritual-psychic in its potential to be open to others as it was to them. It is the realization of this potential that Steiner invites practitioners to share.

Steiner's experience is that Christ has dispelled the barrier the fall of man posed to human thinking, keeping it from moving beyond the world of faith into that of the spirit. In this Steiner moves beyond the limits of faith accepted by St. Albert and St. Thomas. For Steiner the redemptive action of Christ can be accepted into the thinking of those humans willing to undergo the transforming practices to receive it. "We must consider anew, in a completely factual way, the spiritual-psychic content of man, the thought-world which receives into itself the transforming Christ-principle, in order that, through Christ in us, that is, in our thought world, we may discover again the spiritual world."[16] Steiner explains the way to this transformation of thinking in two major works, *Intuitive Thinking as a Spiritual Path* and *How to Know Higher Worlds*, for those who will take up the difficult practices he recommends. Isn't it significant that Steiner entitled his book on Thomas Aquinas *The Redemption of Thinking*? Throughout his writing Steiner's many references to Meister Eckhart, John Tauler, Henry Suso and others influenced by them indicates that his approach to the spiritual life is very much in resonance with that of St. Thomas, St. Albert and their immediate successors. Steiner challenges us to recover for our times the capacities through which these spiritual giants of the medieval world left such a rich heritage for the West.

My own conviction that the spiritual science flowing from the thought life of St. Albert and St. Thomas as developed seven hundred years later through Rudolf Steiner could recapture the true greatness of the Western world as it reaches out to the best in the East for an earth-friendly revisioning of science and spirituality.

Acknowledgements

*M*any persons, mentors, leaders, family and friends, living and dead, have helped me stay the course in bringing to fruition my long time search for the Truth that would set me free and the sharing of it in this earth-friendly revisioning of science and spirituality. My gratitude stretches back over much of my life as I take this opportunity to express my appreciation and gratitude to:

Marguerite Sanders Hofstetter, my mother whose deep faith gave meaning and direction to my early life; Oscar Bernard Hofstetter, Sr., my father who with integrity, faith and courage nourished and educated a large family during the depression - an example to me of St Matthew's "Set your mind on God's [kindom] and justice before everything else, and all the rest will come to you." 6:33. My brother, Oscar Jr who was able to make my father's law profession a better provider of the family and thus make possible much of the travel, peace and justice work that enriched my search.

Dominican Sisters who gave me a scholarship to a small Catholic college in Memphis TN where I satisfied my thirst for a more connected, less fragmented approach to education than I found in high school. There Sr. Aquinata Martin, op came into my life as teacher, friend, and mentor. Her dedication to mind-stretching intellectuals of all ages, to a critical approach to the history of the church and the world, her love of the saints and mystics invited me to further my pursuit of truth as a member of her Ky Dominican community.

Dorothy Day in her courageous stand for the poor through widespread Catholic Worker Houses offered a tempting alternative to religious life, but the latter provided the opportunity to teach as well as to continue the work of peace and justice in which Dorothy Day and Thomas Merton were such significant leaders.

Dr Vincent Edward Smith, my mentor during biological study at the University of Notre Dame, who was ever ready to share the wealth of his love of the philosophy of science of Thomas Aquinas; to Sr. Nona McGreal,op who clued me into the wealth I would find in Dr.Smith, my brother Robert Hofstetter also studying at Notre Dame who joined me at the well of truth in St. Thomas.

My Dominican community which supported me even when my ministry was not well understood. Among the sisters who were special friends and often involved themselves in some avenue of my ministry were Verona Weidig, Dorothy Briggs and particularly my blood sister, Margaret Marie Hofstetter, as well as Betsy Lunz. Also special are those who participated in the many workshops on earth spirituality which Laura Miller and I presented at our Motherhouse and in a variety of cities where Dominicans ministered.

Dr. Martin Luther King Jr who through the civil rights movement called me to keep my promise to God to pursue the truth by marching with him, with the garbage workers in Memphis, with Caesar Chavez, and other human rights activists.

Sr. Margaret Ellen Traxler a significant supporter of Dr Martin Luther King Jr.with whom I was a founding member of the National Coalition of American Nuns to speak out on social issues.. Margaret Ellen, as Director of the National Catholic Conference for Interracial, provided the funds and leadership for me to coordinate a project in Memphis after King was killed. Her travelling workshop offered me one summer of giving workshop in support of racial justice in a variety of cities across the US, and with her plan our search for justice for women in cities round the world.

Rev. Ramzi H. Malik, op who read Scripture to me while I was studying at the University of Notre Dame. As a member of our Ky Bethany community, he provided spiritual guidance and the needed background for Bethany members as we assumed leadership of the Kentucky Dominican's Center of Ecumenism and Reconciliation to promote dialogue among Jews, Christians and Muslims, and to foster better relationships among Dominican women and men. This work evolved into my making six peace missions to the Middle East.

Anne Shafer and Ruth Thone, who through their friendship, prsence, and leadership have enriched my life in our struggles for a more just and peaceful world.

Clare Danielsson, a godchild of Dorothy Day, with whom I coordinated a Home Sharing Project at Boughton Place in upstate New York. Along with finding homes for and with seniors, we gave dream, myth and fairy tale workshops in various local centers. Many years of psychodrama training at Boughton Place with Clare and Zerka Moreno deepened my understanding of human nature, especially my own.

Janet Abels, director of the private retreats I made at her Seven Meadows Farm where in a dream I was given confirmation of the work I felt called to do. In the dream I was holding a beautiful infant while standing behind me a handsome young man, a Christ figure, reminded me that the baby was also his.

Laura Miller, a Ky Dominican Associate who for the last 20 years provided me a home away from home where we could laugh, cry, pray and meditate together. Sharing her home I found a place to learn to garden on the grounds where 50 years earlier Father Divine and his peace mission folks had a productive garden, two barns still standing and a motel long ago burned down. Along with a quiet home for thinking and meditating, Laura provided the equipment for writing and gardening, time for human rights involvement and workshops on earth spirituality which Laura directed with me.

Father Thomas Berry whose friendship and books awakened me to the desperate plight of the earth and at whose invitation I gave a Teilhard lecture on Barbara McClintock at his Riverdale Center for Religious Research and thus began my second stint at writing.

Arthur Fabel, editor for Teilhard Perspectives who was always willing and ready to edit my writing, sometimes more than once, and to provide encouragement and ideas for many of the articles which were written after 20 years away from this ministry.

Richard Tarnas, my longtime mentor (by phone and email) whose book, The Passion of the Western Mind and friendship have been an immense support of my commitment to a renewal of the wisdom of Aristotle and St. Thomas and my hopes of finding a way to get it published.

Jean Houston who gave me scholarships to participate in three years of her Mystery School, a unique opportunity for body, soul and spirit enrichment. This experience simulating the riches found in ancient mystery centers, was enhanced by a visit to West Africa with Jean, Peggy Rubin and a Mystery School group and later in another to Greece and the Greece islands.

Walter Alexander and his study group at the Steiner Book Store in Manhattan where I deepened my knowledge of Owen Barfield who confirmed my confidence that a path to truth was available in the science of Rudolph Steiner and Thomas Aquinas.

Georg Kühlewind whose workshops, books and friendship have opened to me a new depth of what it is to be a Christian.

Aristotle, St. Thomas Aquinas, Johann Wolfgang von Goethe, and Rudolph Steiner for the heritage they left the Western world now being claimed in support of a spiritual science for the 21st century.

John Barnes whose remarkable poetic writing about Goethe gave me the courage to ask him as editor of Adonis Press to publish my writing. He suggested trying Steiner Books for publication.

Christopher Bamford whose awesome wisdom and scholarship made his acceptance to publish my work at Steiner Books a very special gift and to Sarah Gallogly for her fine editing.

Notes

Introduction:

1. G. B. Tennyson, *A Barfield Reader: Selections from the Writings of Owen Barfield* (Wesleyan University Press, Middletown, CT, 1999), p. 150.
2. Owen Barfield, *Owen Barfield and the Origin of Language* (St. George, Spring Valley, NY, 1976), p. 12.
3. Georg Kühlewind, Stages of Consciousness (Lindisfarne Press, 1984), p. 138.
4. Cf. Rudolf Steiner, *What Is Anthroposophy?* (SteinerBooks, 2002), p.25.
5. Thomas F. O'Meara, O.P., *Thomas Aquinas, Theologian* (University of Notre Dame Press, South Bend, 1997), from back cover.
6. Josef Pieper, *Guide to Thomas Aquinas* (Ignatius Press, San Francisco, 1991), pp. 123, 124.
7. Matthew Fox, "Thomas Aquinas: Mystic and Prophet of the Environment," *Creation Spirituality* (July/August, 1992), p. 33.
8. Rudolf Steiner, *Goethe's World View* (Mercury Press, Spring Valley, NY, 1985), p. 53.
9. Rudolf Steiner, *Truth and Science* (Mercury Press, 1993), p. iii.
10. Steiner, *Redemption of Thinking* (Anthroposophic Press, 1983), pp. 102, 103.
11. *Ibid.,* pp. 112, 113.
12. *Ibid.,* p. 115.
13. Robert McDermott, *The Essential Steiner: Basic Writings of Rudolf Steiner* (Harper San Francisco, 1984), pp. 1–4.
14. G. B. Tennyson, *A Barfield Reader,* p. 150.
15. Owen Barfield, *Saving the Appearances* (Wesleyan University Press, Middletown, CT, 1988), p. 85.
16. *Ibid.,* p. 105.
17. *Ibid.,* p. 141.
18. Walter M Abbott, SJ ed., *The Documents of Vatican II* (Guild Press, New York, 1966), p. 662.
19. Richard Tarnas, *The Passion of the Western Mind: Understanding the Ideas That Have Shaped Our World View* (Ballantine, New York, 1991), p 176.
20. *Ibid.,* p. 433.
21. Theodore Roszak, *Ecopsychology: Restoring the Earth, Healing the Mind* (Sierra Club Books, San Francisco, 1995).
22. Owen Barfield, *Saving the Appearances,* p. 91.
23. Ita Wegman, *The Mysteries* (Temple Lodge, London, 1995), p. 111.
24. Rudolf Steiner, *Intuitive Thinking as a Spiritual Path: A Philosophy of Freedom* (Anthroposophic Press, 1995), p. 25.
25. Rudolf Steiner, *The Origins of Natural Science* (Anthroposophic Press, 1985), p. 2.
26. Rudolf Steiner, *Mystics after Modernism: Doscovering the Seeds of a New Science in the Renaissance* (Anthroposophic Press, 2000), p. 7.
27. Rudolf Steiner, *The Redemption of Thinking,* p. 58.
28. *Ibid.*
29. Richard Tarnas, *The Passion of the Western Mind,* p. 444.

30. Rudolf Steiner, *The Origins of Science,* p. 70.

31. Rudolf Steiner, *Goethe's World View,* p. 86

32. Rudolf Steiner, *Goethean Science* (Mercury Press, 1988), p. 119.

33. *Ibid.,* p 122.

34. Richard Tarnas, *The Passion of the Western Mind,* p. 445.

Chapter One

1. Carolyn Merchant, *The Death of Nature* (Harper, San Francisco,1980), p. 1.

2. Wendell Berry, *The Unsettling of America: Culture and Agriculture* (Sierra Club Books, 1986), p. vi.

3. Berry, "Farming and the Global Economy," delivered at the Earth Summit on Sustainable Development (Louisville, KY, May 25, 1993).

4. Berry, *The Unsettling,* p.143.

5. *Ibid.,* p. 169.

6. *Ibid.,* p. 143.

7. *Ibid.,* p. 170.

8. *Ibid.,* p. 147.

9. Jerry Mander, *In the Absence of the Sacred* (Sierra Club Books, San Francisco, 1991) ch. 14.

10. *Ibid.,* p. 386.

11.Thomas Berry, "Ecology and the Future of Catholicism" in Albert J. LaChance and John E. Carroll, *Embracing Earth: Catholic Approaches to Ecology,* (Orbis Books, Maryknoll, NY, 1994), p. xi.

12. Wendell Berry, *The Gift of Good Land: Further Essays Cultural and Agricultural* (North Point Press, San Francisco, 1981), p. 281.

Chapter Two

1. Stanislav Grof, ed., *Ancient Wisdom*

and *Modern Science* (SUNY Press, Albany, 1994).

2. Robert M. Hutchins, *The Great Conversation* (William Benton, Encyclopedia Britannica, Chicago, 1952), p. xii.

3. *Ibid.,* p. 18.

4. *Ibid.,* p. 26–28.

5. *Ibid.,* p. xii.

6. *Ibid.,* p. 1.

7. *Ibid.,* p. 2.

8. *Ibid.,* p. xxvi.

9. *Ibid.,* p. 23.

10. Edwin A. Burtt, *The Metaphysical Foundations of Modern Science* (Doubleday, NY, 1924), p. 20.

11. *Ibid.,* p. 23.

12. E. F. Schmacher, *Small is Beautiful* (Harper, NY, 1973), pp. 91, 92.

13. Jose Ortega Y Gasset, "The Revolt of the Masses," in *Great Essays in Science,* ed by Martin Gardner (Pocket Books Inc., NY, 1957), p. 112.

14. *Ibid.,* p. 113.

15. *Ibid.,* p. 124.

16. Erwin Schrödinger, *What is Life? and Other Scientific Essays* (Doubleday, NY, 1956), p. 95.

17. Pitirim Sorokin, *The Crisis of Our Age* (Dutton, 1941), pp. 80–132. Sorokin refers to an idealistic culture. In later works he refers to his ideal culture as an integral culture which I use in this essay.

18. *Ibid.,*p 13.

19. Paul William Roberts, "Blood Feud" (*Saturday Night,* Dec., 1992), pp 53–105; Stephanie Hiller, "A New Answer to Cancer," (*Yoga Journal,* Sept/Oct.1993), pp 40–47; Steven R. Elswick, 1994, "The Amaxing Wonders of Gaston Naessens," (*Nexus,* 2, 18, 1994), p 40–45.

20. D. H. Lawrence, "Apropos of Lady Chatterley's Lover", in *Sex, Literature and Censorship,* ed H. T. Moore (Viking Press, New York), p. 106.

21. Schrödinger , *What is,* pp. 100, 101.

22. *Ibid.,* p 97.

23. *Ibid.,* p. 133.

24. *Ibid.,* p. 107.

25. *Ibid.,* p. 178.

26. *Ibid.,* p. 100–101.

27. Arthur Zajonc, "The Two Lights" in "Lindisfarne Letter" author sent to me, p. 53.

28. Aristotle, *Physics,* Book II, Ch.2, 194b, 24–30.

29. Thomas Berry, "The Wild and the Sacred," in (*Teilhard Perspectives* 26, 2, 1991), pp. 1–3.

30. Rupert Sheldrake, *The Rebirth of Nature: The Greening of Science and of God* (Bantam Books, New York, 1991), p. 223.

31. Joan Chittister, *Illuminated Life* (Orbis, Maryknoll, NY, 2000), p. 86.

32. Rudolf Steiner, 1956, *The Redemption of Thinking* (Anthroposophic Press, 1956), p.105.

33. R. D. Laing, *The Reenchantment of the World,* by Morris Berman (Bantam Books, NY, 1981), on cover.

34. Richard Tarnas, *The Passion of the Western Mind* (Ballantine Books, NY, 1991), p 178.

35. *Ibid.,* p. 443.

36. *Ibid.,* p. 445.

37. William J. Bennett, *The Book of Virtues* (Simon and Schuster, NY, 1993), P. 17.

38. Adrian M.Hofstetter, "The New Biology: Barbara McClintock and an Emerging Holistic Science." (Anima, PA, 1992).

39. Arthur Zajonc, "New Wine in What Kind of Wineskins? Metaphysics in the Twenty- First Century," in *New Metaphysical Foundations of Modern Science,* ed Willis Harman (Inst. of Noetic Science, CA, 1994)

40. George Wald, "The Cosmology of Life and Mind," *Ibid.,* p. 129.

41. Ilya Prigogne & Isabelle Stengers, *Order Out of Chaos,* (Bantam Books, NY, 1994), p. 40.

42. Berman, *The Reenchantment,* p 3.

43. Prigogne and Stenger. *Order,* p. xii.

Chapter Three

l. Bede Jarrett, op, *The Life of St. Dominic* (Burns Oates & Washbourne, London, 1934), p 129.

2. Robert Maynard Hutchins, *No Friendly Voice* (University of Chicago Press, IL, 1936), p. 8.

3. *The Great Conversation in The Great Books of the Western World* (*Encyclopedia Brittanica,* Chicago, 1952), p. 5.

4. *International Dominican Information* (I.D.I.) Jan 1996, p. 2.

5. *The Learning Society* (Frederick A. Praeger Publishers, NY, 1968), p. 109.

6. *Ibid.,* p. 108.

7. *Education for Freedom* (Louisiana State University Press, Baton Rouge, 1943), p. 25.

8. *The Conflict in Education In a Democratic Society* (Harper, New York, 1953), p. 107.

9. *Education for Freedom,* p. 23.

10. Josef Pieper, *Guide to Thomas Aquinas* (Ignatius Press, San Francisco, 1991), p. 62.

11. *Ibid.,* pp. 63, 64.

12. *Ibid.*, p. 81.

13. *The Passion of the Western Mind* (Ballantine, New York, 1991), pp. 189, 190.

14. ed. by Geraldine Van Doren (Macmillan, New York, 1990)

Chapter Four

1. In the foreword of *Night* by Elie Wiesel (Hill & Wang, New York, 1958), p. 7.

2. Quoted in *Great Essays in Science,* ed. by Martin Gardner (Pocket Books, New York, 1957), p. 262.

3. Barbara Ward, *Faith and Freedom* (Image Books, 1958), p. 14.

4. Gerald Vann, O.P. *The Water and the Fire* (Sheed & Ward, New York, 1954), p.13.

5. Rene Dubos, *Mirage of Health* (Harper, New York, 1959), p. 27.

6. Walter Grompius, "The Curse of Conformity" in *Adventures of the Mind* ed. By Richard Thruelsen and John Kobler (Knopf, 1959), p. 265.

7. "Auguries of Innocence," 11, 1– 4.

8. J. B. S. Haldane, *Possible Worlds and Other Papers (*Harper, NY, 1928), pp. 221, 214.

9. Hamlet, II, 2, 315–320.

10. Susanne K. Langer, *Philosophy in a New Key* (Mentor, NY, 1942), p. 16.

11. From *God is Not a Mathematician,* in C. Stanley Ogilvy, *Through the Mathescope* (Oxford, NY, 1958), p. 8.

12. Lewis Carroll, *Alice in Wonderland and Through the Looking Glass* (Kingsport, TN, 1946), pp. 66, 67.

13. *Modern Science and the Nature of Life* (Harcourt, Brace, 1957), pp. 71 –78.

14. *Ibid.,* p. 76.

15. *Ibid.,* p. 77.

16. Barbara Ward, *Faith and,* p. 281.

17. Julian Huxley, *Man in the Modern World* (Mentor, NY, 1944), p. 133.

18. René Dubos, *Mirage,* pp. 172, 173.

19. *Apropos of Lady Chatterley's Lover,* p. 83.

20. "The Arsenal at Springfield," 11. pp 32–36.

21. Gerald Vann, O.P. *The Water,* p. 44.

22. Joseph Wood Krutch, *The Great Chain of Life* (Houghton Mifflin, MA,1956), p. 143.

23. "The Tables Turned," v. 2.

24. Frederick Wilhelmsen, *Hilaire Belloc: No Alienated Man* (Sheed and Ward, NY, 1953), p. 22

Chapter Five

1. John Gribbin, *In The Beginning: The Birth of the Living Universe* (Little Brown, NY, 1993), p.19, 20.

2. Leon Lederman & Dick Teresi, *The God Particle* (Dell, 1993), p. 402.

3. Paul Davies, *The Mind of God* (Simon & Schuster, 1992), p. 57.

4. John D. Barrow, *Theories of Everything* (Fawcett Columbine, New York, 1991), p. 71.

5. Paul A. Laviolette, *Beyond the Big Bang* (Park Street, VT, 1995), p. 282.

6. Luc Brisson and Walter Meyerstein, *Inventing a Universe* (State University of New York, Albany, 1995), p. 1.

7. John D. Barrow, *Theories of Everything: The Quest for Ultimate Explanation* (Oxford University Press, NY, 1991), p. 239.

8. In *Meditations with Hildegard of Bingen,* by Gabriele Uhlein (Bear & Co., NM, 1982), p. 91.

9. Uhlein, p. 65.

10. Uhlein, pp. 78, 79.

11. Matthew Fox, *Meditations with*

Meister Eckhart (Bear & Co., NM, 1983), p. 90.

12. Fox, pp. 16, 17.

13. Tarnas, *The Passion of the Western Mind* (Ballantine, 1991), p.178.

14. Rupert Sheldrake in foreword to *Sheer Joy* (Harper San Francisco,1992), p. xvii.

15. Rudolf Steiner, *The Redemption of Thinking* (Anthroposophic Press, 1956), p.105.

16 Christopher Fry, *A Sleep of Prisoners* (Oxford University Press, New York, 1951), in the epilogue by A. P. Shephard.

Chapter Six

l. Adrian M. Hofstetter, OP, "New or Traditional Earth Spirituality" in *Sisters Today*, 69 (Jan. 1997), p. 15–20.

2. Stephen Hawking, *A Brief History of Time* (Bantam Books, 1988), p. 140.

3. Hawking, *Black Holes and Baby Universes* (Bantam, 1993), p. 144.

4. *Ibid.*, p.111.

5. Thomas O'Meara, op, *Thomas Aquinas Theologian* (Notre Dame University Press, 1997), p. 202.

6 William E. Carroll, "Aquinas and the Big Bang" (Iowa: Internet 1998) www.cornellcollege.edu// science_religion/list.htm.

7. Paul Davies, *God and the New Physics* (Simon & Schuster, 1983), p. viii.

8. Hawking, *A Brief History of Time*, p. 174.

9. Brian Swimme & Thomas Berry (Harper San Francisco, 1992).

10. Steven Weinberg, *The First Three Minutes* (Basic Books, 1988), p. 154.

11. Daniel D. Dennett, *Darwin's Dangerous Ideas* (Simon & Schuster,

1995), p. 320.

12 John Horgan, "The End of Cosmology" in *The End of Science* (Broadway Books, 1995), p. 94.

13. *A Syntopicon of the Great Books of the Western World,* ed Robert M. Hutchins (Encyclopedia Brittanica, Chicago, 1952), p. 159.

14. Vincent Smith, *The General Science of Nature* (Bruce Publishing, Milwaukee, 1958), p. 3.

15. *The Higher Learning in America* (Yale University Press, 1986), p. 81.

16. Cf., Lynn Margulis, "Big Trouble in Biology" in *Doing Science,* ed John Brockman (Prentice Hall, 1991), p. 214; Catharine Halkes, *New Creation* (John Knox Press, Louisville, KY, 1991), p. 3.

17. Ruth Hubbard, *The Politics of Women's Biology* (Rutgers University, New Brunswick, 1990), pp. 18, 19.

18. (Pocket Books, 1989), pp. 20.

19. *Ibid.,* p. 73.

20. Elisabet Sahtouris and Willis W. Harman, *Biology Revisioned* (North Atlantic Books, CA, 1996), p. 20.

21. Adrian M. Hofstetter, "The New Biology: Barbara McClintock and an Emerging Holistic Science" (Teilhard Studies No. 26, spring, 1992).

22. (One World, NY, 1992), p. 107.

23. Pitirim Sorokin, *The Crisis of Our Age* (One World, NY, 1992), p. 85.

24. Sorokin, p. 216.

25. Richard Tarnas, *The Passion of the Western Mind* (Ballantine Books, NY, 1991), p. 421.

26. Willis Harman with Jane Clark (Institute of Noetic Science, Petaluma, CA, 1994).

27. Jeremy Naydler, *Goethe on Science* (Floris Books, Edinburgh, 1996), p. 48.

28. Arthur Zajonc, "New Wine in What Kind of Wineskins? Metaphysics for the Twenty-First Century" in *New Metaphysical Foundations of Modern Science* (note 26), p. 335.

29. Rudolf Steiner, *Goethe's World View* (Mercury Press, 1985), p. 59.

30. Naydler, Goethe on, p. 110.

31. Rudolf Steiner, *The Redemption of Thinking: A Study in the Philosophy of Thomas Aquinas* (Anthroposophic Press,1983), p. 102.

32. *Ibid.,* p. 115.

33. In "Thomas Aquinas, Mystic and Prophet of the Environment" by Matthew Fox (*Creation Spirituality* July/August, 1992), p. 33.

34. Arthur Fabel, "Teilhard 2000: The Vision of a Cosmic Genesis" (*Teilhard Studies* No. 36 Spring 1998).

35. Richard Tarnas, "The Great Initiation" (*Noetic Sciences Review*, No. 47, 25th Anniversary, 1998), p. 25ff.

36. St. Paul, 2 Romans 8:22.

Chapter Seven

1. W. Stanley, "The Structure of the Viruses," in *The Cell and Protoplasm,* ed. H. Moulton (Washington, 1940), p. 135.

2. Salvador Luria, *General Virology* (John Wiley & Sons, NY,1953), p. 113. 3. *Ibid.,* p.115.

4. *Biology: The Human Approach* (Philadelphia, 1950), p. 1.

5. *The Human Use of Human Beings* (Boston, 1954), p. 31.

6. Carl L. Wilson, *Botany.* (The Dryden Press, 1952), p. 14.

7. E. Racker, "Metabolism of Infected Cells," in *Cellular Metabolism and Infections,* ed. E. Racker (NY, 1954), p. 138.

8. *Biology: Its Human Implications,* 2nd. ed. (CA, 1952), p. 9.

9. L.ibbie Hyman, The Invertebrates (McGraw-Hill, NY, 1940), v, I, p. 4.

10. *De Anima,* 412a.l – 415b28.

11. Cf. De Part. *Animal.,* 641a18 – 33.

12. *De Anima,* 414a13 – 14.

13. *Ibid.,* 413b10.

14. For St. Thomas this is an a posteriori demonstration, since the reason the soul is the principle of living activities is that it is the form of the body. The more formal cause is in the conclusion. In *De Anima,* 3, n. 253. Cajetan points out that St. Albert accepted this proof as propter quid demonstration. *De Anima,* ed. P. Coquelle, O.P., pp. 78, 79, 103. If the soul or the principle "by which" is thought of as the final cause of the body, not just as the subject of the operations characteristic of living things, then Cajetan claims, this proof is a priori and a propter quid demonstration. *Ibid.,* ch. 2. "...*quoniam `ideo anima, non solum actualiter, sed etiam in seipsa essentialiter, est actus et perfectio corporis susceptivi vitae quia in seipsa essentialiter est res cui debetur primo quod sit ratio nostrae vitae et non e converso."* *Ibid.,* p. 102 Cajetan explains that St. Thomas interprets *"quo vivimus"* according to actual exercise and thus the demonstration for the latter is mainfestly a posteriori, *Ibid.,* p. 101.

15. *De Anima,* 412b18–22.

16. *Ibid.,* 415b8–11.

17. W. Gregory, "Fish Skulls: A Study of the Evolution of Natural Mechanisms," in *Transactions American Philosophical Society*

(Philadelphia, 1933) New Series 23, p. 443.

18. Thus we see Aristotle move surely from principles to logical conclusions. His modern counterparts, the twentieth-century leaders in the field of biology, J. S. Haldane, E. S. Russell, and others, more slowly and falteringly, have likewise rejected the peelings of mechanism and vitalism and are exposing a core of conclusions which look amazingly like Aristotle's. For a statement on the view of Haldane and Russell on the matter cf. *Hyman, Invert.,* pp.17, 18.

19. *De Anima,* 413a20–30.

20. *Ibid.,* 7, n. 311; Summa Theol., I, 69, 2 ad 1.

21. *Ibid.,* 416b24.

22. Wilson, *Botany,* p. 324.

23. S. Cohen, "Comparative Biochemistry and Virology," in *Advances in Virus Research,* ed. K. Smith & M. Lauffer (New York, 1955). III, 15; H. Epstein, "The Properties of Bacteriophages," in *Advances in Virus Research,* ed. K. Smith and M. Lauffer (New York, 1953), p. 6.

24. *Ibid.*

25. The Angstrom Unit, "A," used in measuring light waves, equals one ten-thousandth of a micron or one hundred-millionth of a centimeter.

26. Andre Lwoff said that "the United States are now *par excellence,* the holy land of bacteriophage." "Lysogeny" in *Bacteriological Review,* ed. P. Wilson (Baltimore, 1953), p. 271.

27. A. Polson and C. Shephard interpreted their results of a diffusion study on T3 and T4 to indicate that the virus exhibited independent motility. "On Diffusion Rates of Bacteriophages," in Biochimica et Biophusica *Acta* (New York, 1949), p. 137. Epstein says this would mean that the extracellular particle is metabolizing to supply energy for self-motion. Although the evidence against such extracellular metabolism is not extensive, he thinks it probably valid. *op. cit.,* pp. 7–8.

28. Gunther S. Stent, "The Multiplication of Viruses" in *Scientific American Reader,* ed. D. Flanagan (New York, 1953) p. 349.

29. Epstein, *The Properties,* p. 3.

30. *Ibid.,* pp.18 –20. A. Hershey, "Some Central Problems of Viral Growth," in *International Symposium–the Dynamics of Virus and Rickettsial Infections,* ed. F. Hartman, F. Horsfall, Jr., J. Kidd (New York, 1954), p. 13.

31. D. Bauer, "Metabolic Aspects of Virus Multiplication," in *The Nature of Virus Multiplication; Second Symposium of the Society for General Microbiology held at Oxford University, April 1952,* ed. P. Fildes and W. Van Heyningen (Cambridge, 1953), pp. 46, 47.

32. Lwoff, *"*Lysogeny,*"* p. 322.

33. *Ibid.,* p. 8.

34. R. Matthews and J. Smith, "The Chemotherapy of Viruses," in *Advances in Virus Research,* ed. K. Smith and M. Lauffer (New York, 1955), III, 73.

35. Lwoff, *"*Lysogeny*"* p. 331.

36. S. Luria, "Bacteriophage: An Essay on Virus Reproduction," in *Science,* ed. B. Wilson CXI (Washington, 1950), p. 510.

37. *Ibid.*

38. Epstein, *The Properties,* p. 11.

39. Lwoff, "The Nature of Phage Reproduction," in *The Nature of*

Virus Multiplication; Second Symposium of the Society for General Microbiology held at Oxford University, April 1952, ed. P. Fides and W. Van Heyningen (Cambridge, 1953), p. 149.

40. Epstein, *The Properties,* p. 17.

41. William Kane, O.P., Personal communication, 1956.

42. Cohen warns that some of the data collected on viruses may be misleading as they were obtained mainly from a few of the easier to isolate plant viruses and from a group of "nonrepresentative viruses selected by historic accident, such as T2, T4 and T6 bacteriophages." *Comparative,* p.11.

43. Lwoff, "Lysogeny," p. 332.

44. Stent, *The Multiplication,* pp. 347–354.

45.John Donohoo, S. M. in a symposium at Notre Dame University, Spring 1956. After a confusing presentation, Luria reaches the same conclusion. General Virology, p. 114.

46. *De Anima,* 416b24.

47. Luria, "Bacteriophage; An Essay on Virus Reproduction," p. 511.

48. Cohen, *Comparative,* pp. 3, 4.

49. *Ibid.,* p. 3.

50. *Ibid.*

51. *Ibid.,* p. 43.

53. *Ibid.,* p. 8.

53. H. Ephrussi-Taylor, "Current Status of Bacterial Transformations," in *Advances in Virus Research,* ed. K. Smith and M. Lauffer (New York, 1955) III, 306.

54. Stanley, p. 135.

55. Lwoff, "Concluding Remarks," in *Cellular Metabolism and Infections,* ed. E. Racker (NewYork, 1954), p. 175.

56. Forrest Fulton disagrees with those who claim that the virus does not multiply by binary fission. At least, according to him, it has not yet been decisively disproved. "A Venerable Hypothesis," in *The Nature of Virus Multiplication; Second symposium of the Society for General Microbiology held at Oxford University, April 1952,* ed. P. Fildes and W. van Heyningen (Cambridge, 1953), p. 263.

57. Matthews and Smith, *The Chemotherapy.* p. 61.

58. Lwoff, "Lysogeny," p. 332; "The Life Cycle of a Virus," in *Scientific American,* ed. D. Flanagan CXC (New York, 1954), p. 34.

59. *De Anima,* 5, no. 288.

60. "'Supremum enim inferioris naturae attingit id quod est infimum superioris.'" *Summa Theol.,* I, 78, 2. "In this way we are able to perceive the wondrous connection of things. For we always find the lowest in the higher genus touching the highest of the lower genus: thus some of the lowest of the animal kind scarcely surpass the life of plants, such as oysters which are immovable, have only the sense of touch, and are fixed to the earth like plants. Hence Blessed Dionysius says (Div. Nom. *vii)* that Divine wisdom has united the ends of higher things with the beginnings of the lower." Sum. Cont. Gent., II, 68.

61. Lwoff, "The Nature of Phage Reproduction, p. 162.

62. De Part. Animal., 644a5, in *The Basic Works of Aristotle,* ed. R. McKeon (New York,1941)

63. *Ibid.,* 644b5.

Chapter Eight

1. *The History of Herodotus,* Bk. 3, in Great Books of the Western World, ed. R. Hutchins (Chicago, 1952), VI, 112, 113.
2. 608b5–611a5; 611b30–612b5.
3. *Seneca ad Lucilium Epistolae Morales,* transl. R. Gummere (New York, 1920), II, p. 397.
4. Julian Huxley, "Darwinism Today," in *On Living in a Revolution* (New York, 1944), p. 103.
5. *Ibid.,* p. 10.
6. *Ibid.*
7. Asa Chandler (New York, 1955), p. 1.
8. Toynbee (New York, 1956), p. 4.
9. Huxley, *Darwinism,* p. 102.
10. Charles Darwin, *The Origin of the Species*, ed. R. Hutchins (Chicago, 1952), XLIX, p. 46, 47.
11. *Ibid.,* p. 37.
12. *Ibid.,* pp 95, 98.
13. *Ibid.,* pp 7, 39, 62.
14. *Ibid.,* p. 40.
15. *Ibid.,* p. 39.
16. (NewYork, 1950), p. 108.
17. *Ibid.*
18. *Ibid.,* p. 123.
19. *In appendix of Mutual Aid,* P. Kropotkin (Boston, 1955), pp. 329–341.
20. *Ibid.,* pp. xiv–xv.
21. *From quotation in Animal Aggregations,* by W.C. Allee (Chicago, 1931), pp. 352, 353.
22. *Ibid.*
23. *Ibid.,* p. 355.
24. *Ibid.*
25. Allee, *Cooperation Among Animals* (NewYork, 1951), p. 29.
26. *Ibid.,* p. 49.
27. *Ibid.,* pp. 63–68.
28. *Ibid.,* pp. 79–82.
29. *Ibid.,* p. 17.
30. The term "nonsocial" is used in referring to animals that do not live specialized community lives as to bees, ants, and termites. Biologists refer to the latter as "social" animals. Cf. Allee, *Ibid.,* p. 154.
31. *Ibid.,* p. 63.
32. *Ibid.,* p. 18.
33. *Ibid.,* p. 24.
34. *Ibid.,* p. 27.
35. *Ibid.,* p. 29.
36. *Ibid.,* p. 17.
37. *Ibid.,* pp 11, 57, 211.
38. Allee, *Animal Aggregations,* p. 356.
39. Allee, *Cooperation Among Animals,* p. 213.
40. Ashley Montagu, *On Being Human* (NewYork, 1951), pp. 73, 76.
41. *Ibid.,* p. 109.
42. Montagu, *Darwin, Competition and Cooperation* (NewYork, 1952), p. 41.
43. *Ibid.,* p. 70.
44. *Ibid.,* p. 72.
45. Montagu, *On Being Human,* p. 109.
46. *Ibid.,* p. 101.
47. *Ibid.,* p. 115.
48. *Ibid.,* p. 98.
49. *Ibid.,* p. 101.
50. *Ibid.,* p. 98.
51. Allee, *Animal Aggregations,* p. 355.
52. Montagu, *On Being Human,* p. 29.
53. Herbert Spencer, *First Principles* (NewYork, 1958), pp. 571–573.
54. Simpson, *The Meaning of Evolution* (New Haven, 1949), p. 218.
55. *Ibid.,* p. 219.
56. *Ibid.,* p. 95.
57. Transl. A. Mitchell (New York, 1911), p.222.
58. Cf. The bibliographies and reading

lists in their works cited.

59. *The Meaning of Evolution*, p. 221.

60. *Ibid.,* p. 230.

61. *Ibid.,* p. 292.

62. Huxley, *Evolution in Action* (NewYork, 1953), p. 38.

63. Huxley, "Religion as an Objective Problem, in *Man Stands Alone* (New York,1941), pp. 276–279; J. B. S. Haldane, Daedalus (New York, 1924), pp. 91–93; J. Huxley, *Evolution in Action* (NewYork,1953), p. 38.

64. Montagu, *On Being Human,* p.109.

65. Allee, *Cooperation Among Animals,* p.191.

65. Percy Shelley, "Queen Mab," in *The Poetical Works of Percy Bysshe Shelley,* ed. E. Dowden (NewYork, n.d.), p.33.

67. Alfred Tennyson, "Balin and Balan," in *The Poetic and Dramatic Works of Alfred Lord Tennyson* (New York, 1898), p. 364.

68. *Ibid.,* p. 274.

69. *Cooperation Among Animals,* pp. 3, 4.

70. (New York, 1954), pp. 110, 111.

71. Cf. Thomas Aquinas, *Phys.,* I & II.

72. P. 3.

73. E. Schrödinger , extracted in *What is Life? and Other Scientific Essays* (NewYork, 1956), pp. 89–109.

74. *Ibid.,* p. 100.

75. *Ibid.,* p. 100, 101; cf. foreword by Louis de Broglie in Causality and Chance in *Modern Physics,* by David Bohm (New York, 1957), pp. ix – xi.

76. *The Nature of Natural History,* p. 236.

77. II Phys., 8, 198b10–199b33.

78. *Meta.,* L, 10.

79. *Summa Theol.,* II–II, 26, 3; II–II,

26,4 ad 3; I –II, 109, 3.

80. *Ibid.,* I, 15, 2.

81. *Meta.,* L, 10.

82. *Summa Theol.,* I, 15, 2.

83. C. Adams, *Space Flight* (New York, 1958), p. 237.

84. *Rockets and Space Travel* (New York, 1947), p. 307.

85. *Ibid.,* p. 251.

85. *Ibid.,* p. 259.

86. "Weightlessness" in *Air University Quarterly Review,* X (1958), 135.

87. Adams, *Space Flight,* P. 259.

Chapter Nine

1. "DNA: Key to All Life," LV (1963), 70–90.

2. E. Tatum, "A Case History in Biological Research," *Science,* CXXIX (1959), 1711, 1714.

3. Life, op. cit., p. 90.

4. "Cellular Dynamics," in *Biophysical Science: A Study Program,* ed. J. L. Oncley, F. O. Schmitt et al., p. 24.

5. *Ibid.,* p. 6.

6. *Ibid.*

7. 1(1961), p. 75.

8. "In Defense of Biology," *Science,* CXXXIII (1961), 1745–1748.

9. Brachet, "The Role of the Nucleic Acids in the Processes of Induction, Regulation, and Differentiation in the Amphibian Embryo and the Unicellular Alga, Acetabularia Mediterranea," in *Biological Organization at the Cellular and Subcellular Level,* ed. by R. J. C. Harris (NewYork, 1963*),* p. 179.

10. Robert Zuck.

11. Cf. N. Weiner, *The Human Use of Human Beings* (NewYork, 1956), pp. 22, 23. Weiner does not distinguish the sense organs of man from the

"sense organs" of machines.

12. J. C. King, "The Fourth Moment of a Character Distribution as an Index of the Regulative Efficiency of the Genetic Code," in *Biological Organization at the Cellular and Subcellular Level, op. cit.,* pp. 136, 137.

13. W. M. Elasser, "Quanta and the Concept of Organismic Law," J. Theoret. *Biol.* (1961), I, p. 55.

14. Clifford Grobstein, "Cytodifferentiation and Macromolecular Synthesis," in the book of the same title, ed. by Michael Locke (NewYork, 1962), p. 4.

15. E.g., Otto H. Schmitt, "Biological Transducers and Coding," in *Biophysical Science—A Study Program, op. cit.,* p. 492.

16. "Properties of Large Molecules That Go Beyond the Properties of their Chemical Sub-Groups," J. Theoret. *Biol.* (1961), I, pp. 342–344.

17. P. Weiss, op. cit., p. 18; L. Picken, *The Organization of Cells* (Oxford, 1962), p. 492; C. Grobstein, "Differentiation of Vertebrate Cells," in *The Cell,* ed. J. Brachet and A. E. Mirsky (NewYork, 1959), 1, p. 489.

18. F. O. Schmitt, "Molecular Biology and the Physical Basis of Life Processes," in *Biophysical Science: A Study Program,* op. cit., p. 5.

19. H.Kacser, "The Kinetic Structure of Organisms," in *Biological Organization at the Cellular and Subcellular Level, op. cit.,* p. 27.

20. F. O. Schmitt, *loc. cit.*

21. "Intermediate States in Enzymatic DNA Synthesis," in *J. Cell and Comp. Physiol. Suppl.,* LXII (1963), p. 61.

22. "Environmental Biology," in *BioScience,* XIV (1964), p. 13.

23. *Time's Arrow and Evolution* (New York, 1962), p. 123.

24. *De Caelo,* 306b6.

25. *De Generatione et Corruptione,* 316a5–11.

26. T. Schwann, "Microscopical Researches," in *Great Experiments in Biology,* ed. by M. L. Gabriel and S. Fogel (New Jersey, 1955), p. 15.

27. CL B. Glass, "Indeterminacy and Causality," in *Philosophy of Science,* ed. by W. L. Reese (New York, 1963), pp. 245, 246.

28. Schwann, "Microscopical, p. 15.

29. This problem has been ably exposed and discussed by Lwoff in *Cellular Biology, Nucleic Acids and Viruses* (ed. O. S. Whitelock), a special publication of the New York Academy of Sciences (New York, 1957), pp. 300–301.

30. Arthur Konigsberg who has succeeded in getting a muscle cell to proliferate and differentiate into striated muscle tissue, thinks that "failure to obtain normal differentiation of a particular cell type in a synthetic environment might merely reflect inadequate reproduction of *in vivo* conditions." Cf. "Clonal Analysis of Myogenesis," *Science,* CXIL (1963), 1276.

31. Account in P. R. White, "The Cell as Organism, 'Tissue Culture,' Cellular Autonomy, and Cellular Interrelations," in *The Cell,* ed. by J. Brachet and A. E. Mirsky (New York, 1959), I, p. 294.

32. "Differentiation of Vertebrate Cells," in *The Cell,* I, p. 477.

33. Cf. note 30 and F. C. Stewart, M. O. Mapes, and l. Smith, "Growth and Organized Development of Cultured Cells," *American Journal of*

Botany, XLV (1958), 705–708.

34. Levintow and H. Eagle, "Biochemistry of Cultured Mammalian Cells," *Am. Rev. Biochm.,* XXX (1961), p. 623.

35. *Ibid.,* p. 624.

36. *Ibid.*

37. A. A. Moscona, "Analysis of Cell Recombinations in Experimental Synthesis of Tissues in Vitro," *J. Cell. Comp. Physiol. Suppl.,* LX (1962), pp. 65–81.

38. *Op. cit.,* p. 627.

39. H. Eagle, "Applications and Limitations of Mammalian Cell Culture," in *New Developments in Tissue Culture,* ed. by 1. W. Green (New Jersey, 1962), pp. 65, 66.

40. "The Potential Use of Plant Tissue Cultures in Physiological and Biochemical Investigations," in *Plant Tissue Culture and Morphogenesis,* ed. H. D. Brown (New York, 1963), pp. 28–29.

41. "How Cells Divide," *Sci. Amer.* (1961), 119.

42. Moscona *"Analysis.,* p. 67.

43. *Ibid.*

44. P. Weiss and G. Andres, "Experiments on the Fate of Embryonic Cells (Chick) Disseminated by the Vascular Route," *J. Exptl. Zool.,* CXXI (1952), pp. 449–468.

45. C. Grobstein, "Levels and Ontogeny," *Am. Sc.,* L (1962), p. 50.

46. A. A. Moscona, "How Cells Associate," *Sci. Amer.* (1961), p. 144.

47. T. Yamada, "The Inductive Phenomenon as a Tool for Understanding the Basic Mechanism of Differentiation," *J. Cell. Comp. Physiol. Suppl.,* LX (1962), p. 49.

48. "Cellular Dynamics," *op. cit.,* p. 19.

49. A. H. Haber, "Morphogenesis and the Cell Theory," in *Plant Tissue Culture and Morphogenesis, op. cit.,* p. 87.

50. *Ibid.*

51. "Studies of Living Shoot Apices," in *Plant Tissue Culture and Morphogenesis, op. cit.,* p. 47, 78.

52. *Ibid.,* pp. 72, 73.

53. *Ibid.,* p. 73.

54. F. O. Schmitt, *op. cit.,* p. 7.

55. *Ibid.*

56. N. Bohr, *Atomic Physics and Human Knowledge* (NewYork, 1958), pp. 98 ff.

57. "Blood Screening for Phenylketonuria," *J. Am. Med. Assoc.,* CLXXVIII (1961), p. 863.

Chapter Ten

1. Erwin Schrödinger, *What is Life?* (Doubleday, NY, 1956), p. 120.

2. Development of Aristotilean science may be found in *The Science of Nature: An Introduction,* by Vincent Edward Smith (Bruce Pub., Milwaukee, 1966)

3. William Harvey, *Anatomical Exercises on the Generation of Animals* (Great Books of the Western World, Chicago, 1952), vol. XXVIII, p. 332.

4. Aristotle, *Physics,* book II, ch. 3, 194b, 24–30.

5. *Ibid.,* ch. 7, 198a, p. 23.

6. Lynn Margulis, "Big Trouble in Biology" in *Doing Science,* ed, John Brockman (Prentice Hall, NY, 1988), p. 213..

7. Lewis Thomas, *The Lives of a Cell* (Bantam, New York, 1974), p. 118.

8. James Lovelock, "Small Science" in *Doing Science, op.cit.,* p. 177.

9. John P. Briggs, and F. David Peat, *Looking Glass Universe* (Simon &

Schuster, 1984), p 32.

10. William Beck, "The Complementarity Argument, Physical Reductionism and Other Philosophical Problems Implicit in the New Biology" in *Philosophical Problems in Biology,* ed. Vincent E. Smith (St. John's University Press, New York, 1966), pp. 25–54.

11. William Irwin Thompson, *Gaia: A Way of Knowing* (Lindesfarne Press, 1981), from book jacket.

12. *Ibid.,* p. 19.

13. *Ibid.*

14. *Ibid.,* pp 20, 21; see also H. Maturano and Francisco Varela, *The Tree of Knowledge,* (Shambala, Boston, 1987)

15. Reference to the remarkable story of alchemy in Morris Berman, *The Reenchantment of the World* (Bantam, 1984), pp. 61–105, 314–19, and other references in index

16. Briggs and Peat, *Looking Glass.* The creative work of these three physicists is summarized.

17. Gregory Bateson, *Mind and Nature: A Necessary Unity* (Bantam, 1979), pp 235–236.

18. *Ibid.,* p 4.

19. Bateson, in "Men are Grass" in *Gaia A Way of Knowing,* p. 39.

20. Kabir, "The Simple Purification", in *News of the Universe,* ed. Robert Bly (Sierra Club Books, 1980), p. 271.

21. *Ibid.,* p. 38.

22. Gregory Bateson & Mary Catherine Bateson, *Angels Fear* (Bantam, 1987), p. 8.

23. *Ibid.,* p. 2.

24. Morris Berman, *The Reenchantment,* p. 19l. I have relied on Berman's fine account of William Bateson's life and work.

25. Evelyn Fox Keller, *A Feeling for the Organism* (Freeman, New York, 1983), p. 204. I rely mainly on this volume along with resource materials that Barbara McClintock sent to me.

26. *Ibid.*

27. *Ibid.,* p. 203.

28. M. Berman, *Reenchantment,* pp. 191–196.

29. *Ibid.,* p. 307.

30. John Briggs, and F. David Peat, *Turbulent Mirror* (Harper and Row, 1989).

31 Aristotle, *Physics,* bk I, 184a, pp. 22, 23.

32. *Ibid.,* bk II, ch. 7, 198a 23.

33 Aristotle, *On the Heavens,* bk I, ch. 4, 271a, 10.

34. Keller,. *A Feeling,* p. 139.

35. Marilyn Ferguson, *The Aquarian Conspiracy* (St. Martin's Press, 1980), p. 150.

36. Margulis,"Big Trouble", p. 219.

37. Keller, *A Feeling,.* p. 69.

38. *Ibid.,* p. 136.

39. References to these physicists in Ferguson, *The Aquarian,* ch 6.

40. *Ibid.,* p. 69.

41. Gregory Bateson, *Steps to an Ecology of Mind* (Ballantine Bks, NY,1972), p 246.

42. Keller, *A Feeling,* p. 198.

Chapter Eleven

1. Lynn Margulis, "Kingdom Animalis: The zoological malaise from a microbial perspective," *Amer. Zool.,* 1990, 30 [4]: p. 867.

2. Margulis, "Big Trouble in Biology" in *Doing Science,* ed. John Brockman (Prentice Hall, 1991), p. 220–224.

3. John Scott Haldane, *The Philosophical Basis of Biology* (Doubleday, 1931), pp.147, 148.

4. Libbie Hyman, *The Invertebrates* (McGraw Hill, 1940), pp. 17, 18.

5. Rupert Sheldrake, "Morphogenetic fields: Nature's Law," in R. Weber, *Dialogues with Scientists and Sages* (Routledge and Kegan Paul, New York, 1996), p. 79.

6. Horace F. Judson, *The Eighth Day of Creation* (Simon and Schuster, NY, 1976), p. 205.

7. *Ibid*, pp. 209, 220.

8. *Science* 1968, pp. 160, 395.

9. Ilya Prigogne and Isabelle Stengers, *Order Our of Chaos* (Bantam, 1984), pp. 30, 31.

10. *Ibid.*, p. 174.

11. *Ibid.*, p. 40.

12. *Ibid.*, p. 55.

13. *Ibid.*, p.xii.

14. Macmillan, p. 40–41.

15. Rudolph Steiner, ed., *Goethe, The Metamorphosis of Plants* (Manfred Associates, 1978), p. 7.

16. Roger Lewin, *Complexity: Life at the Edges of Chaos* (Macmillan, 1992), p. 41.

17. Gregory Bateson, *Mind and Nature* (Bantam, 1979), p. 8.

18. *Ibid.* 16–17

19. Evelyn Fox Keller, *A Feeling for the Organism* (Freeman, New York, 1983), p.198; Adrian Hofstetter, *The New Biology* (Anima Press, PA, 1992), pp.11–15.

20. *Ibid.*, p. 97.

21. *Ibid.*, p.136.

22. N. Fedoroff, and D. Batlstein, *The Dynamic Genome* (Cold Spring Harbor Laboratory Press, Woodbury, NY, 1992).

Chapter Fourteen

1. Thomas S.Kuhn, *The Structure of Scientific Revolutions* (University of Chicago Press, IL, 1970).

2. Helen Longino, "Subject, Power and Knowledge" in *Feminism and Science,* ed by Evelyn F. Keller and Helen Longino (Oxford University Press, NY, 1996), p. 264.

3. Ruth Ginsburg, "Uncovering Gynocentric Science" in *Feminism and Science* (Indiana University Press, Bloomington, 1989), p. 82.

4. Ruth Hubbard, *The Politics of Women's Biology* (Rutgers University. Press, NJ, 1992), p. 18.

5. *Reweaving the World,* ed. by Irene Diamond and Gloria F. Orenstein (San Francisco, 1990); *Ecopsychology,* ed. by Theodore Roszak, Mary E, Goomer, and Allen D. Kanner (San Francisco, 1995).

6. Betty Roszak, "The Spirit of the Goddess" in *Ecopsychology, Ibid.,* p. 288.

7. Brian Swimme, "How to Heal a Lobotomy" in *Reweaving the World* (cf, note 5), p. 17.

8. Andrea Nye, *Philosophy and Feminism* (Twayne Publishers, New York, 1995), p. 89.

9. Donna Haraway, "Situated Knowledges: The Science of Feminism and The Privilege of Partial Perspective" in *Feminism and Science* (cf, note 2), p. 253.

10. Ruth Hubbard, "Science, Facts and Feminism" in *Feminism and Science* (cf, note 3), p. 128.

11. Hubbard, *The Politics,* p. 11.

12. Genevieve Lloyd, "Reason, Science and the Domination of Matter" in *Feminism and Science* (cf., note 2), p. 47.

13. Ruth Bleier, *Science and Gender* (Pergamon Press, NY, 1984), p 205; *The Death of Nature,* by Carolyn Merchant, (Harper San Francisco,

1980), p. 170.

14. Ynestra King, "Healing the Wounds" in *Reweaving the World* (cf, note 5) p 118.

15. Ruth Bleier, *Science and.,* p. 8.

16. Sandra Harding, *The Science Question in Feminism* (Cornell University Press, Ithica, 1989), p. 139; Helen Longino, "Can There be a Feminist Science? in *Feminism and Science* (cf, note 3), p. 56.

17. Elizabeth Schussler Fiorenza, "In Search of Women's Heritage" in *Weaving the Visions,* by Judith Plaskow and Carol.P. Christ (Harper San Francisco, 1989), p. 36.

18. Harding, *The Science Question,* p. 251.

19. Mary Tiles, "A Science of Mars or a Science of Venus?" in *Feminism and Science* (cf, note 2), p. 221.

20. Helen E. Longino, "Can There Be a Feminist Science?" in *Feminism and Science* (cf, note 3),p. 56.

21. Ginsberg, *Uncovering,* p. 70.

22. Evelyn FoxKeller, *Reflections on Gender and Science* (Yale University Press. CT, 1995), p. 126.

23. Keller, "The Gender/Science System" in *Feminism and Science* (cf, note 3), p. 36.

24. Keller, *Reflections on,* p. 171.

25. Adrian M. Hofstetter, "The New Biology: Barbara McClintock and an Emerging Holistic Science," *Teilhard Studies* No. 26 (Anima Books, PA, 1991).

26. Vincent E. Smith, *The General Science of Nature* (Bruce Publishing, Milwaukee, 1958)

27. Andrea Nye, *Philosophy and,* p. 3.

28. Harding, *The Science Question,* p. 136.

29. *Ibid.,* p. 41.

30. *Ibid.,* p. 231.

31. Keller, *Reflections on,* p 21.

32. Charlotte Witt, "Feminist Metaphysics" in *A Mind of One's Own,* ed. Louise M. Antony and Charlotte Witt (Westview Press, Boulder, 1993), pp. 273, 276.

33. Marcia Homiak, "Feminism and Aristotle's Rational Ideal" in *A Mind of One's Own,* p. 15.

34. Andrea Nye, *Philosophy and,* p. 119.

35. Lloyd, *Reason, Science* (cf, note 12), p. 45.

36. Erwin Schrödinger, *What Is Life? and Other Scientific Essays* (Doubleday, 1956), p. 101.

37. *Ibid.,* p.103.

38. Werner Heisenberg, *Physics and Philosophy* (Harper & Row, 1958), p. 169.

39. Martha C.Nussbaum, *The Fragility of Goodness* (Cambridge University. Press, 1986), p. 250.

40. *Ibid.,* p. 245.

41. *Ibid.,* p. 287.

42. *Ibid.,* p. 250.

43. *Ibid.,* p. 299.

44. Keller, 1983. *A Feeling for the Organism: The Life and Work of Barbara McClintock* (Freeman, New York, 1983), p. 198.

45. *Ibid.,* p. 202.

46. Nussbaum, *The Fragility,* p. 258.

47. *Ibid.,* p. 249.

48. *Ibid.,* p. 371.

49. *Ibid.,* p. 258.

50. Keller, *A Feeling,* p. 203.

51. *Ibid.,* pp. 178, 9.

52, Nussbaum, *The Fragility,* p. 259, 260.

.53. Keller, *A Feeling,* p. xii.

54. Nussbaum,. *The Fragility,* p. 247.

55. *Ibid.,* p. 260.

56. *Ibid.,* p. 278.

57. *Ibid.,* p. 259.
58. Keller, *A Feeling,* p. 101.
59. *Ibid.,* p. 97.
60. Benjamin Farrington, *Aristotle, Founder of Scientific Philosophy* (Wednesday & Nicolson, London, 1965), p. 83.
61. Nussbaum, *The Fragility,* p. 265.
62. *Ibid.,* p. 259.
63. Keller, *A Feeling,* p. 200.
64. Richard Tarnas, *The Passion of the Western Mind* (Ballantine Books, NY, 1991), p.188, 189.
65. *Ibid.,* p. 178.

Chapter Fifteen

1. Sandra M. Schneider, "Leadership and Spirituality in Postmodern Religious Congregations" (Rochester NY, 1997), unpublished. This dilemma was not referred to in her *Religious Life in the New Millenium,* vol. I (Paulist Press, 2000)
2. Bede Griffiths, "The Vision of Non-Duality in World Religions" in *Spirit and Science,* ed David Lorimer (Floris Books, UK, 1998), p. 320, 321.
3. Karl Jaspers, *The Origin and Goal of History* (Routledge & Kegan, London, 1953), pp. 1, 3.
4. Simon Tugwell, ed. *Albert and Thomas: Selected Writings* (Paulist Press, 1988), p. 81.
5. Bede Griffiths, *Universal Wisdom: A Journey Through the Sacred Wisdom of the World* (Harper Collins, London, 1994), p. 8.
6. Richard Woods, *Mysticism and Prophecy: The Dominican Tradition* (Orbis Book, Maryknoll, New York, 1998), pp. 77, 78.
7. Karl Rahner, *Concern for the Church: Theological Investigation* XX (Crossroads, New York, 1981), p. 78.

8. Tugwell, *Albert and,* p. 93.

Epilogue

1. Owen Barfield, *Saving the Appearances* (Wesleyan University Press, 1988), p. 164.
2. Christopher Bamford, in Rudolph Steiner, *What is Anthroposophy?* (SteinerBooks, 2002), p. 5.
3. Rudi Lissau, *Rudolf Steiner: Life, Work. Inner Path and Social Initiatives* (Hawthorn Press, U.K., 1987), p. 73.
4. *Ibid.,* p. 19.
5. Barfield, *Saving,* p. 168.
6. Collosians, 1:15–20.
7. Richard Woods, *Mysticism and Prophecy: The Dominican Tradition* (Orbis Books, Maryknoll, New York, 1998), p. 43.
8. *Ibid.,* p. 79.
10. *Ibid.,* pp. 78–79. Bernard McGinn, ed., *Meister Eckhart and the Beguines Mystics* (Continuum, New York, 1994), p. 160.
11. G. B. Tennyson, *A Barfield Reader: Selections from the Writings of Owen Barfield* (Wesleyan University Press, Middletown, CT, 1999), p. 147.
12. Rudolph Steiner, *The Redemption of Thinking: A Study in The Philosophy of Thomas Aquinas* (Anthroposophic Press, 1956), p. 73.
13. Rudolph Steiner, *The Origins of Natural Science* (Anthroposophic Press, 1985), p. 7.
14. Steiner, *The Redemption,* p. 102.
15. *Ibid.,* p. 72.
16. *Ibid.,* p. 114.